SAGITTARIUS RISING

SAGITTARIUS RISING

by

Cecil Lewis

LONDON
PETER DAVIES

First Impression . . *June 1936*
Second Impression . . *August 1936*

Printed in Great Britain for PETER DAVIES LTD. by T. and A. CONSTABLE LTD.
at the University Press, Edinburgh

CONTENTS

SAGITTARIUS

NINTH SIGN OF THE ZODIAC, THE
ARCHER, GOVERNING VOYAGES AND
WEAPONS AND ALL SWIFT THINGS.
A FIERY BUT DIVIDED SIGN, DOMI-
NATED BY JUPITER, DENOTING IN
THE CHARACTER GAIETY AND A LOVE
OF SPORT ON THE ONE HAND, AND
ON THE OTHER A POWER OF PRO-
PHECY AND PHILOSOPHY: WHICH
SIGN OCCURS IN THE HOROSCOPE
OF THE AUTOBIOGRAPHER, RISING.

THERE are fortunate men to whom life is a continuous developing pattern, whose education leads them on to a career that carries them, almost in spite of themselves, to a place in the world from which, as their powers desert them, they withdraw to ease and seclusion, and whose final demise is as quiet and completing as the full stop at the end of a long and well-constructed sentence. Worthy men; good, useful men, no doubt; perhaps lucky men. There are many of them. In spite of the chaos of our time you constantly find them, self-insulated from doubts and speculations, from anything which might upset the steady flow of their little stream: complacent, comfortable, corpulent. There are moments when I envy them their unassailable security.

No such life has been mine. For to me, and thousands like me, that easy developing pattern was completely thrown out of symmetry by the first World War. It took me from school at sixteen, it destroyed all hope of University training or apprenticeship to a trade, it deprived me of the only carefree years, and washed me up, inequipped for any serious career, with a Military Cross, a Royal handshake, a six-hundred-pound gratuity, and—I almost forgot to say—my life.

There were men older than I whose education was complete. To them the War was a setback, disastrous but not irremediable. There were others, older still, who had positions to which they could return. But we very young men had no place, actual or prospective, in a peaceful world. We walked off the playing-fields into the lines. We lived supremely in the moment. Our preoccupation was the next patrol, our horizon the next leave. Sometimes, jokingly, as one discusses winning the Derby Sweep, we would plan our lives " after the War." But it had no substantial significance. It was a dream, conjecturable as heaven, resembling no life we knew. We were trained with one object —to kill. We had one hope—to live. When it was over we had to start again.

I do not complain of this. It was a fine introduction to life; but now, a step beyond the half-way house, that immense experience begins to fall into perspective as merely an episode. A great episode, of course; one that was to change the whole shape of civilization; but so different, so complete in itself, that now, at a distance of twenty years, my personal memories of it are quite detached—as if they belonged to another life.

No doubt the psychologists have decided to what extent the shape of a man's life is dependent on the impact of his first adult experience. I observe (for what it is worth to them) that mine seems to fall into short complete blocks, that it is a repetitive not a running design, Chinese not Japanese; a theme, if you like, with variations. And in moments of depression, when I wish for a longer sweep to carry me safely into the sober years and find that, strangely, it eludes me, I console myself with the futile reflection : It's the War, my boy, it's the War.

This book is concerned with the first two of these lives, blocks, variations, or what you will. Both were over before I was twenty-four. Each, as I have said, was complete in itself, and might, from its remoteness to my present everyday life, have happened to somebody else. Did I, in fact, fly all through the long months of the Somme battle? Did I dive headlong, guns stuttering, into the Richthofen Circus that night Ball was killed? Did I range over darkened London, nervous under the antennae of her searchlights, hunting for Gothas? And did I, all that behind me, celebrate my twenty-first birthday four months after the Armistice? It seems I did.

Equally remote seem my two years in China. Two glorious, perfect years! Those crumbling palaces, those breathless courtyards, and the ghostly herons circling the Forbidden City in the dawn, did I, with these eyes, see all those things?

Well, here is my logbook lying on the desk. One thousand hours flying . . . fifty-three types of machines. . . . Here is my blackwood table, my lacquer, my jade. . . . It must be so.

Now both those lives are over. In London the April rain drenches the roofs. The curtains are drawn. Within my study all is quiet and peaceful. The paper on which I write lies in a little pool of light, and my hand moves laboriously, back and across, back and across. . . . Back and across the years! It is not easy. I kept no diaries, and memory, that imperfect vista of recorded thought, eludes and deceives. As in distorting mirrors at a fair, I can see myself long or stumpy, lean or fat, at will. Never my true self. Mercifully, no doubt.

Still, I can convey something after all. Not a connected narrative of adventure and heroism;

3

rather, in a series of incidents and impressions, all that my mind remembers of the shape of those six years. Some of it perhaps will be inaccurate in detail, but broadly it is true. In case such things should be of interest, before they escape me further let me set them down.

I

TRAINING

I stood with Maynard Greville on the stone terrace outside the School House studies at Oundle in the spring of 1915.

" I vote we chuck all this at the end of term and join up," said he.

" Wouldn't it be fine !—but they won't let us."

" Why not? We're almost seventeen."

" But old King says you can't get a commission in anything until you're eighteen."

" Rot! What about the Flying Corps? They'll take you at seventeen. They want young chaps."

" Shall we speak to Beans? "

" No, he might stop us. I vote we write to the War Office and see what happens."

" All right! Oh, Maynard, wouldn't it be ripping ! "

*

It took us a long time to get those letters right.

" We mustn't let it look too much like kids ; but it wants to sound keen and all that."

" We ought to type it, really."

" What's the good of saying that when we haven't got a typewriter? "

" Ashworth might lend us his."

" And tell the Head afterwards ! No, thanks."

At last the letters were sent off. An agonizing wait followed. In our impatience and excitement it seemed incredible the War Office didn't reply by return of post. Surely the chance of getting two keen young chaps was not to be missed?

When the buff envelopes arrived, a week later, we had given up all hope. We retired excitedly to our study and shut the door. We might have been conspirators. Certainly no spies ever observed greater secrecy in opening their official instructions than we did in concealing our intention to serve our country. The paper heading was enough to start the heart pounding: " WAR OFFICE, WHITEHALL." And then the formal opening: " DEAR SIR, I am in receipt of your communication of the — inst. . . ." We raced through the rest; then with a whoop began to dance wildly round the study.

" They'll see us! They'll see us! They haven't turned us down. Good egg ! "

" And I say, look at this : ' I have the honour to be, sir, your obedient servant —' Isn't that comic? He wouldn't finish up like that unless he really wanted us."

" Rot ! All those johnnies end their letters like that. They have to."

" We're going to be pilots ! We're going to be pilots ! Hurrah ! "

*

In retrospect it seems to have been lightly decided. Actually I suppose it was the last link in a long subconscious chain of wish fulfilment. For, now I come to think of it, I hardly remember a time when I was not air-minded. At prep. school I was already making gliders out of half-sheets of paper, curving the plane surfaces, improvising rudders and ailerons, and spending hours launching them across the room from chairs and tables. I devoured the pages of *Flight* and *The Aero*. I could tell all the types of machines—Latham's Antoinette, Blériot's monoplane, the little Demoiselle. I followed the exploits of the Wright brothers in America and Cody on Laffan's Plain. I remember well my disappointment when Latham set off to fly the Channel only to fall into the sea a mile from the Folkestone Cliffs. I remember my annoyance when Blériot actually did it, for to my youthful aesthetic sense Blériot's stubby little machine was not to be compared with Latham's lovely bird.

A year later I met Hill. Then model-making started in real earnest. Hill's attic in his parents' house at Hampstead was full of models. Models hung on hooks from the ceiling and on the walls; models stood on the tops of chests, on tables, on the floor. The bench was a gorgeous muddle of tools and glue, veneer and solder, florists' wire and elastic. He taught me the mysteries of hollow spars, bracing, and rigging. He explained how to make planes from wire frames, cunningly soldered together and covered with jap silk stretched tight as a drum, how to do fine thread lashings and make them fast with varnish, how to use a twist drill, and many other tricks of the model-maker's trade. I acquired then a love of making things that needed accuracy, patience, and precision, and never to this day can I see a shoddy finish in anything without offence to a sense of fine workmanship that I learned at the age of thirteen.

But, whereas I only made models copied from or based on Hill's, he was continually designing new types and was already deep in the mathematics of thrusts, lifts, propeller pitches, etc. He, too, joined the Flying Corps, and though I never saw him again, I believe he later became a designer at the Royal Aircraft Factory at Farnborough and is still in the Force.

But, in spite of this passion for " aeronautics " —as they were then called—it never occurred to me that I might be actively concerned in them. That I myself might fly a real full-sized aeroplane was beyond the bounds of the wildest possibility. Then came the War. Warneford brought down a Zeppelin. The importance of the air began to be realized. An immense impetus was given to aircraft design and manufacture. The opportunity opened, and the onlooker became participant.

★

If you choose a misty morning to take a stroll across the bridge over the lake in St James's Park, you will see to the east one of the most magical views in London. For the Horse Guards, the War Office, and the black pyramidal roofs of Whitehall Court beyond form a composite group which mounts, with all the majesty of some legendary castle, cupola above cupola, roof over roof, up from a frame of mist and plane trees to the palest of pale heavens. It has, on such a morning, all the mystery of some faerie citadel, and seems to have been materialized out of air a moment since for the amazement of the passer-by.

Certainly nobody could have held it in greater

awe or deemed it more unapproachable than we two who were bidden to keep an appointment at Room 613A that spring morning. The great staircase of the War Office was, if anything, less impressive than the bearing of the commissionaire at whose gesture the inevitable buff forms were filled up. Then interminable staircases, interminable corridors, a series of blue-clad messengers, a brief intimation, "Wait here, please," and behold Room 613A materialized before our eyes: the Mecca of a month's waiting, the place where we were to play that scene, so often rehearsed, in answer to the questions: "Who are you? What can you do?"

Up to that moment it had somehow never occurred to us that any one else had thought of joining the Royal Flying Corps. It was our own brilliant and original idea, no one else could have had it. So great was our dismay to find a long queue of young men waiting ahead of us. Our hope, buoyant till that moment, dropped, deflated.

"Are all these chaps trying to get in too?"

"Looks like it."

"Oh Lord!"

Then silence and the slow shortening of the queue, each of us staring anxiously at the faces of those leaving, trying to read from their eyes: "Has he got in?" "Shall I?"

*

Lord Hugh Cecil, Staff-Captain, interviewing applicants to join the R.F.C., was bald and mild, with good hands and a most charming manner.

9

" So you were at Oundle? "

" Yes, sir."

" Under the great Sanderson? "

" Er—yes, sir." (Old Beans the great Sanderson! Well, I'm blowed!)

" Were you in the Sixth? "

" Yes, sir—Upper Sixth. Er—a year under the average, sir."

" I see. How old are you? "

" Almost eighteen, sir." (Liar! You were seventeen last month.)

" Play any games? "

" Yes, sir. I got my School Colours at Fives, and I captained the House on the river. I should have got my House Colours for Rugger this year if I'd stayed; but——"

" Fives, you say? You should have a good eye, then."

" Yes, I suppose so, sir." (Does Fives need a good eye? Well, he seems to think so. I'm getting on all right.)

" You're very tall."

" Six foot three, sir."

" I don't think you could get into a machine."

" Why, sir? " (Oh Lord! He's going to turn me down. He *mustn't* turn me down!)

" Well, they're not built for young giants like you, you know."

" Couldn't I try, sir? "

A slow smile, a pause, then : " Yes, I suppose so. I'll write a note to the O.C. at Hounslow. And if it's all right, come and see me again."

" Oh, thank you so much, sir. I'm awfully keen, sir, to——"

" I'm glad." He wrote rapidly. " Here, take
this with you and show it to the O.C. Hounslow."
" Thank you, sir. Good morning, sir."

*

In the Piccadilly Grill, dinner was in full swing.
Waiters bustled among the tables, the confused
chatter of three hundred people baffled De Groot's
attempt to render a selection from *Pagliacci*. My
mother and a friend were waiting for me. I arrived
late and, I suppose, rather flushed and excited.
" Well, dear, how did you get on? "
" Pretty well."
" Did you go up? "
" Yes! "
" Oh! " There was a faint tremor in her voice.
(Not already! This only son, in the war, in the
air, and a moment ago he played at her feet. Not
already! Not to be snatched away already . . .)
" It was ripping, Mother. When I got down
there, they let me get into a machine—a Maurice
Longhorn it's called. You have to climb up under
the wires, stand on the tyre, heave yourself up
on to the plane, and over into the nacelle [1]—
that's a sort of shoe you sit in. Oh, it was so
exciting! You know, I couldn't understand why
that johnnie at the War Office said I might be too
tall; but, you see, there's a sort of a pair of handle-
bars that work the ailerons, and if I'd been a bit

[1] I have used French terms here and elsewhere in the book because,
though they are now obsolete, they were current at this time. Thus
Nacelle=car, Fuselage=body, Longerons=tail booms, round which
the body was constructed, Ailerons=hinged flaps in the trailing edge
of the main planes to give lateral control.

11

taller I couldn't have got my knees underneath them—but it was all right. The officer said so."

" I'm so glad, dear." (The Germans have the supremacy of the air, too. . . . The papers admit it even. . . . Perhaps the training will take a long time. . . . Perhaps . . .)

" And then I waited about for ages—that's why I'm so late—because the Captain, awfully decent he was, said he'd give me a flip if I liked, so he lent me a helmet and goggles and gloves and everything, and I climbed up behind him——"

" Weren't you frightened, darling? "

" No! much too excited! The engine went off with a roar and we bumped along over the ground —taxying, they call it—and then we took off! I didn't feel it when we left the ground. The bumping stopped, that's all. And then I saw everything below. The Thames and all the houses and people looked like little dots and he went round twice and a cucumber frame looked the size of a matchbox I happened to notice it and then we landed I hardly felt it touch and I'm to go back to the War Office to-morrow the Captain gave me a note. Oh, I hope I'll be able to do it all right. It's a marvellous feeling! "

" I expect you will, dear."

*

But, though I was admitted to the R.F.C., the months went by, summer blossomed and faded, and still no orders came to join up. I grew impatient and bearded the War Office again. Again the staircases, the corridors, the waiting.

" The age for joining the R.F.C. has been raised to eighteen. I'm sorry."

" But, sir, when you put me down, the age was seventeen, wasn't it ? "

" Yes."

" Then this regulation came in after I joined up ? "

" Yes."

" Oh, sir, can't you let me through ? I've counted so much on it ! "

" I'll see what I can do. Let me see, you first came in April. . . . H'm . . ." He consulted a ledger. " Yes. Leave it to me. Good-day."

★

" Report Brooklands fifteenth " ran the magic telegram. The moon-faced boy disappeared on his red bicycle between the tall pines. Surrey autumn, westering sun, bronze-plated tree-trunks, the scent of resin, matted pine-needles, toadstools, and out and away along the flanks of the hills the blazon of gold bracken and the crumbling dustiness of dead heather . . . " Report on the fifteenth . . ." A faint hum drifted over from Farnborough ! Somewhere aloft there in the distance a machine, a pilot, a comrade, sworn to the same fellowship of daring and loneliness in the high cold airs of evening. " Report on the fifteenth. . . ."

★

Longhorn. . . . Shorthorn. . . . Seventy-horse Renault. . . . Hundred-horse Mono. . . . BE 2c. . . . Avro. . . . The theory of aileron control.

13

. . . Put your nose down before shutting off. . . . Watch the Pitôt tube.[1] . . . Taxi slowly. . . . Such phrases as these come to my mind when I think of my six weeks' training at Brooklands that winter. Day after day, rain, high winds, " No flying ! " Day after day, up from Weybridge on the motor-bike, under the track, round the sheds, only to stand about shivering, gazing with awe into the Sopwith hangars, and sometimes, on finer days, watching Hawker fly his " Pup " under the Byfleet bridge. Long hours of idleness, waiting, talking, grumbling at our status as civilian cadets which laid us open to attack from officious patriotic old ladies who haunted the streets of London at that time.

" Why aren't you in uniform, my boy? " said such an old busybody to one of us. He lifted his hat. " Madam, excuse me. My mother always warned me against speaking to strange women in the street."

★

I took my ticket (*i.e.* learned to fly and obtained my pilot's certificate) on a Maurice Farman "Longhorn." It was a biplane and, judged by present standards, a museum piece. The main planes had a span of about fifty feet. Four longerons (tail booms) ran out behind the centre section to the box tail, which had two rudders. In front of the main planes was a pair of giant skids. These started below the

---

[1] The Pitôt tube was a column of pink liquid which rose and fell, like a thermometer, in a glass tube, under the pressure of the air, and so registered the speed of the machine. The standard clock form of Airspeed Indicator was not in use on training machines in 1915.

planes and formed the undercarriage (where they carried four wheels) and ran forwards and upwards, like the prow of an enormous toboggan, to carry the elevator between them at their upper tips. On the lower main plane rested the nacelle, a long shoe, where a 70-h.p. Renault engine pushed behind in the heel and two passengers sat in tandem in the toe, which projected out in front of the plane. The controls (which were duplicated for instructor and pupil) consisted of pedals for the rudders, a stick to push and pull for the elevator, and at the top of this a pair of handle-bars, which, when swivelled up and down, worked the ailerons. The whole contraption was held together with piano wire, with which it was festooned in every direction— lift wires, landing wires, drift wires, bracing wires: we used to say you could safely cage a canary in a Longhorn without fear of losing it.

However, it had advantages. If you crashed it, there was such a lot between you and the ground that you were unlikely to get seriously hurt. Also it had no vices. It was docile and well behaved. It climbed at forty-five, flew level at sixty, and settled down like a kite when landing.

The Longhorn (of beloved memory) had a sister, the "Shorthorn." This had dispensed with the skids and elevator forward, and had a somewhat more workmanlike appearance. (It was impossible to take the Longhorn seriously. It was an aerial joke, like the Daddy Long Legs). Pupils were only allowed to fly the Shorthorn after taking their tickets. We used to " put in time " on them. I actually flew about two hours on one. It was a sturdy machine, and even a year later, on visiting a

15

French aerodrome, I found these machines, slightly modified and with more powerful engines, still being used for Artillery Reconnaissance.

★

One and a half hours' dual stood to my credit. I had trundled round the aerodrome with Sergeant Yates, my instructor, doing left-hand circuits, and made a few indifferent landings.

" You'd better go solo this afternoon, if the wind drops."

" Yes, sir."

" Remember to take plenty of room to get off."

" Yes, sir." (Last week George had neglected that important point, caught the upper lip of the concrete, and gone arsy-tarsy down into the meadow on the other side.)

" Get your tail well up before you try to take her off. Don't climb under forty-five, and when you come down, keep her at fifty-five until you want to land. If you're at three hundred feet over the Members' Bridge you'll get in all right." (Sandy had misjudged it two days ago, and flown into the sewage farm. What a mess he was in when he came back to the sheds! How we had laughed!)

" Yes, sir."

Alone in the nacelle of the Longhorn, the engine ticking over, the instructor leaning over the side. " Run her up." Stick back, throttle slowly forward. Twelve hundred. " She'll do." Chocks away. Taxi slowly. Away over the bumpy ground. How difficult to steer right down the aerodrome with a following wind! Give her a bit of throttle, rudder

16

. . . round she comes. Throttle back. Take a deep breath. Try the controls. Rudder—Elevator —Ailerons. . . . God! Who said they wanted to fly? How the heart pumps! Waiting for the pistol at the school races last year! Just the same—sick, heart pumping, no breath. . . . Well, come on! Can't stay here all night! Throttle full open, elevator forward. . . . We're hardly moving. The revs are all right. Why doesn't the tail lift? What's the speed? Thirty! . . . Forty! . . . Ah! It's coming up! . . . She'll never get up, though. . . . We shall fly into the track! . . . Steady now. Don't pull her off too soon! Forty-five! Fifty! Now! Ease back the stick! Gently, gently. . . . Bounce . . Bounce . . . Bounce. . . . She's lifting! She's away! Forty-five! Keep her down, man! For God's sake keep her down, we shall stall! Easy does it. Ah, we'll clear the track after all. . . . Steady now. . . . There it goes, well underneath. Now I can breathe. Keep her at fifty. That's it. Good. . . . Now, what about a turn? Just a little left rudder. Bank. Ease her round. . . . I'm getting on all right. What's the height? Five hundred. That'll do. That's safe enough. . . .

And so round the track, getting confidence, turning, turning, always left. . . . Try a right turn now. Now . . . oh, she's shuddering. There's something wrong! Straighten! Quick! Straighten! . . . No, it's all right. . . . Funny, that vibration. Must report it when I get down. When I get down! How the hell do I get down? (Young Johnson, a week or two back, was frightened to come down, flew round and round the aerodrome for an hour until his petrol gave out, and then crashed on landing.) The engine keeps me up. If I shut it off we shall fall. . . . What did he say? Put your nose down before shutting off. Let's try it. . . . God! Stomach in your mouth like a scenic railway! How I hate scenic railways! Horrible things. Try again. Throttle back and nose down together. . . . That's better! That's it! Keep her at fifty-five. . . . How quiet it is without the engine! Look out! Sixty, sixty-five. . . . Nose up a bit. Shall we get in? Yes. No. A bit more engine. That's it. There go the pines underneath. Lovely woods look from the air! Mossy. Now shut off again. Steady. . . . Now . . . Now! Hold your breath. Ease her back. Gently . . . Quick! You're flying into the ground! Pull her up! Up! . . . Not too much. . . . That's it. Now . . . Why don't we land? We're stalling. Engine, quick! Bang! Bounce! Bounce! Bounce! Rumble! Rumble . . . rumble. . . . We're down! Hurrah! We're down! I've done it! I haven't crashed! I've done it! . . .

Pause for a minute to get your breath. Good boy! You've done it! Phew! Thank God, it's over! . . . Now, come on! Taxi up to the sheds in style. Confidence. That's the way! Show 'em. Good! Switch off.

Mechanics examine the undercarriage. " Any damage? "

" Nao! These 'ere airioplanes 'll stand anything! "

★

GEORGE, by the Grace of God, of the United Kingdom of Great Britain and Ireland, and of the

British Dominions beyond the Seas, King, Defender of the Faith, Emperor of India, Etc.

To Our Trusty and well beloved *Cecil Lewis* Greeting.

We reposing especial Trust and Confidence in your Loyalty, Courage, and good Conduct, do by these Presents Constitute and Appoint you to be an Officer in Our Special Reserve of Officers. You are therefore carefully and diligently to discharge your Duty as such in the Rank of 2*nd Lieutenant* or in such higher Rank as We may from time to time hereafter be pleased to promote or appoint you to, of which a notification will be made in the *London Gazette*, and you are at all times to exercise and well discipline in Arms both the inferior Officers and Men serving under you and use your best endeavours to keep them in good Order and Discipline. And We do hereby Command them to Obey you as their superior Officer and you to observe and follow such Orders and Directions as from time to time you shall receive from Us, or any your superior Officer : according to the Rules and Discipline of War ; in pursuance of the Trust hereby reposed in you.

Given at Our Court at Saint James's, the twenty-eighth day of December, nineteen hundred and fifteen, in the Sixth Year of Our Reign.

By His Majesty's Command.

*

Christmas ! Three days' leave ! And the new uniform arrived ! How tight the field-boots were ! Agony, walking to the station ! And every one surely staring at the " trusty and well beloved "

young man in a tunic too small and breeches too
big. And the Sam Browne belt! Let me tell you
a Sam Browne belt is full of pitfalls for the ignorant.
It is supplied with two shoulder-straps; but you
only wear one. Which? It has extra links, and
hooks for swords, and buckles, and clips—and it
all looks so new!

At the hotel many officers. Decent chaps, ready
to take a young man under their wing. " The belt
goes this way. Undo that clip. You needn't wear
it for dinner. Put on a pair of slacks."

Then Mother, gay and fond, " doing her bit "
as quartermaster of a hospital over the moors near
by, bringing a young nurse to tea. Nurse Baxter,
tall, dark, and pretty. Very demure, being taken
home in the dark, along the sandy lanes of the
heath, between the high gorse hedges.

" It's so dark. Would you mind taking my
arm? It's silly of me to have put on these high-
heeled shoes."

" Certainly." Pressure of her arm against mine.
The back of my hand touching the softness of her
side. I, an officer in the R.F.C., taking a girl
home, alone with her on the heath at night!
Strange and new, this sense of mastery and elation.
She stumbled. I held her closer. She stopped.

" Look at the lights down there in the valley.
Isn't it quiet? "

" Yes." Heart thumping. Her head so near.

" And look! Over there, too! " The head closer,
hair brushing my cheek, a faint scent of violets.

" Yes." A long, long pause, a distant dog-bark,
a car grinding up the hill. . . .

" Why don't you kiss me? "

20

Miracle! She offers herself! Lovely; sensed in the dark—only sensed, close and strange. . . . I, turning to her, kissed her lightly, gently, shyly. She laughed intimately, quietly, rubbing her cheek against mine. . . .

We moved on, a strange new bond between us, and the question in my mind, bright, butterfly-like: Why me? Why me? Why me?

The lights of the hospital nearer. We stopped again.

" Why did you want me to kiss you? "

" I wanted you to."

Then back through the darkness, alone. I ought to have . . . If I had . . . Why didn't I . . .? Tumultuous thoughts, racing, dancing, and written over the stars : " I wanted you to! I wanted you to! "

*

After taking my ticket on the Longhorn and putting in a couple of hours on the Shorthorn, I was posted to Gosport for final training on Avros and BE 2c's. When I could fly those machines adequately I should be able to put up my " Wings "— that coveted little badge, without which the double-breasted R.F.C. tunic looked bare and unfinished, and which marked the probationer's graduation to the status of a fully-fledged pilot.

The training squadron's Mess and quarters at Gosport were in a disused coastal defence fort, star-shaped, with quarters for the troops in the hollow ramparts and the empty centre used as a drill ground. A strange new life began to open up.

Mess etiquette, Mess manners, Mess bills. The King's health, drunk in port, every night after dinner. "Gentlemen, you may smoke." Drill, kit inspection, the duties of orderly officers. Southsea, with its cafés, restaurants, theatres, and girls. An easy camaraderie with men whose uniform seemed to have robbed them of all other status. So-and-so has a car : he's always in town. So-and-so is a Regular, seconded to the R.F.C. So-and-so has done nine months in France, got his D.S.O., but his nerve's gone; they've made him an instructor. So went the gossip; but among all those men I had no sense of contact. Faces peer out from the heavy folds of my memory, and are gone. They are wraiths who talked the "shop" of the aerodrome, the chances of flying to-morrow, the news from the Front—a nebulous and trivial background against which my growing passion for the air stands out in high relief.

*

Up over Southampton Water doing "dual" in an Avro, I thought it would be fun to make a mild left turn. I started it, left stick and rudder, in the usual way. The machine canted over, the turn got steeper and steeper. Evidently the instructor wanted to show me vertical turns. I knew the theory of it : over forty-five degrees the rudder becomes the elevator and the elevator the rudder. All right : I held on, began to slack off the rudder and pull in the stick, keeping the nose on the horizon. The turn became vertical. Then, slowly we came out of it and went into one on the opposite

bank. I followed the instructor's movements carefully, remembered the directions so often rehearsed.
After all, these vertical turns were not so very
difficult, I thought, if you took them quietly; but
how beautifully and easily he did them. It would
take me months to learn it properly. The instructor
switched off. We came down and landed.

" You can go solo to-morrow," he said. " Those
turns were beautiful. Beautiful! "

" But I didn't do them, sir. You were doing
them."

" I? I never touched the stick at all, and in the
second one I had my feet off the rudder! "

" Well, I'm damned! "

*

Next day, I took the Avro off on solo. The
machine was beautiful to fly, light and responsive,
and an excellent training machine (for which it was
used, almost exclusively, throughout the war). I
came down, made a good landing, and taxied up to
the sheds, before which a dozen machines were
standing. Just as I reached them, the button
switch, controlling the engine, situated in the head
of the joystick, broke. That meant the engine
could not be switched off, and being an 80-h.p.
Mono,[1] it had only one way of running—full out!
Under such circumstances an experienced pilot

[1] Mono, an abbreviation for Monosoupape (single valve): a seven-
cylinder French rotary engine. The explosive mixture entered the
cylinders from the crankcase through a perforated skirt (in the manner
of 2-stroke engines), and was discharged through the single valve in the
head. The admission of the mixture into the cylinders could not be
accurately controlled, and the engine had always to run at full throttle.

would have immediately cut off his main switch or closed his petrol. But the unfortunate novice, panic-stricken, in a machine with a runaway engine, was deserted by the clear thinking necessary to act so quickly. The engine roared out threateningly. I jammed on the rudder, with the vague idea of turning to take off again. But the tail flew up in the air, spun round, and the machine, like an angry wasp in its death-agony, careered round and round in a small circle at full speed within fifty yards of £20,000 worth of aircraft. The next moment there would be a nasty crash. Round and round went the machine, the frantic instructor shouting orders quite inaudible above the roar of the engine, the pupil paralysed! I felt as helpless as a man at the wheel of a car in an uncontrollable skid; worse, for this skid was not just once round, it had already been at least six. Men rushed out of hangars, waving the juggernaut away from the other machines to which, with every angry spin, it was coming closer. Frantic signs and gesticulations flashed past my eyes; but by now I was dizzy, paralysed, helpless.

Suddenly, by the mercy of heaven, the engine coughed and stopped. Praise be to God! Only a burst tyre.

" What the bloody hell d'you think you're up to? " shouted the irate instructor, leaning menacingly over the cockpit. I was trembling, exhausted.

" My button switch broke."

" Well, God Almighty, haven't you got a petrol tap, and a needle valve, and a main switch? "

" Yes; but it was so sudden, I didn't quite know . . ."

" Well, for Christ's sake know next time. These bloody little button switches are always going wrong. Oughtn't to be fitted, in my opinion. Petrol off at once, see? "

★

The FE 2b was a pusher (that is, the engine pushed it from behind), a development of the Vickers Fighter, made by the Royal Aircraft Factory. It had a 160-h.p. Beardmore engine and an Oleo telescopic undercarriage. This, in the air, hung down like a pair of stilts on wheels ; but when you touched the ground, it shut up, taking the weight and the shock of uneven landings and settling the machine on to the ground in a long comfortable rumble. It was a fine machine, slow, but very sturdy, and carried a pilot, with an observer before him, in a boot which stuck out in front of the machine (in the manner of the Shorthorn). Forward, therefore, it had a fine arc of fire and, attacked head on, was extremely formidable. Attacked from the rear, it was necessary for the pilot to stand up in his seat, hold the stick with his knees and use his own gun, which fired backwards over the top plane—not an easy job, but frequently resorted to in a dog-fight. With good battle tactics, a flight of these machines was very deadly, even to an enemy with far greater speed and manœuvrability. FE's were used for bombing raids and long reconnaissances, and time and time again they would fight their way home from twenty miles beyond the lines, continually circling to protect each other's tails, surrounded by enemy scouts. It's no joke to be shot up by a dozen machine guns for half an hour, engaged in a

25

running fight in which the enemy can outpace you, outclimb you, and outturn you. It needs a lot of guts and a cool head; but the FE's were manned by stout fellows. They soon had the respect of the Huns,[1] who would never risk attacking unless they outnumbered them by two to one, and did wonderful work right through 1916 and on into the summer of 1917, when the FE's were scrapped as obsolete and the DH 4's and Bristol Fighters took their place.

But at this time the FE was the last word in aircraft, and these machines began to arrive at Gosport: a squadron of them was preparing for overseas. Strange Flight-Commanders and pilots appeared. Observers, gunnery officers, equipment officers, and air mechanics were drafted in. There was activity up at the sheds, and tension in the Mess. We were excited. We talked of nothing but the FE. For we were all bound for the Front. Small wonder if we discussed long hours together the merits of the machines we might have to take over the lines. Some were considered safer than others. Some, like the Moranes and DH 2's, were death-traps. Some only did defensive patrols. Others did long bombing raids far into the enemy country. Our chances were closely bound up with the machine we flew and the work it was detailed for. So we took a

---

[1] It has been suggested that this word has an ugly connotation, and that I should not use it. But we always referred to our friends the enemy as "Huns," just as the Infantry knew them as "Fritz" or "Jerry," and nothing derogatory was, or is, intended. When they captured our pilots or observers they treated them with courtesy and gallantry, as I think we did them. I do not remember, except on one occasion over London in 1917, ever having any feelings of animosity against the Germans. They were simply "the enemy"; their machines had black crosses, and it was our job to bring them down.

very personal interest in the FE, watched how she climbed and turned, and inquired closely into the reliability of the Beardmore engine (for we didn't relish the idea of engine failure twenty miles over in Hunland). We got the pilots to take us up as passengers to get the feel of the machine in the air. She was heavy, but stable, easy to land, and very reliable. The general verdict was that we should any of us be lucky to be posted to an FE squadron.

At last, after a month's preparation, the squadron was ready. The machines were lined up by Flights in front of the sheds, three rows of four each. They looked very imposing. The February sun glistened on their new white wings. The streamers fluttered from the rudders of the Flight-Commanders. The Lewis guns stood cocked up on their mountings. The pilots and observers, muffled up in their leather coats, stumped about in their sheepskin boots, strapping up their haversacks, looking over their machines, polishing their goggles. They collected round the Major for final instructions, consulted their maps, and then went off, pulling on flying-caps and mufflers, climbed into their cockpits, settled down and strapped themselves in. The mechanics kicked the chocks more firmly against the wheels and sucked in the engines. Contact! The pilots spun their starting magnetos, and one by one the engines sprang into life. Three minutes to warm them up, and then a heavy roar, which rose and fell as pilot after pilot ran up his engine, tested his magnetos, and then, satisfied, throttled down again. At last they were all ready, engines ticking over, and a deep thrumming of the planes and wires vibrating filled the air. The Major dropped his hand, and

A Flight Flight-Commander opened his engine up, turned, and taxied away down the aerodrome. The others followed him, single file, and one by one they headed to the wind, pushed their throttles open, rose, swaying in the ground gusts, and sailed up towards the sheds.

We stood on the tarmac watching them go. And still, after twenty years, my heart swells at the memory of the sight. I can hear the strong engines and smell the tang of the burnt oil. I can see them as they came hurtling up, their goggled pilots and observers leaning down to wave a last farewell before they passed in a deafening flash of speed and smoke fifty feet overhead. One by one they came up as if saluting us—drum roll crescendo, cymbal crash, rapid diminuendo. One by one they disappeared behind the sheds.

It was a prelude to action in that noble and tragic adventure of the world's youth; the first visible instance of collective farewell; the first realization of a grim purpose behind that casual and carefree life. It caught at my heart then, as a stage show catches its audience, which weeps, almost with pleasure, at the tragedy of others; which shares, at a remove, an agony it need not undergo. I was an onlooker that day; they were a symbol of the time: young men who rose up, passed with a cry and a gesture, and were gone. When my turn came I did not feel it so.

Once in the air, the squadron took formation. The three flights, each a diamond (Flight-Commander leading, numbers two and three to right and left, fifty yards between wing-tips, number four a hundred yards directly behind the leader and slightly above to avoid his slipstream), wheeled, a moving arrow-head (A Flight leading, B and C to right and left), over the green fields and the white cliffs of England, passed majestically away in the sunlight, growing smaller and smaller as they climbed, the roar of their engines sinking to a murmur, and the murmur dying to silence before we lost them. At last, straining our eyes, we could see them no longer. They were twelve remote and splendid spirits who had gone.

*

A month later, on March 20th, 1916, to be precise, the scene repeated itself, for another FE squadron, No. 22, left for France. I did not see them go, for I had been posted to the squadron as a spare pilot, and had left the day previous with the Major, Adjutant, and all the rest of the personnel, by boat to Rouen.

By this time I was, of course, a fully-fledged pilot. I had passed out on the Avro and BE 2c. I had put up my " Wings "—which had expanded my chest measurement by at least six inches—and was ready for anything.

My mother came down to say good-bye. She behaved as all good mothers should, gave me a cigarette-case, talked of everything except the Front, adjured me to write regularly, said she was not going to worry as I was quite certain to come through all right, and said good-bye at the station without breaking down. Seventeen is not a grateful age. So much is taken for granted. The parent's care and solicitude become a burden to be cast off. So I record with some remorse how little that parting meant. I was full of the new life, and utterly failed to grasp the blank my going would leave, the daily searching through the long casualty lists, the daily listening for the knock which might mean a word, a line, some message, however meagre, from "somewhere in France." I was rather relieved to have her gone, for I dreaded a scene. I was as certain as she that I should come through all right, and that being so, why get emotional over a temporary separation? But, all the same, the truth was that the average length of a pilot's life at that time was three weeks. I was hopelessly inequipped and inexperienced. Later, no pilot was allowed to cross the lines before he had done sixty hours' flying —I had done thirteen. There was every excuse for a last farewell; but, mercifully, we did not know it. It is only now I can look back, judge of the hazards, and get a vague idea of the miracle that passed me through those years unscathed. She had made me have my photograph taken, too, and I hated it! The only one I cared about showed the "Wings" prominently; but, of course, she liked another, in profile, where they did not show at all—liked the expression, she said. Sentimental, mothers were; but she was proud too. I was not to know that photo was to stand on her desk if "anything happened," for her to say, "This was my son!" and try to find something to justify a belief in the worthiness of my death when, in her heart, she knew that the world could never be richer or nobler for butchering a million of its sons.

She was gone, leaving me for my last evening to

the care of Eleanor. It was to be a champagne dinner, her new frock, a box at the theatre, and, after, I was to take her home. She was the love-liest girl in the neighbourhood, very much sought after, with a full engagement book, a large heart, and a big sofa before the fire.

Smile at this innocent parting if you please. I confess to a sigh of regret, not at a lost opportunity, but at something inevitably lost, something which, to me, seems precious—the idealism, the directness, the simplicity of youth. I lived with a secret image of perfection in my heart. My hope, my belief in myself and in life, was boundless, vague and vast as a cloud horizon before sunrise. The prosaic and worldly things—money, position, self-interest —out of which men build their little sand-castles of vanity and power, meant nothing. They slipped by, ignored. Everything you did should be the best possible. You should live gloriously, gener-ously, dangerously. Safety last!

As time went by, the outlines of this picture blurred. The fresh colours, hastily laid on, dimmed, cracked, and peeled off. Also the world slung mud at it, ridiculed it, or smiled patronizingly, in a worldly-wise way: Pretty, but, of course, quite impracticable. Alas, they were right. Con-siderations with which ideals have little to do loom large to-day. However, I still have the picture knocking about. Occasionally I give it a rub up. It's surprising how fresh it keeps, all things con-sidered.

All of which sounds so pretentious that some-thing in Sir Galahad's best manner should follow. It doesn't. There is nothing in this little fireside scene the night before I went to France. It might have ended differently. Because I was young it didn't. That's all.

We went back, after the theatre, to her house. In the warm gloom of the sitting-room she threw off her cloak and stretched herself on the big sofa before the fire. I sat at her feet. We didn't talk much. I took her hand and gazed at her. She was beautiful. I was going to the Front. I wanted, I suppose, some memory to take with me, some talisman, some hold on life, something to remember and be remembered by; but I didn't know her well, and I was young.

"Don't be angry with me; but, may I kiss you . . . once?"

She smiled teasingly at me. Little I knew. . . . I suppose there may have been something touching in this humility, this awkwardness, this lamentable lack of anything approaching a lover's technique. She drew my head down to her breast.

"Silly!"

"I'm sorry I'm going away."

"You'll soon be back."

"Yes."

I raised my head. She smiled. I kissed her forehead. She moved a little on the sofa and patted it with her hand. "Come!" I lay beside her, her shoulders caught in my arm. The scent of her hair drifted up to me, the delicate turn of the cheek with its silken down caught the firelight. We lay still for a little. I wonder what she was thinking of. Somebody else, probably.

"You must go now."

"No! Not yet!"

32

" Yes.   It's late."

" Kiss me again ! "

She submitted to the rough, dry kisses, and smiled again, sphinx-like.   Poor innocent !

" Now go.   It's late.   Mother will be wondering . . ."

" I shall never see you again."

" Oh yes, you will."

" When I come back on leave, will you . . .? "

" Of course I will."

" Darling, do you . . . like me a bit? "

" Should I have let you kiss me if I hadn't? "

That seemed conclusive.   She yawned delicately, and hid it behind her hand.

" I'm sleepy."

I pulled on my greatcoat.   She was arranging the squashed cushions.   " Oh ! " she laughed, " if that sofa could talk ! "

If that sofa could talk !   Ought I to have been bolder, then?   What did the phrase mean?   I pulled her to me.

" No.   No more.   She's sleepy."

" Of course.   I'm greedy.   Sorry !   Good-bye ! "

" Good-night !   Good luck !   Good-bye ! "

II

THE SOMME

THE transport glided steadily up the river from Havre to Rouen. As a child I had spent a summer holiday at St Briac; but all I remembered of it was the myriads of sand-fleas hopping on the beach. France was new and strange. It all seemed on a bigger scale, a broader canvas. God was painting miniatures when He filled in England: He bought a bigger brush for France. And it was nostalgic too. England can be mournful, dreary, cold, damp, miserable, dead; but it is not melancholy. For melancholy implies a certain pensive sweetness, a romantic sadness, and that is not an English quality. It was spring, too. The weeping willows swung their tresses down on to the water. The poplars pointed at the overcast day. The grass and the crowded undergrowth rose from the river banks in lovely curves, rich and sensual curves, making little hills where black-slated châteaux stood, dark and ugly under a melancholy dove-grey sky.

And such squalor and poverty in the villages! Hideous little huts, ramshackle tin-roofed sheds, rusty cans, rubbish. Funny that the French should be so bitterly patriotic and yet have so little pride in their countryside! Now England would be gay, with the almonds out, the promise of pear blossom, and crocus in the gardens. The cottages would be neat, cared for ; poor, perhaps, but never squalid.

Later, on the Somme, I grew to love that French river landscape ; but that day, with so much left behind, so much at hazard, it oppressed me, and I was glad at last to see Rouen, magnificent in the dusk, with its façade of shuttered houses and its long grey lines of docks, its tugs, barges, and, towering above them, the silhouettes of cranes.

A case of typhoid had developed on the transport, and so the whole ship was quarantined for ten days. We officers were not kept in the isolation camp, but allowed to go to a hotel. We spent the time wandering about the city, visiting the cathedral, the spot where St Joan was burnt, the theatres, the cafés. I celebrated my eighteenth birthday there, and next morning came a curious birthday present. I was not to go with 22 Squadron. I was to proceed to No. 1 Aircraft Depot, at St Omer.

*

No. 1 Aircraft Depot was the base through which all machines had to pass on their way to the front. The squadrons proceeding overseas landed there, and then went on to their allotted aerodromes. The ferry pilots, whose job it was to take machines overseas and bring others back, fly generals about, test reconditioned aircraft, etc., were all stationed at St Omer. It was also used as a park for the erection and testing of machines sent over from England in parts, and as a pool which retained spare machines to replace those damaged beyond repair at the squadrons, or lost beyond the lines. It overhauled engines, tested guns, swung compasses, sent out component parts, and when enemy aircraft were captured intact, they were always sent up to the depot to be flown.

St Omer was also the headquarters of the General Officer Commanding the R. F. C. — " Boom " Trenchard—his staff, his cars, and his queer A.D.C. (for men thought him queer until they knew him), Maurice Baring. They were quartered in a small château near the aerodrome, which stood on a hill south of the town.

St Omer was small, rather too narrow when the wind was north or south, and unfit for the larger, heavier, and faster machines used later in the war. It was scrapped as a depot then, and Marquise took its place. But in March 1916 it was simply buzzing with activity. When I came up to the sheds, the O.C. said : " There's a BE 2c. Look on it as your own. Do all the flying you want." A machine of my own ! I had been used to taking my turn with the others, flying the training machines at Brooklands and Gosport, machines belonging to nobody, just machines. But now it was to be " my machine." I could get it rigged as I liked. I could tune up the engine. I could take a pride in it. And, best of all, I could fly it as much as I liked !

In those days I lived for the air. There was nothing in life to compare with taking a machine off the ground, wheeling away into the sky, trying turns, spirals, dives, stalls, gliding, zooming, doing all the stunts a pilot needs to give him confidence and nerve in a tight corner. So far I had been content if I could get off and down again without smashing anything. If I bounced across the aerodrome like a frisky elephant, it didn't matter: I was down. Now I was determined to master the three-point landing (wheels and tail skid touching the ground at the same moment, the correct, slow, safe landing, which, when you can do it every time, is the sure sign of a first-class pilot). I would land and land that 2c. I would choose a spot on the aerodrome and land on it. I would learn to judge distance. I would learn how to S-turn in, so as to lose height without turning out of the wind. I would practise forced landings by switching off the engine at a thousand feet and getting down on the mark without using it again. Then, I had never been above a thousand feet, now I would go up and up, five thousand, ten thousand, as high as the machine would go, to get confidence over height and security in every manœuvre.

"The higher, the safer," said Patrick to me. He was the O.C. of the testing and ferry pilots, and one of the finest fliers in the Force. "Get up to five thousand and throw her about. You're strapped in. You can't fall out. It doesn't matter what happens, whether you're on your back or on your ear, she'll always fall out of it. Shut off your engine and straighten your controls and she'll put her nose down. Bound to: it's the heaviest part of the machine. Don't try any tricks near the ground. Only fools who want to show off do that. They always kill themselves in the end."

"And if she spins?"

"Let her. Only keep your head. All you young pilots are frightened of spinning. A machine spins because you've got the controls in such a position

37

that she can't get flying speed. Push your stick forward, get her nose down, and you'll be out of it in a brace of shakes. Come on! Stick on my tail!"

And with this he jumped into his machine. I followed in mine. We took off and climbed together up to five thousand feet. Then he waved to me and dived over to the left. I followed. It was steep and fast. He turned and zoomed up again to the right, standing his machine on her tail till I thought she would stall. I followed again, my heart pumping, sweating with nervous excitement and exhilaration. It was glorious! A sort of loosening up of my aerial joints. Hitherto I had turned carefully, gingerly, watching the indicators, the speed, the engine revs. Now there was no time to watch anything except where Patrick was going next. I kicked on the rudder to get round. I pulled on the bank, using strength and pressure to make her answer quickly. I became oblivious of everything, the ground, the speed, the height—nothing mattered except to follow the man ahead of me, who kept looking round and waving encouragement. And, strangely, the machine didn't seem to mind. I had always felt a wholesome respect for the frailness of an aeroplane. What was it, after all? A few pieces of wood, some linen, steel wire, and a roaring engine. Surely it couldn't stand rough treatment? But it could. It did. It vibrated a bit and shuddered at times; but that, I found afterwards, was my own lack of skill. Use it properly, give it the correct bank for the amount of rudder, never yank at the controls, but move them firmly and steadily, and any amount of aerobatics will do no harm to the machine. Only ham-fisted pilots pull their machines out of shape.

So we careered about the sky. Actually, I suppose, they were very mild turns and twists, for Patrick was teaching and encouraging me; but to me they seemed hair-raising, breath-taking, and when I began to be able to stick close to him I was as proud as Punch. He straightened up and waved me level. I caught up with him, and we waved and laughed to each other fifty yards apart a mile above the ground. Then he made a sign for me to separate, and put his nose down. I watched him shoot ahead on a steepish dive, engine full on. Then his nose went up, and the machine rose in a beautiful curve. Up and up it went, while I watched it, breathless. Now it was vertical, now it had passed the vertical, it was leaning on its back, it was upside down, a hundred feet above my head, now it was plunging downwards vertically, flattening out, and at last level, and beside me again! A loop! Marvellous it had been to see it so close, so smooth and effortless, so easy! Now I should never rest until I had done one too! But Patrick was off again, summoning me to follow. He had throttled down. We followed each other in a wide spiral, down and down, back to the insignificant earth. Patrick had taught me what flying meant. It was more marvellous than I had ever imagined. There was nothing like it. There never could be.

" What a marvellous loop! How do you do it? " We had taxied in and were walking down to the Mess.

" Get her up to a hundred, pull up steadily, and throttle down when you see the earth again."

When you see the earth again! That sounded a bit frightening. "It's the easiest stunt of all. Far easier than a tight spiral. All you need is enough speed. If you funk it and pull up too soon, you won't have enough way to get over the top and you'll hang there upside down—and probably fall out in a spin. Plenty of speed, and it's easy."

"Can I try one?"

"Why not? You were pretty good just now. How much time have you done?"

"Fourteen hours."

"Fourteen! It's absolutely disgraceful to send pilots overseas with so little flying. You don't stand a chance. I'll speak to the Major and try to keep you here for a bit. You must fly all day. Another fifty hours and you might be quite decent; but fourteen! My God, it's murder!"

*

So I flew and flew on the old 2c. You would have to go to South Kensington Museum to see what it was like now. A biplane with staggered wings, dihedral, inherently stable (so they said), fitted with two separate cockpits for pilot and observer, the pilot behind, and pulled through the air by a ninety-horse R.A.F. air-cooled engine using a four-bladed propeller. I remember, while I was training at Brooklands, one came over, and to our unaccustomed eyes it was wonderful, elegant, beautiful. Rumour, which exaggerated, said it actually touched eighty on the level. We admired its streamline wires. What an improvement on the Longhorn, whose piano wire sang like a jew's-harp every time it touched sixty! To think that one day, with luck, we might fly one! Well, for me the day came at Gosport.

"Look out!" said the Major. "She's rather fond of chasing her tail." This seemed a very flexible thing for an aeroplane to do. A cat, perhaps; but an aeroplane. . . . He must have seen my puzzled expression. "When you put on rudder to turn, she's supposed to take up the correct bank herself—that's what they mean by ' inherently stable.' Don't you believe it. Get her banked correctly on your bubble, otherwise you'll turn flat and chase your tail—spin, I mean."

Spin! I suppose nobody reading this to-day who is at all familiar with flying thinks anything of spinning. In 1916, to spin was a highly dangerous manœuvre. A few experts did it. Rumour had it that once in a spin you could never get out again. Some machines would spin easier to the left than to the right; but a spin in either direction was liable to end fatally. The expression "in a flat spin," invented in those days, denoted that whoever was in it had reached the absolute limit of anger, nerves, fright, or whatever it might be. So spinning was the one thing the young pilot fought shy of, the one of two things he hoped he might never do—the other was, catch fire in the air. Now that I have done both, I assure you there is no comparison. Spinning is a mild stunt. It makes you a bit giddy if you go on long enough. It's a useful way of shamming dead when a Hun is on your tail; but fire in the air! That's a holy terror!

So at Gosport and then at St Omer I had a certain respect for the old 2c. She might " chase her tail." Patrick cured me of that in one or two games of follow-my-leader. Actually she was as docile and dull as a motor-bus—and about as heavy to handle—and it was very difficult to get her to spin at all. So I flew and flew the old 2c. I learned to make three-point landings five times out of six. I learned to make vertical turns, keeping my nose on the horizon and not losing height. I learned to do a " split-arse " spiral—coming down in a tight corkscrew, and being careful not to look at the ground, which made you giddy. I learned—or rather I got up my nerve, for there was nothing to learn—to stall : that is, to pull the machine up on her tail and cut the engine off and wait there till she lost flying speed and fell out of it. This was the way to start a spin ; but if you kept your controls central she didn't do it. At last I made up my mind to loop.

" I'm going to loop," I said to Patrick, much as a man might announce he was going over Niagara in a bath-tub.

" Oh ! " he said, quite unconcerned. He was busy with a compass. I walked away, rather huffed. He might encourage · a chap. Apparently he woke up to the fact that something more was expected of him. He called after me : " Hey ! Plenty of speed ! Put her well up to a hundred ! And remember, when you cut off your engine at the top you'll need some right rudder to counteract the torque. Otherwise you'll fall out of it sideways. If you come out square the first time, I'll stand you a drink—a couple of drinks," he added, as an afterthought.

I took off and climbed to three thousand. Then

I put the nose down. How she screamed, diving with the engine full out! Eighty-five, ninety, ninety-five. . . . She was screaming and vibrating like hell. I lost my nerve. I wouldn't try it. I hadn't intended to do it. I was only seeing what it felt like to go fast with the engine on. After all, I hadn't got to do the beastly stunt. It was no earthly use, anyway. I'd do it to-morrow, when the machine had been trued up and didn't vibrate so. I'd . . . But, of course, old Pat would be watching. How could I come down and face him? "Lost your nerve?" he would inquire, and I should go down, right bang to the bottom, in his estimation. Well . . . I'd have another try. Throttle full open. Eighty-five, ninety, ninety-five. . . . She's not shaking quite so much . . . a hundred . . . a hundred and five. . . . Now! I pulled back the stick. The horizon disappeared. Everything was sky. Up and up I went. I must be over now, I thought. But there was nothing. I hung on to the stick, looking upwards. At last, there, right above me, was the rim of the horizon! I was over! Engine off! The 2c came shooting down on the dive, I kept the stick back, and gradually the speed fell off. I'd done it! And what's more, I'd remembered the rudder and come out straight—or I thought I had. Pat would owe me a drink—a couple of drinks. By this time I was down to a thousand. I opened the throttle to get the right side of the aerodrome to come in. Nothing happened. I shut it and opened it again. Not a splutter. Plenty of pressure in the tank. Try the gravity. Quick, switch over! No good. Not a cough. This means a forced landing. I must have oiled the plugs up at the top

43

of the loop. Damn! I can't get back to the aerodrome. Where's the wind? I've only got five hundred feet. This ploughed field will have to do. This *would* happen just when I've looped. Hell! Here goes! And I settled her down into the furrows of the plough without accident. My first loop and my first forced landing all in one. I sat there in the middle of the field, cooling off, for both those things had required the limit of my skill and nerve at that time. Soon a tender came down the road. In it were Patrick and a couple of mechanics. I was out of the machine, examining the engine.

"What's the matter?" shouted Pat as he came up.

"She cut out, after the loop. I must have oiled the plugs up."

"Funny!" He walked round to the cockpit. "Did you switch off on the top of that loop? It was a good one, by the way."

The horrible truth dawned on me. "Why, yes—I suppose I did. You told me to."

"I said, cut your engine off. With the throttle, not the switch, you lunatic. You never switched on again, did you?" He laughed. "You're a damn fine pilot! Contact!" The mechanic had been spinning the prop. Now he gave a sharp jerk and away she went. "Fancy fetching me all the way out here for that! You forfeit those drinks. They're on you, my boy. Jump up, I'll flip you back." We popped over the hill and down on to the aerodrome.

"Actually, you didn't do so badly," said Pat, as we walked into the bar. "You didn't smash the machine up, and that's more than a lot of chaps could say on their first forced landing. And the loop was a beauty. I'll stand you a gin, after all."

*

Follow-my-leader with Patrick gave me my first taste of aerial fighting, getting your nose and your guns on the enemy's tail and sitting there till you brought him down. It was a year later before I actually did any; but, from the first, the light fast single-seater scout was my ambition. To be alone, to have your life in your own hands, to use your own skill, single-handed, against the enemy. It was like the lists of the Middle Ages, the only sphere in modern warfare where a man saw his adversary and faced him in mortal combat, the only sphere where there was still chivalry and honour. If you won, it was your own bravery and skill; if you lost, it was because you had met a better man.

You did not sit in a muddy trench while some one who had no personal enmity against you loosed off a gun, five miles away, and blew you to smithereens —and did not know he had done it! That was not fighting; it was murder. Senseless, brutal, ignoble. We were spared that.

As long as man has limbs and passions he will fight. Sport, after all, is only sublimated fighting, and in such fighting, if you don't "love" your enemy in the conventional sense of the term, you honour and respect him. Besides, there is, as everybody who has fought knows, a strong magnetic attraction between two men who are

45

matched against one another. I have felt this magnetism, engaging an enemy scout three miles above the earth. I have wheeled and circled, watching how he flew, taking in the power and speed of his machine, seen him, fifty yards away, eyeing me, calculating, watching for an opening, each of us wary, keyed up to the last pitch of skill and endeavour. And if at last he went down, a falling rocket of smoke and flame, what a glorious and heroic death! What a brave man! It might just as well have been me. For what have I been spared? To die, diseased, in a bed! Sometimes it seems a pity.

So, if the world must fight to settle its differences, back to Hector and Achilles! Back to the lists! Let the enemy match a squadron of fighters against ours. And let the world look on! It is not as fanciful as you suppose. We may yet live to see it over London.

My secret longing, then, was for a scout, and at St Omer it fixed on the Bristol Bullet, a tiny machine, much too small for my long legs. Only a few of these machines were made. They were given to the best pilots in 2c squadrons to do a bit of fighting on the side—for at that time special scout squadrons had not been organized. I asked if I could take up the Bullet. It was foolish, for the dashboard fouled my knees, and I could hardly use the rudder. Besides, she was light as a feather on all controls, and before I got used to them I came down on a gusty day, slipped out of the wind through being slow on the rudder, bounced, broke a Vee-piece on the undercarriage, and crunch! over she went on her back. I clambered out from my first

crash feeling a fool, furious with myself. But
not so furious as all the other pilots were with me,
for the Bullet was the only scout at St Omer. They
had enjoyed taking her up, and now I had written
her off. " You'd better stick to the 2c," they said,
" and not try to run before you can crawl." So
back I went, with my tail between my legs.

★

But not for long. There was a machine standing
quietly in a corner of the hangars which had been
pointed out to me casually, as one points to a rattle-
snake at the Zoo and passes on to more congenial
creatures, as a Morane. I had heard of it, of course.
It was one of the recognized death-traps which
pilots in training prayed they might never have to
fly. And the chances were in their favour, for only
two squadrons in the Force flew them : No. 1 and
No. 3. Pilots trained on ordinary Avros and 2c's,
when turned loose on Moranes killed themselves
with alarming rapidity. The authorities decided
that this must stop. Dead pilots and smashed-up
machines: it was costly and wasteful, and bad for
the morale of the squadrons concerned. Result :
an old Morane was sent to the Depot to train
pilots on. But as the machine was not fitted with
dual control, even when it was used for training,
it was difficult to see what advantage was gained,
beyond the fact that it may have been more convenient to kill a pilot at the base than at the
front. On that point the pilots were presumably
indifferent.

Of course you have already guessed the sequel.

One morning the machine was wheeled out and Patrick called me over: "Come on! You'd better learn to fly the Parasol." I suppose I didn't jump with joy, for he went on: "It's not a bad kite really. Morane squadrons have to have the pick of the pilots. That's why I chose you." I was always susceptible to compliment; but this was a back-handed one with a vengeance. "Have a look over her. I'll run up the engine." Well, there was nothing else for it. I had a look over her, and the more I saw of her the less I liked her. It was certainly not love at first sight, nor even at second or third sight; but I did come to love the Morane as I loved no other aeroplane. She carried me right through the Somme battle. I did all my best work on her. I got my M.C. and my mentions in despatches for that work. I flew her for over three hundred hours, and never during all that time did I have a crash of any kind, and only one case of engine failure. Good old Parasol!

But I had better describe her to you, for, like the Pterodactyl, the type is extinct now. Moranes were French machines. You could see that as soon as you looked at one. It was something in the design, difficult to put a finger on. Rakish, rather stylish, and yet somehow different—in the way that a Bugatti or a Delage is different. There were three types: a little single-seater scout, the Monocoq, a devil to fly (it landed at about seventy); the Biplane, a venomous-looking brute of a two-seater, like a dragon-fly, with a long thin body and two square-cut wings well forward (it was sometimes mistaken for and attacked as a Hun); and the Parasol.

The Parasol was the queerest-looking of the lot. She was a two-seater monoplane. The wing was carried above the body, well above it—hence the nickname—and you sat under the wing in the fattish circular fuselage, which looked rather like the stump of a good cigar. She was a tractor, of course, and carried a rotary engine in the red-hot end of the stump. The rotary was an 80-h.p. Le Rhône. It was a beauty, the sweetest-running rotary ever built. It throttled down and ticked over like a water-cooled stationary, and was as smooth as silk over its whole range. At full out it had a happy note like a homing bee. Also it was as reliable as a sewing-machine.

None of the Moranes had any tail plane. Most aeroplanes (this for the uninitiated) have a fixed tail plane with a movable flap on the back of it—the elevator. So, if you take your hand off the elevator control (the stick), the elevator just remains where it is, streaming out behind the tail plane, and if the machine is adjusted correctly it will fly on level, hands off. But the Morane contented itself with the elevator, the movable flap, only. And this elevator was a balanced elevator—that is, it carried some of its surface ahead of its fulcrum. The technicalities really don't matter : the result was that the elevator was as sensitive as a gold balance ; the least movement stood you on your head or on your tail. You couldn't leave the machine to its own devices for a moment ; you had to fly it every second you were in the air. The other controls, just to make it more difficult, were practically non-existent. There was a rudder, too small to get you round quickly, and ailerons which were so inefficient that sometimes, if you got a bump under one wing taking off, it was literally seconds before you could get the machine on an even keel again. As a final complication, the stick, which in any respectable aeroplane stands up straight and at a comfortable height to get hold of, was short. It did not come above the knees and had a grip on top, like half a shooting stick, into which you slipped your hand. If you were foolish enough to let go of this in the air, the stick fell forward with a crack against the tank and the machine went straight into a nose-dive. Never, even when you knew the machine inside out, could you relax for a second.

I think I have said enough for the reader, whether he knows anything about flying or not, to realize that the Morane really was a death-trap, thoroughly dangerous to fly, needing the greatest care and skill, the lightest hands, and the most accurate judgment to land. After nineteen hours solo, mostly on 2c's and Shorthorns, I did not relish the job. Subsequently I flew every machine used by the Air Force during the war. They were all child's play after the Morane.

★

Patrick had run up the engine, found it O.K. and called me to climb up behind him. " I'll give you a flip round," he said. " You can get the feel of her, and see how the engine controls work." I swung up into the cockpit beneath the plane. It was cosy once you were inside. You sat well down into the body, the seats were comfortable, there was plenty of room. The passenger's seat was immediately behind the pilot: he had to sit with his knees open to keep clear of the curved back of the pilot's seat. It was the first time I had ever been in a monoplane, and I had a sense of insecurity in the air at first, through having no plane beneath me. It was funny to look down on space. But this was actually the Parasol's strongest point, for the uninterrupted view below made it perfect for ground observation. It was used for spotting for the Artillery and for Contact Patrol (of which more anon), and throughout the war I never flew a machine to equal it for this. Above you could see nothing.

We took off and climbed. I leant over the back of Patrick's seat and watched him; but you can't tell what an aeroplane is like to fly until you fly it. In the hands of another man, particularly if he is expert, everything looks easy. But I noticed that he treated it with respect. He didn't throw it all over the sky. It climbed pretty well, flew level at about seventy-five; but as soon as you throttled down, it fell like a brick out of the sky, floated in a peculiar way before landing, and bounced like the devil if you didn't sit it down just right. Patrick, of course, sat it down perfectly. He got out, and we changed places.

"Remember," he said, "watch your elevator. As soon as you open up, push the stick forward; the tail will lift at once, and then you can ease her off."

Easier said than done, for when I obeyed these instructions I found the tail shot up over my head in a flash; and when I jerked back the stick in a panic, it slumped down on to the ground with a heavy crunch. I pushed the stick forward again. Up went the tail. I pulled it back. Down it came. By this time I had flying speed, so the last pull back did not bring the tail down on to the ground with a thud, it lifted the machine into the air, pretty well stalling it. So I staggered bucketing across the aerodrome, giving a passable imitation of a scenic railway. Oh, that balanced elevator!

" Don't turn under five hundred feet," said Patrick. I was up to a thousand before I had got the hang of the elevator. But when I got to the squadron I found that one of the unwritten orders. No pilot, however experienced, however elated, would take any liberties with a Parasol under five hundred. I flew on. Once the breathless excitement of getting off was over, I began to feel easier. The machine was snug and warm. It seemed fairly normal on turns. I wandered about for a bit, tried the gliding angle, played with the engine controls, and came down to land.

I don't believe the Schneider Trophy racer is any more difficult to land than a Parasol was. There was just one place, and one only, in the float, where the stick had to be firmly and quickly drawn back to your stomach. If you missed that point you bounced, the undercarriage was weak, the Vee-pieces buckled, and over you went. In a high wind, even when you were down, a gust would lift the Parasol right off the ground again and blow it over like a toy. To prevent this, the mechanics used to come running out on to the aerodrome, judge where you would land, and rush to catch hold of the lift wires under the wings, where they hung on, swinging, one on each wing-tip, while you taxied in.

However, I was lucky that day, for I got down with only a couple of bounces. The Vee-pieces held. I taxied in.

*

Great excitement in the Depot! A Fokker had been captured undamaged. Early in 1916 the Fokker was the menace of the R.F.C. Hearsay and a few lucky encounters had made the machine respected, not to say dreaded, by the slow, unwieldy machines then used by us for Artillery Observation and Offensive Patrols. A sort of mystery surrounded the Fokker. Nobody knew whether it had a rotary or a stationary engine. Few having been attacked by it had come back to tell the tale; but one pilot had seen the long black block of the cylinder heads nestling along the cowling: it must have a stationary engine. To-day I cannot see why this should have been so important to us. At the time it was. We wanted, I suppose, to have a specification of that machine. Rumour credited it with the most fantastic performance! It could outclimb, outpace, and outmanœuvre anything in the R.F.C. You were as good as dead if you as much as saw one . . . and so on. In short, our morale wanted bucking up.

All we knew was that it was an evil-looking monoplane scout, connected with the already famous name of Richthofen. So anxious were Headquarters to have some details of the machine that one 2c pilot, just about to be attacked, deliberately let the machine come within range, took out his Kodak and made a snapshot of it. I have always regarded this as one of the minor heroisms of the war. Unfortunately the snap was out of focus.

53

And now a Fokker had delivered itself into British hands! An enemy ferry pilot, bringing a new machine from the base in Germany, had flown right over the lines without knowing it, and made a perfect landing on an Allied aerodrome to ask where he was! He was told. To balance it up, I must record that about the same time a British ferry pilot, taking the latest FE 2b to France, did exactly the same thing and landed perfectly in Germany. So we were quits.

It turned out that the Fokker had a rotary engine (the long black block of cylinder heads was the air-cooling barrel of the machine gun). Otherwise it was perfectly orthodox, and there remained only to put it up against a British scout to judge its performance. The Morane Bullet was chosen, and the two machines were run out on the aerodrome, side by side. All the General Staff assembled to watch the tests. Both machines took off together, and it was immediately clear that the Morane was all over the Fokker. It climbed quicker, it was faster on the level, and when the two machines began a mock fight over the aerodrome, the Morane had everything its own way. A cheer went up from the ground. The bogey was laid. A description of the machine, its size, power, capabilities, was circulated at once to every one in the Corps. It did a great deal to raise the morale and prepare the way for the Allied air supremacy later that year.

*

After the tests were over, four of us were sent up to have a go at the Fokker—a Morane Biplane, the

Parasol, the Nieuport (another excellent French scout), and the 2c. All of them gave quite a good account of themselves except the 2c, which, in performance, was nowhere. Besides, I was flying it, and when experienced pilots were really on their mettle I was left a long way behind. Soon all the others came down and landed; but as my engine was running beautifully, and it was a lovely evening, I decided to see the sunset from ten thousand feet.

At five thousand over the aerodrome I turned north. The flat country stretched to the four horizons. To say it looked like a map was a cliché. There was a resemblance, of course, as between sitter and portrait; but the real thing had a bewildering amount of extra detail, a wealth of soft colour, of light and shade, that made it, at first, difficult to reconcile with its printed counterpart. Main roads, so importantly marked in red, turned out to be grey, unobtrusive, and hard to distinguish from other roads. Railways were not clear black lines, but winding threads, even less well defined than the roads. Woods were not patches of green, except in high summer; they were dark browns and blacks, merging, sometimes imperceptibly, into the ploughed fields which surrounded them. Then there were cloud shadows, darkening patches of landscape and throwing others into high relief; ground mist, blurring the horizon and sometimes closing in around you to a few miles, or even a few hundred yards, an impalpable wall of vapour, mysteriously receding as you advanced. It was not always easy to find your way, or read your map. You could get lost in the air as easily as in a forest, and you were just as likely to fly in circles as walk in them on the ground. True, you had a compass to give you a general sense of direction; but compasses in those days, owing to the vibration of the machine, had a maddening habit of spinning like tops. Once lost, there was a tendency to panic. One or two sharp turns to try to pick up a landmark, and you lost all sense of direction. North, south, east, or west might be anywhere. The sharp turns set the compass spinning. Within a minute you grew quite bewildered. There was only one thing to do: keep your head, choose a distant landmark and fly on it, give your compass time to settle, and then try to pick up unmistakable landmarks—lakes, towns, or important railway junctions—and fit them to your map. It was easier high up than low down; but, whatever the height, the pilot had to have a sense of scale. Ten miles on the map looked very different in reality at a thousand or ten thousand feet, so you had to take your height into consideration when locating your position. It needed experience, and it was the lack of this experience that led pilots to do apparently imbecile things like flying machines across the lines and landing them in Germany. The final resort, of course, was to land and ask where you were; but that was a terrible confession of incompetence, except in foul weather —besides, you might be told: Berlin!

But on this particular evening no such danger threatened the novice with his twenty hours of flying. There to the north was the coastline— unmistakable landmark—Boulogne, Calais, Dunkerque. Beneath were the straight French roads, with their avenues of poplars. Calais itself nestled under the right wing-tip, compact and cosy, one tall church spire and ten thousand chimneys, breathing a vague bluish vapour which hung pensive in the sky. Beyond the harbour was the Leave Boat, starting for England: two white furrows and a penn'orth of smoke. An escort of destroyers flanked her; and beyond the steel-grey sea, almost hidden in the evening haze, was the outline of the Dover cliffs, white beyond the water. The Dover cliffs! England! Home!

I turned south towards Boulogne, climbing, always climbing. Already I was two miles above the earth, a tiny lonely speck in the vast rotunda of the evening sky. The sun was sinking solemnly in a black Atlantic cloud-belt. To the east, night crept up: a lofty shade drawn steadily over the warring earth. The earth, so far below! A patchwork of fields, browns and greys, here and there dappled with the green of spring woods, intersecting ribbons of straight roads, minute houses, invisible men. . . . Men! Standing, walking, talking, fighting there beneath me! I saw them for the first time with detachment, dispassionately: a strange, pitiable, crawling race, to us who strode the sky. Why, God might take the air and come within a mile of earth and never know there were such things as men. Vain the heroic gesture, puny the great thought! Poor little maggoty men!

The upper rim of the circle of fire dipped finally behind the clouds, and a bunch of rays, held as it were in some invisible quiver, shot a beam high into the arc of heaven, where it turned a wraith of cirrus cloud to marvellous gold. The lofty shade had covered the visible earth, and beauty

lingered only in the sky. It turned colder. . . .
I remembered suddenly the warmth of the Mess fire
and the faces of friends. It would be good to be
down again. I turned towards home and throttled
down. The engine roar died. The wind sang
gently in the wires. A long steady glide carried
me inland. Now that the engine was off and the
warm air did not blow through the cockpit, I grew
chilly and beat my hands on my thighs. It was
cold at ten thousand in March. I opened up the
engine again to feel its warmth. Slowly the aerodrome rose up through the gauzy swathes of mist
spun by the invisible hands of twilight. Above,
the cirrus turned copper, faded to pink and mauve,
and at last drifted grey and shroudlike in the vast
arena of the darkening heaven. I must hurry. It
would be night before I was down. Over the sheds
at four thousand I went into a vertical bank and
rushed earthwards in a tight spiral. At a thousand
I pulled out, feeling a bit sick, burst my engine
to make sure of the plugs, and then cautiously felt
my way in over the hangars and touched with that
gentle easy rumble which means a perfect landing,
turned, and taxied in.

★

I walked down to the Mess and was greeted by
the O.C.
   " Hullo, you're down at last. Orders are just
through that we're to send you to No. 9 Squadron—2c's."
   " But . . . I was to be a Morane pilot . . ."
   " Well, if you ask me, you're well out of that.

They're too damn dangerous. Nos. 1 and 3 have killed a hell of a lot of pilots lately."

" When am I to go? "

" Right away. They want you urgently. I think you'll find there's a train for Amiens to-night. Better slip along and see the Adjutant. Get your batman to pack your kit."

A squadron at last! But, 2c's. . . . That meant artillery observation, dawdling up and down the lines while Archie [1] took pot shots at you; that meant photography; that meant beastly long reconnaissances, with Fokkers buzzing about on your tail. The obscure future date on which I should at last go into action had always been remote in my mind, imperfectly realized, even, I suspect, deliberately shut out. Now, suddenly, with a brief order, it had become startlingly clear and close at hand. For months after, with a few brief moments of respite, I was to live hypnotized not so much by the dread of death—for death, like the sun, is a thing you cannot look at steadily for long—as by the menace of the unforeseen. Friends, Mess companions, would go out on patrol and never come back. Archie, hostile aircraft, and machine-gun fire from the ground all took their toll. As the months went by it seemed only a matter of time until your turn came. You sat down to dinner faced by the empty chairs of men you had laughed and joked with at lunch. They were gone. The next day new men would laugh and joke from those chairs. Some might be lucky and stick it for a bit, some chairs would be empty again very soon. And so it would go on. And always, miraculously, you

[1] The common slang for an Anti-Aircraft Battery.

were still there. Until to-morrow. . . . In such an atmosphere you grew fatalistic, and as time went by and left you unscathed, like a batsman who has played himself in, you began to take liberties with the bowling. You took unnecessary risks, you volunteered for dangerous jobs, you provoked enemy aircraft to attack you. You were invulnerable: nothing could touch you. Then, when one of the old hands, as seemingly invulnerable as yourself, went West, you suddenly got cold feet. It wasn't possible to be sure—even of yourself. At this stage it required most courage to go on—a sort of plodding fatalism, a determination, a cold-blooded effort of will. And always alone! No friends right and left, no crowd morale. The lot of the P.B.I.[1] was hopeless enough; but each in his extremity had at least some one at hand, some one to cheer and to succour.

Besides, we were always at the mercy of the fragility of the machine and the unreliability of the engine. One chance bullet from the ground might cut a thin wire, put the machine out of control, and send us, perfectly whole, plunging to a crash we were powerless to prevent. So, in the later stages, we had to win victories over ourselves long before we won any over the enemy, for it was not impossible to turn back, to tell a lie—not always easy to verify— of faulty engine, bad visibility, jammed guns, and so stave off the inevitable for one day more. We came in for some admiration at that time, just because we were pilots, just because we flew. But flying is pleasurable enough, in short doses, and was even in those days reasonably safe. Truth-

[1] P.B.I.: Poor bloody infantry.

fully, there was little admirable in that. But to fly on a straight line, taking photos of the enemy trenches, an easy Archie target, within range of the ground machine guns, bumped by the eddies of passing shells and pestered by enemy scouts, that required nerve. And it would have to be done twice a day, day after day, until you were hit or went home. Small wonder if, under this strain, pilots lived a wild life and wined and womanized to excess. Stanhope in *Journey's End* summarizes it perfectly : " To forget, you bloody little fool, to forget. Do you think there's no limit to what a man can bear? "

The squadron tender met me at Amiens. The driver loaded up my kit. We picked up three other pilots in the Square. They had dined well, and came bundling into the tender with much laughter and began singing songs at the top of their voices. As the tender bumped and slithered over the pavé they began to sober up a bit, found out who I was, and looked me over like a new boy at school, answering all my questions about work, machines, casualties, with airy unconcern. It was only later I found out that when you went on a "blind" to Amiens, talk about the job was taboo. You had come in specifically to forget it. Arrived in the tumble-down village (smell of mud and manure), they took me over to the Mess to report to the O.C., who gave me a drink while I told him all about the Fokker, the details of which had not yet reached the squadron. The news was good, and as one of their pilots had been shot down by a Fokker two days previously they were glad of it, and we had another round of drinks. Then I was given a billet at a farm along the muddy street: a musty-smelling room with the windows hermetically sealed and dry rot in the big feather bedstead. I lay for a little before sleeping, wondering about it all. It seemed curious that my training should land me in a stuffy little room in some obscure village in France, and that from here my personal war should begin.

★

Next morning I was allotted a machine and given my orders. I was to put in time—the old story. My Flight-Commander was scandalized at my lack of experience. Twenty hours, the total my logbook showed, was no good to him. I was to take my machine and fly it all day. I was to get the lie of the land, go up with a map and locate all the landmarks, so that I could find my way back from the lines in any weather, like a homing pigeon. I was particularly to familiarize myself with the advance landing-ground, so that I could get down safely if the engine should be hit or I should be wounded on patrol. And so on.

So I set off. I browsed round the countryside, visited the FE squadron I had come out with, had my first look at the lines. The next day I went over them at ten thousand, and on my way back got completely lost. I have already explained the difficulties of map-reading. French maps were different from the English ones I was used to. They were nothing like so accurate, and the nomenclature put me off. Still, how I could have missed Amiens with its great cathedral when I was within twenty miles of it at ten thousand feet I don't know. But I did;

and at last resorted to the amateur's refuge—to come down and ask where I was.

So my training went on. Practice at formation flying, locating gun emplacements in a given map square co-ordination, practice at reconnaissance formation, at lamp signalling, at forced landings, and later, several trips with gunnery officers who came down from their batteries and were taken up to see their targets from the air.

*

After ten hours of this came my first real job—to photograph the enemy second-line trenches. The lines, from the air, had none of the significance they had from the ground, mainly because all contours were non-existent. The local undulations, valleys, ravines, ditches, hillsides, which gave advantage to one side or the other, were flattened out. All you saw was two more or less parallel sets of trenches, clearer in some places than in others according to the colour of the earth thrown up in making them. These faced each other across the barren strip of No-Man's-Land, and behind them started a complicated network of communication trenches, second-line trenches, more communication trenches, and then the third-line trenches. The network was more complex at the important positions along the line; but everywhere it was irregular, following the lie of the ground, opening up to a wide mesh at one place, closing up, compact and formidable, at another. As positions were consolidated more trenches were dug, and later, when I came to know my own section of the line as well as the palm of my hand, I could tell at a glance what fresh digging had been done since my last patrol.

The surveying of the German line was difficult from the ground. You couldn't very well walk about with a theodolite and a chain in full view of the enemy, so the making of maps was largely a matter of aerial photography. In the spring of 1916, with the big offensive on the Somme preparing, the accuracy of these maps was of the greatest importance. So our job that day was to go over the front line at 7500 feet and fly all along the enemy second-line trenches from Montauban, round the Fricourt salient and up to Boisselle, photographing as we went.

If there was ever an aeroplane unsuited for active service, it was the BE 2c. The pilot sat slightly aft of the main planes and had a fair view above and below, except where the lower main plane obscured the ground forward ; but the observer, who sat in front of him, could see practically nothing, for he was wedged under the small centre section, with a plane above, another below, and bracing wires all round. He carried a gun for defence purposes ; but he could not fire it forward, because of the propeller. Backwards, the centre-section struts, wires, and the tail plane cramped his style. In all modern machines the positions are reversed ; the pilot sits in front, leaving the observer a good field of fire aft and using his own guns, which can be fired through the propeller, forward. But in 1916 the synchronized gear enabling a machine gun to be fired through the whirling propeller and still miss the blades had not been perfected.

The observer could not operate the camera from his seat because of the plane directly below him, so it was clamped on outside the fuselage, beside the pilot; a big, square, shiny mahogany box with a handle on top to change the plates (yes, plates!). To make an exposure you pulled a ring on the end of a cord. To sight it, you leaned over the side and looked through a ball and cross-wire finder. The pilot, then, had to fly the machine with his left hand, get over the spot on the ground he wanted to photograph—not so easy as you might think—put his arm out into the seventy-mile-an-hour wind, and push the camera handle back and forward to change the plates, pulling the string between each operation. Photography in 1916 was somewhat amateurish.

So I set out on that sunny afternoon, with a sergeant-gunner in the front seat, and climbed up towards the lines. As I approached them, I made out the place where we were to start on the ground, comparing it with the map. Two miles the other side of the front line didn't look far on paper; but it seemed a devil of a way when you had to fly vertically over the spot. The sergeant knelt on his seat, placed a drum on the Lewis gun, and faced round over the tail, keeping a wary eye open for Fokkers. But the sky was deserted, the line quiet. Jerry was having a day off. I turned the machine round to start on my steady course above the trenches, when two little puffs of grey smoke appeared a hundred feet below us, on the left. The sergeant pointed and smiled: "Archie!" Then three others appeared closer, at our own height. It was funny the way the balls of smoke appeared magically in the empty air, and were followed a moment later by a little flat report. If they didn't range us any better than that they were not very formidable, I thought, and began to operate the camera handle.

There are times in life when the faculties seem to be keyed up to superhuman tension. You are not necessarily doing anything; but you are in a state of awareness, of tremendous alertness, ready to act instantaneously should the need arise. Outwardly, that day, I was calm, busy keeping the trenches in the camera sight, manipulating the handle, pulling the string; but inside my heart was pounding and my nerves straining, waiting for something, I did not know what, to happen. It was my first job. I was under fire for the first time. Would Archie get the range? Would the dreaded Fokker appear? Would the engine give out? It was the fear of the unforeseen, the inescapable, the imminent hand of death which might, from moment to moment, be ruthlessly laid upon me. I realized, not then, but later, why pilots cracked up, why they lost their nerve and had to go home. Nobody could stand the strain indefinitely, ultimately it reduced you to a dithering state, near to imbecility. For always you had to fight it down, you had to go out and do the job, you could never admit it, never say frankly: " I am afraid. I can't face it any more." For cowardice, because, I suppose, it is the most common human emotion, is the most despised. And you did gain victories over yourself. You won and won and won again, and always there was another to be won on the morrow. They sent you home to rest, and you put it in the background

66

of your mind; but it was not like a bodily fatigue from which you could completely recover, it was a sort of damage to the essential tissue of your being. You might have a greater will-power, greater stamina to fight down your failing; but a thorough-bred that has been lashed will rear at the sight of the whip, and never, once you had been through it, could you be quite the same again.

I went on pulling the string and changing the plates when, out of the corner of my eye, I saw something black ahead of the machine. I looked up quickly: there was nothing there. I blinked. Surely, if my eyes were worth anything, there had been something . . . Yes! There it was again! This time I focussed. It was a howitzer shell, one of our own shells, slowing up as it reached the top of its trajectory, turning slowly over and over, like an ambling porpoise, and then plunging down to burst. Guns fire shells in a flat trajectory; howitzers fling them high, like a lobbed tennis ball. It follows that, if you happen to be at the right height, you catch the shell just as it hovers at its peak point. If you are quick-sighted you can then follow its course down to the ground. I watched the thing fascinated. Damn it, they weren't missing the machine by much, I thought; but I was left little time to consider it, for suddenly there was a sharp tearing sound like a close crack of thunder, and the machine was flung upwards by the force of the ex-plosion of an Archie burst right underneath us. A split second later, and it would have been a direct hit. A long tear appeared in the fabric of the plane where a piece of shrapnel had gone through. There was a momentary smell of acrid smoke.

" Ess ! Ess ! " shouted the sergeant. " They've ranged us ! " I flung the machine over and flew west, then turned again, and again, and again. . . . The Archie bursts were distant now. We had thrown them off.

" How many more ? " shouted the sergeant, with a jerk of his head to the camera box.

" Two."

Flying on a steady course is the surest way to get caught by Archie, and we had been, right enough. If we were quick we might snatch the other two photos and get away before he ranged us again. I turned back over the spot, pulled the string and flew on to make the last exposure, when the sergeant suddenly stiffened in his seat, cocked his gun, and pointed : " Fokker ! "

I turned in my seat and saw the thin line of the monoplane coming down on our tail. He had seen the Archie bursts, no doubt, had a look round to see if we were escorted, and, finding it all clear, was coming down for a sitter.

I got the last photo as he opened fire. The distant chatter of his gun was hardly audible above the engine roar. It didn't seem to be directed at us. He was, I know now, an inexperienced pilot, he should have held his fire. We replied with a chatter that deafened me, the muzzle of the Lewis gun right above my head. The Fokker hesitated, pulled over for a moment, and then turned at us again. The sergeant pulled his trigger. Nothing happened. " Jammed ! Jammed ! " he shouted. He pulled frantically at the gun, while the stuttering Fokker came up. I put the old 2c right over to turn under him. As I did so, there was a sharp crack, and the little wind-screen a foot in front of my face showed a hole with a spider's web in the glass round it.

It was Triplex: no splinters; but another foot behind would have put that bullet through my head —which was not Triplex. A narrow shave. Instinctively I stood the machine on its head and dived for home. At that moment, as if to cap it all, the engine set up a fearful racket. The whole machine felt as if it would fall to pieces.

" Switch off! Switch off! " yelled the sergeant. " The engine's hit."

I obeyed, still diving, turning sharply as I did so to offer a more difficult target to the Fokker. But, luckily for us, he decided not to pursue. In those days the Huns did not adventure much beyond their own side of the lines, and now we were back over ours.

We saw him zoom away again. He had us at his mercy, had he known. There was a moment of wonderful relief. We laughed. It had all happened in much less time than it takes to tell, and we were still alive, safe!

" Make for the advance landing-ground," shouted the sergeant. He was furious with the gun jamming, jumpy at our narrow shave, and, anyway, didn't relish his job with inexperienced pilots like me, just out from home.

I spotted the advance landing-ground—thank heaven I had been down on it previously—and circled to make my landing. It would have been a fine thing, I thought, if that had happened a few miles farther over and I had been forced down in Hunland on my first patrol. I skimmed over the telegraph poles, got down without mishap, and jumped out to examine the machine.

The sergeant was apostrophizing the gun: " These bloody double drums ! " he said. " Always jamming ! He had us sitting, God dammit ! "

I pulled over the prop. There was a hollow rattle from the inside. Something serious, a big end gone, or a smashed connecting-rod, probably. Anyway, they would have to send out another engine. . . . But we were down ! Here was the ground under my feet ; the sky above, serene, impersonal ; the machine solid beneath my touch, swaying slightly in the wind. All that remained to bear witness of our escape was the rattle of the engine, the tear in the plane, the smashed windscreen, and the tiny perforations of the bullet holes in the body, two down behind my seat, more in the tail. The sergeant came up.

" Are you all right, sir ? "

" Fine ! And you ? "

" Quite, thank you, sir. I thought he'd got us with that second burst. Always turn, sir, as soon as a machine attacks. It can't get its sights on you so easy. And it has to allow for the traverse. . . . If you'll phone the squadron, sir, and order out a tender and a repair squad, I'll dismount the camera and get a guard put over the machine. You got all the photos, didn't you, sir ? "

" Yes. Twenty-two in all."

" The Corps will be pleased. They wanted them badly."

Well, we'd got away with it ! We'd done the job ! If you'd heard me phoning the squadron ten minutes later, you might have imagined from my casual manner I'd been through that sort of thing every day for a month.

*

" Et si par hasard
Tu vois ma tante,
Compliments
De ma part."

Three men were walking back along the dusty moonlit road, with a cold wind on their foreheads, singing this idle song. Their voices sounded small and empty as they echoed back from the copses that flanked the valley and dwindled over the rolling furrows of the fields. They were walking home, all the way from Amiens to the aerodrome, in the small hours of the morning, and they were tired. Sometimes they would sit and rest at the foot of roadside shrines with their iron crosses, their gutted votive candles, and dead offerings of flowers.

" Et si par hasard
Tu vois ma tante,
Compliments
De ma part."

They sang gaily to keep their spirits up. Partly because two of them were proud of this new accomplishment of singing a song in French, partly because . . . Well, it had all begun in a café in Amiens.

A high room, panelled with fly-blown mirrors, studded with marble-topped tables, buzzing with the conversation of French and English officers, alive with waiters, white-aproned, greasy-haired, whisking round drinks on trays.

71

" Garçon ! "

" M'sieu ? "

" Trois fines."

" B'en, m'sieu."

A web of grey smoke leaked upwards from the cigarettes in the hands of this chattering crowd. The atmosphere was rank and heavy. The floor reeked of spilt wine-slops.

Suddenly one of the trio, a little French-Canadian, he who had taught them the song, made a dart towards the door and returned with two girls, triumphant. The five sat down round a large smelly table. Neither of the two Englishmen could speak more than a word or two of French, but this didn't matter much, for the Colonial interpreted and there was always " Vive la France ! " to fall back on, to which the girls responded with " Vive l'Angleterre ! " and this was the cue for another round of drinks.

An hour passed in growing hilarity. It was dinner-time. They all decided to dine in a private room upstairs. The girls were very concerned at the odd number. " We must," they said, " trouver une de nos amies pour ce joli garçon." The young man referred to was embarrassed. The world of cocottes and demi-mondes was new to him. Could one find women as one finds sixpences in the street? Apparently one could. There were whispered conversations outside the door, and at last one of the girls, a heavy brunette, returned. She explained that next door there was a girl who . . .

" Come and see her." They slipped out of the room, and peeping through the half-opened door of the next, saw a pale child with a cloud of light hair sitting very demurely opposite a fat French officer. The officer had his back to the door. From either side of his thick neck the points of his enormous waxed moustaches stuck out. His hair was black and oily, bald on the crown. He gesticulated with his hands, waving a piece of crust in one as he talked. The girl sat with her eyes fixed on him, giving not the slightest sign that she was being watched. The French-Canadian explained : " She is the mistress of an officer who is in Paris, and this fat man is his friend and is looking after her ; but she, as you can see, is very bored, and that is why she would be glad to entertain you after dinner. You must not be seen to speak to her, and, of course, you cannot go out of the café with her. You must follow her—at a distance of fifty metres."

After this somewhat mathematical assignation they returned to finish dinner. Then the party broke up in couples, the men arranging to pick up the tender at half-past ten in the Square. The girl slipped in through the door and whispered to him :
" Suivez-moi, mais soyez discret."
" Follow her," the French-Canadian translated, " but don't make a bloody fool of yourself."
She slipped out again, and the other two couples went off down the stairs, waist-in-waist.
" Allons ! allons ! " cried one. " Nous ferons des petites cochonneries, Albert, tu veux ? "
The roads were dark and deserted. Over the black puddled pavé occasional lorries rumbled by, feeling their way in the glimmer of oil lamps. She clung close to the shadows of the houses. He followed, trying to remember as best he could the maze of twisting, featureless streets through which

he would have to find his way back. At last she
stopped at a doorway and waited for him to come up.
She did not speak, looked furtively up and down
the street, put her fingers to her lips, and turned
her key in the lock. The house smelt warm. The
door clicked behind them. They felt their way up
the dark narrow stairs. She opened a door, went in
and lit two candles on the mantelpiece, and poked
up the fire. He followed her. It was not a large
room, and most of it was taken up by a huge double
bedstead, of the variety with a black shiny frame
surmounted by brass knobs. The coverlet was of
coarse crochet-work. The bed had not been made.
A blue blind was pulled down in the single window.
Lace curtains hung at either side of it, and on the
table stood a fern in a pot and a small tray, on which
lay a coffee-cup with its dregs, a piece of bread and
butter, bitten into, and an empty egg-shell in a blue
cup, flanked by a soiled spoon.

She took off her hat and coat and shook out her
bobbed hair. Like all very young men, he thought
there was some magic about French girls. To him,
Paris was not the beautiful city of elegance and
gaiety, of palaces, fountains, and boulevards where
you sat under the chestnuts, munched *fraises des
bois* floating in cream and sipped a *vin rosé* as
clean and heady and good for the soul as anything this side of paradise. No, Paris in 1916
was to him a sort of gigantic brothel where women
wore nothing but georgette underwear and extra
long silk stockings. In the Mess at the aerodrome
hung half a dozen Kirchner drawings, showing
exquisite creatures in various states of nudity—but
never, of course, quite nude, or all the illusion

would be gone. And she was like one of these drawings. She had the same disobedient hair, the same impudent nose and credulous mouth, the same large, blue-shadowed eyes.

Conversation was going to be difficult. He sat on the bed.

" Quel . . âge . . avez . . vous? " he began.

She dropped on to his knee unconcernedly and put an arm round his neck.

" Dix-huit! Aighteen! " She giggled. " I do not speak English very good."

With a good deal of gesticulation and laughter he managed to understand that she did not have friends to see her usually. She had one particular friend, but he had been away a long time now and she was bored.

" C'est très dangereux, mon petit, but you are a joli garçon, et—voilà! "

She stood up and went to the fire. " Tu veux rester? " she said, as if she were quite prepared to hear that he did not want to, as if she were not sure whether her charms were sufficient to make any one want to stay.

" Yes," he said, and took off his greatcoat. She saw the Wings on his tunic.

" Ah! Tu es pilote! Que j'aime les pilotes! "

" Yes? "

" Yais! Yais! " she imitated, deftly catching a handful of his hair and tugging at it. " Tu es beau, tu sais." She was on his knee again, and under her open blouse the hollow of her young shoulder seemed infinite in its promise.

" Comme il a froid, mon petit sein," she said, by way of advance. " Il sera mieux dans ta main, coco, dis? "

75

He stayed with her for an age, for a moment, for some period incalculable by the dreary turning of clocks, and at last was ready to go.

" Si tu me vois quelque part, tu ne me reconnaîtra pas, hein? Nevaire speak to me. C'est promis? "

" Yes."

" Mon ami, he kill me if he know. I when I see you, I not know you." (And, indeed, when he saw her again, weeks later, in the same café, with a French officer at her side, she looked at him blankly as one looks at an undesirable stranger.)

" Bonne nuit ! "

" Bonne nuit, mon petit," and again the lithe young body pressed close up to him, and the mouth begged favours.

" Good-naight. Bonne chance, mon petit."

He stole out of the house, found his way back through the blackness of the city, and at last came to the Square. There was not a tender to be seen. At the corner he made out his two friends leaning against the railings.

" That bloody driver," said the Flight-Commander, " has bloody well buzzed off. We shall have to walk it."

" Oh Lord ! "

" Let's have a drink first, anyway."

They went into the hotel, waked the sleepy porter, and managed to wheedle three large brandies-and-sodas out of him. Then they set out. Curiously, they were all three silent about the later part of the evening. Too ordinary a thing? Too precious a thing? Too shameful a thing? It would be hard to say.

Beyond the last Estaminet the road stretched away

in the moonlight. The little French-Canadian began to sing :

> " Alouette, gentille alouette. . . ."

When he stopped for lack of breath, they talked about school, home, parents, a humdrum conversation made only to break the sound of their trudging feet on the white interminable road. But when at last they saw the village their spirits rose, and they walked arm-in-arm up the steep short hill to the church, singing gaily :

> " Et si par hasard
> Tu vois ma tante,
> Compliments
> De ma part."

*

Next day came an order for me to return to St Omer. There was a shortage of Morane pilots. True, I had only flown the Morane once, and then nearly crashed it; but apparently that was better than nothing. The order upset me. I was just settling down to the routine, and now I was to be uprooted again. Besides, Moranes killed off all their pilots. I thought I had escaped that, and now . . . Well, I should see Patrick again, anyway. . . .

I flew the Parasol for ten days, and by that time was fairly familiar with all its tricks and could handle it with passable success. Then a piece of luck came my way. No. 60 Squadron, forming at Gosport, needed a Morane for training. I was detailed to take one home. The chance of returning to Blighty was utterly unexpected. I was wildly excited.

I set off and crossed the Channel at seven thousand feet and landed at Folkestone. The weather looked treacherous, but I filled up and pushed on along the coast. As I went east it got steadily worse, and soon I was down to two hundred feet flying along the beach. It started pouring with rain. I feared the engine would pack up, and saw myself coming down and crashing the precious Parasol on one of the groins along the sands. Inland it was all grey and featureless under the pall of rain. I had no map of England; but of course I should recognize Gosport from training days. But in this weather I was lost. Somewhere on the south coast, but where? Where was the nearest aerodrome? Where should I land? Then suddenly, a landing T.[1] Thank heaven! Down I came. It was Shoreham. Next morning the rain cleared. I set off for Gosport, delivered the machine, and was told to go to Farnborough to ferry an FE back to France. I wired my mother to meet me in town, and took the train for London.

★

In the little cottage on the Surrey hills my mother stood with the telegram in her hand. It had been delivered too late. They had not sent it on from the hospital. She had opened the telegram with such a sinking feeling, for in those days a telegram was a dreadful thing; but it did not contain the cold official intimation : Lieutenant So-and-so killed, wounded, or missing. It said that I was

---

[1] A large white T-shaped windvane set up on the ground and swinging freely so that the upright of the T points always into wind.

back in London and wanted to see her, and now she had missed the train. I should have gone back. She would never see me again. . . .

There was the sound of a motor-cycle at the gate. The engine stopped. She looked out. I saw her there as I came up the path. She rushed to the door and came, half running, half stumbling, down towards me.

" Darling, it's you ! How did you get here ? "

" Well "—I was cheerful and unconcerned, affecting not to notice the tears trickling down my British Warm—" I had to pick up a machine at Farnborough ; but she won't be ready for a couple of hours yet, so I got them to lend me a bike. I thought I'd just slip over and see you before I went back."

" You must have lunch."

She fussed over me and spoiled me. I suppose at the back of her mind was a desire to give me something, some bright memory that would kindle her to vivid life whenever after I might think of her. So she put on a garment of gaiety and courage, a shining garment under which I saw her, as I see her still, gallant and unflinching under the months that were to follow and all the emptiness and grief of later years.

Of course I was full of news. It was all so exciting to me. I had no sense of tragedy. It was a marvellous life, a sport, a game ! And I was there, before her, untouched, unscathed ! Of course ! I was invulnerable, we both knew that. But still . . .

" I must go."

" Must you ? I wish I could come down to the

aerodrome and see you off. I've never seen you fly."

" But how would you get back? "

" I suppose I couldn't—and then, I must go over to the hospital."

She helped me on with my coat and patted me on the shoulder.

" Take care of yourself. Come over again as soon as you can."

" You bet I will."

I pushed off the bike. It started and I swung into the saddle, waved over my shoulder as I opened up, turned the corner and was gone down through the woods. She stood there, she told me afterwards, listening to the sound of the engine until it faded and at last the spring air was lonely and silent; stood there, gazing vacantly at the gravel path, in a sort of trance, feeling nothing.

*

The sturdy FE trundled me back from Farnborough to France, and in two hours I was back in the St Omer Mess. Another week putting in time on the Parasol, and, at last, when my flying time had reached fifty hours, orders to proceed to No. 3 Squadron on the Somme.

The straight main road from Amiens to Albert was the artery which nourished the Somme battle. Troops, guns, ammunition, food, and transport columns of all kinds were continually on the move up and down it. Beyond Albert was the redoubt of Fricourt, the head of the salient against which the offensive was to be launched, and so from Albert the roads forked along the arms of the salient, north towards Boisselle, east towards Montauban. Albert, the junction, came in for a good deal of shelling. There wasn't much left of it. The church was in ruins; but the Virgin at the top of the spire was still intact, though tottering, and it was a common superstition that when she fell the war would end.

The squadron aerodrome stood outside the little village of La Houssoye, right on this arterial road, a single straggling street of tumble-down farm buildings, mud-spattered walls, crumbling plaster, and plenty of rank manure to foster the flies. Most of the personnel were quartered up and down the street, and the three Messes (for the squadron did not mess together, but by flights) stood along it. Beyond the village, towards the lines, where the poplars started again to flank the dusty road, was the aerodrome. A row of Besson-neau hangars (canvas-covered, wooden-framed sheds holding four machines each) backed on to a small orchard where the squadron offices stood. The sheds faced the lines, fifteen miles away; but they were hidden from our direct view by the rolling undulations of the ground. It was that wide featureless landscape typical of northern France, miles and miles of cultivated fields, some brown from the plough, others green with the springing crops, receding to the horizon in immense vistas of peaceful fertility—the sort of country that makes you understand why the French love their earth. A mile or two south of the road, and running more or less parallel to it, lay the shallow valley of the Somme. The lovely river wandered, doubling heedlessly upon itself, through copses of poplar and willow, split into diverse channels where water-weeds streamed in long swathes, lazily curling and uncurling along the placid surface, and flooded out over marshes where sedge and bulrushes hid the nests of the wild-duck, the coot, and the heron. It was always there on our right hand as we left the aerodrome for the lines, an infinitely peaceful companion, basking under a haze at midday, cool and mysterious when mists stole out in the dusk. A sort of contrapuntal theme, it played against our short staccato madness an immortal bass, whose notes, serene and timeless, would ring on when this war was a story of no more moment to the world than Alexander's, dead in the dust of Babylon.

Such were the contours of the earth over which I flew from May until November while the battle raged beneath me, a battle from which two hundred thousand men never returned home.

*

In those days a squadron consisted of twelve machines : three flights of four machines each. No. 3 had two flights of Parasols and one of Biplanes. Our work was Artillery Observation, Photography, and Contact Patrol.

Artillery Observation was the job of correcting a battery's shooting till it had accurately ranged its target. It was carried out in the following manner. The observer (that is, the passenger in the machine who was trained in this work) would call up the battery with which he was detailed to work before leaving the ground, by phone. The commanding officer would tell him the objectives on which he wished to range—an enemy battery, a dump, an important cross-road—and would give their exact map co-ordination on the special large-scale squared maps used for the purpose. They would also agree the time the shoot was to begin. At this time the machine would be in the air over the battery. The observer would then let out his aerial—a long piece of copper wire with a lead plummet at the end— which unwound from a drum in the cockpit, switch on the transmitter, and call up the battery in Morse. In the dugout by the battery the wireless operator would report that all was ready. The machine would call upon the battery to fire, and then watch carefully to see where the shot fell. A code was used to give the exact position of the burst in relation to the objective aimed at: " Over," " Short," " Left," " Right." After a pause to correct sights, the battery, on being signalled, would fire again. By this means, in three or four rounds it was usually possible to get a direct hit on the target, and the airman would send down the triumphant " O.K."

Different types of guns were used for different targets. The field guns took objectives close to the lines (having a flat trajectory and a comparatively short range), the howitzers flung their shells high and far over into the enemy country on targets which it was strategically important to harass in the great offensive which was now in active preparation.

There were also batteries standing by ready to be called up from the air to silence enemy guns. The pilot or observer seeing the flash of a hostile battery, perhaps cleverly camouflaged in a wood or sunken road, would immediately call up and give the map co-ordination. The battery would calculate the approximate range and open fire. If all went well, the H.B. (hostile battery) could be knocked out in a quarter of an hour. All pilots were under orders to report the location of any H.B. seen, no matter what work they were engaged on, and these were then tabulated and circulated to our own gunners by Corps headquarters.

The importance of air supremacy will thus be clear. Unless the gunners could get accurate corrections of their shooting, they were firing, literally, into the blue. True, they might have observation posts on high ground, in church towers, trees, etc., or they might even have their eyes in a kite balloon (of inestimable value in this work); but without air supremacy the balloons would be shot down, the artillery observation machines would be molested at their work, and the value of the guns would be effectively reduced. Such was the Allied supremacy during the Somme battle that we were practically immune from hostile air attack, while the Germans were continually harried by British scouts. It was only in the late autumn that enemy aircraft began to be troublesome.

*

The other main function of the squadron was Contact Patrol. It was an aerial liaison between the front line and the battalion and brigade headquarters, designed to keep them in close touch with each other during the inevitable disorganization of other means of communication during an offensive. At such times, it was realized, the advance would often find itself cut off from its supports and would have difficulty, or sometimes be actually unable, to send back word where they were. But an aeroplane patrolling at low altitude could easily see the red flares which the Tommies carried and were instructed to light at given times. The observer could mark the positions of these flares on the map, write down their co-ordinations on a slip of paper, put it in a weighted message-bag and, swooping down over the battalion headquarters (whose position was known by a semi-circular sheet of white cloth pegged out on the ground), drop the message-bag. As the attack progressed, the latest positions of the flares could be given hour by hour, and as the battalion head-quarters moved up behind the advancing line they would move their ground sheets also, so we should always know where to drop our messages.

Such was the principle of Contact Patrol. It had two other refinements: a signalling ground sheet, which consisted of a black-and-white venetian blind —this, on an elastic return spring, opened white and closed black, and enabled the ground to send Morse messages to the machines above—and a Klaxon horn, which the machines carried, used to call on the infantry for flares and transmit Morse messages to the ground.

This was the theory, and for weeks, when brigades came down to rest from the line, sham attacks were made to practise these new methods of communication. Kindergarten, we called them. The machines called for flares with their Klaxons, the string of Bengal lights went up, the messages were dropped on the ground sheets; everything worked splendidly. At last, one of the greatest anxieties of the infantry had been overcome. But there is usually a gap between theory and practice, and Contact Patrol was no exception, for when the attack was actually launched, the men in the front line (not unnaturally) shrank from lighting fireworks which would give away their position to any German machine gun or battery for miles round. Besides, they had other things to think of—finding cover, digging themselves in, caring for their wounded—and so, during the first phase of the attack, Contact Patrol was pretty useless. Later the co-operation improved; but by this time we had got used to the dangers of low flying over the front line, and used to go right down to a few hundred feet and find the position of our men by actually seeing them in their trenches. It was more accurate; but more dangerous. We lost many good men by direct hits from our own shells, which on their way over struck the machines which were working in their trajectories.

*

Excitement grew as the days went by. Up at the front all was, apparently, quiet. The tremendous massing of guns was carefully camouflaged. Hundreds of batteries took up their positions, and all day and every day we were out ranging them on their objectives; but only a very limited amount of shooting was done, so that the enemy might not suspect the weight of the attack that was being prepared against him.

By day the roads were deserted; but as soon as

dusk fell they were thick with transport, guns, ammunition trains, and troops, all moving up through Albert to take their positions in or behind the lines. We used to lean over the Mess window-sill and watch them, dim and fantastic silhouettes, passing in the flicker of oil lamps, solid-tyred lorries bumping and rattling over the pot-holes, the grinding of gears, the rattle of equipment, the shouted orders, the snatches of song. The noisy nightmare gave us an illusion of victory. We took some pride in this evidence of strength. The sinister ghosts hailed us as they passed, and we shouted back to them catch-phrases of the time, ribald greetings, sardonic cheers —all equally drowned under the clatter of their passing. Endlessly, night after night, it went on. We slept, or tried to sleep, to the sound of it. Yet when dawn came, all signs of it were gone. There was the deserted road, the tumble-down farmhouses, the serene and silent summer mornings. Never do I remember a time when night so contradicted day.

*

One evening the Major came back from Amiens with a case of whisky, a case of champagne, and a large bath sponge.

" To-night," he said, " A Flight will throw a drunk, and B and C Flights are invited."

After dinner the drunk was thrown. The long trestle table, covered with smeared American cloth, stood diagonally across the room : a low room, ill lit, with a rough, red-tiled floor. The gramophone was wheezing, " I'm going back to the shack where the black-eyed——"

87

" Bastards go ! " chipped in the Adjutant. " For Crissake put another tune on the blasted box ! "

" Shampoos ! " shouted the Major. " Who's for shampoos ? "

" Shampoos ! shampoos ! " shrieked the Mess.

Ah, ha ! This was the life ! This was fine ! This *was* a drunk. A row of young men bent their heads over the long table. The Major was mixing neat whisky with champagne in a tin basin. The sponge ! It came in handy that sponge ! A large sponge : it mixed them well !

" Shampoos ! Shampoos ! Hills ! Truefits ! Car ! Guaranteed to curl ! Shampoo, sir ? " Plosh ! He dolloped the sponge on the head of the nearest victim, who raised a dripping head, eagerly licking the liquor streaming down his face. The Mess screamed applause ! " Now me ! Now me ! Now me ! "

" Good old Major ! Dear old boy ! " This was the life ! " Again ! Again ! "

What a waste ! What a drunk ! What a stink !

" Rinse me ! Rinse me ! You silly bastard, you ! "

" Who's a silly bastard ? " said the Major, fixing the company with a watery eye. A lull. No one, apparently, had told the Major he was an illegitimate idiot. No one ! Of course not ! Good old Major ! Fine chap. D.S.O. Retreat from Mons. But, God, how drunk ! Privily he had seized a siphon.

" If it was you said I was a silly bastard," he addressed a dripping, reeling, shampooed wreck, " I'm not. See ? " The siphon spurted. " Rinse you ! I'll rinse you ! "

Squirt ! Squirt !

" Siphons, Orderly ! Siphons ! "

" Yes, sir."

" Sides, take sides! A Flight *v*. B and C Flights. Action all! "

Over went the table. Siphons appeared by magic. The offensive was launched.

Squirt! Scream! Scream! Squirt! Oh you . . . Got him! Right in the . . . More! More! In the mouth! Give me another! Orderly! More siphons! Yes, sir. Silly bastard, eh? God, I'm wet! God, what a life! "

They collapsed, chairs dripping, tunics soaking, walls running, laughing, shouting, swearing, on to the puddled floor. . . .

Under his arm the horn of the gramophone. In his ear the tune of the gramophone; running down, wheezy, good ole gramophone. Poor ole gramophone! Nice ole gramophone! . . .

" Orderly! "

" Yes, sir."

" Whisky. Bott'l whisky."

" Yes, sir."

Down the horn of the poor old, nice old, wheezy old gramophone the whisky poured, dripping on the record, dripping on the floor.

" Jus' givin' the dear ole chap a drink."

" You'll bust it! Wind it! Put it on! Make it go! "

" Dear ole gramophone, doesn't want to go. Wansh shleep! "

> "For she'd a hole in her stocking
> And eyes that were mocking. . . ."

. . . the drunken chorus faded down the street. In his billet one hero found his pillow black, his

bed black, his chairs, table, ceiling, all covered
with a film of soot. For hours and hours the oil
lamp had been smoking.

"Can't shleep here. Goddam batman. Everything shooty." A bright idea struck into his reeling mind: "Shleep with Mam'sel! Shleep with
Mam'sel!"

She was a heavy peasant girl, clogged and
shawled, fruity with the rank odours of the farm-
yard. Her room lay through his. He lurched
over and opened it.

"Mam'sel," he announced, "I—je . . . dor-
mez . . . vous . . . Savey?"

"Oui, oui, venez," said a stupid voice in the
darkness. He groped in the darkness, in the stuffy,
feather-bedded darkness, found her in the darkness.
. . . God, what a drunk! What a bloody wonderful drunk!

*

When I strive to remember the details of my
patrols in those hectic days before the Somme
offensive, it is surprising how little I can recall.
My logbook, where each separate flight is noted,
shows what I was doing, but strangely evokes no
answering ring in my memory.

"*Date*, 28.5.16. *Machine No.* 5133. *Passenger*,
Lt. Brown. *Time*, 1 hour. *Course*, Lines; La
Boiselle. *Height*, 5800 ft. *Weather*, perfect.
Wind, West. *Remarks*, Officer to see segment of
trenches. He saw more than he bargained for—
i.e. 4 Archies right under our tail."

But I do not remember Lt. Brown. I do not
remember the perfect day, nor the Archies under

our tail. And so it is as I look down the remarks
column : " Bumpy—nothing of interest seen."
" Rain, N.b.g. observation. Tried to engage battery—I Target—Poor." " Machine O.K. 5000
feet in 16 minutes."

So much I might have noted, for the trivial
passing impression often serves to unlock closed
vistas in the mind ; but these do not. I am like a
man on a rise, looking back over a plain where white
ground mists lie, seeing isolated trees and roofs,
upthrust haphazard, floating on the sea, without
apparent connection with the lanes and fields
beneath. I remember only incidents, and lose
the vivid landscape of the time.

When the wind blew from the west, strong over
the rolling hill, we had to take off over the sheds.
The heavily loaded Parasol, with its wireless set, its
observer and Lewis gun, its full load of petrol,
lurched reluctantly into the air, skimmed the
canvas hangar tops, and struck the sharp gusts
above them. Then it would put one wing down.
We used to put on opposite stick, holding it hard
against the side of the cockpit ; but without effect.
The wing remained where it was, nothing would
budge it. It was as if some mysterious hand
were deliberately holding it so. Like this we
staggered on over the roof tops. Now if the
engine conked we should be for it ! The rest of
the machine revolted against such unnatural progress, shuddered, slipping sideways to the ground.
Grimly we hung on, waiting for the unseen hand
to be removed, and then breathed more easily as,
at last, the wing came up and, gaining height, we
circled the village and headed out towards the lines.

In summer weather heat bumps used to throw us about up to four and five thousand feet, till we were clear of the haze. It was curious how the most perfect day, seemingly crystal-clear to the four horizons, was, in reality, blanketed with this murky vapour. When at last we rose above it, we saw it had an upper surface, clear-cut and definite, a line like a second horizon, veiling the earthy one beneath. The hotter the day, the thicker and blacker the haze and, by contrast, the purer the air above.

But there were other days when the clouds hung low and we made our way home from the lines dodging the storms. The curtains of rain, bellied by the wind, swung earthwards in sweeping curves. Beyond there would be sunlight, gilding their watery transparency. Blue-black was the under surface of the cloud whence the gold curtain hung, silver-grey the earth where it fell in a flurry of misty splashing. Between these moving screens we threaded our course, watching the dappled surface of the earth, the sunlight polishing the roofs, the trees, the fields, making a newly varnished earth, fresh-scented after the storm.

At last, nearing the aerodrome, the rain would bar our way. Engine off, we would charge at it. The golden curtain became a whirl of flying water, the gentle raindrop a stinging bullet, spinning against the planes, spattering on the wind-screen. Crouching down in the cockpit, we dived, gauging our distance as the earth rose up at us; but even as we landed, the curtain passed, the sun was out again, shining on the last desultory drops, and we leapt out of the machine to marvel at the rainbow!

Such impressions do not dim with passing years.

Though they were only the background against which we worked, they set the tone, filled out the style. The air was our element, the sky our battle-field. The majesty of the heavens, while it dwarfed us, gave us, I think, a spirit unknown to sturdier men who fought on earth. Nobility surrounded us. We moved like spirits in an airy loom, where wind and cloud and light wove day and night long the endless fabric of the changing sky. Hitherto only gallant men with rope and axe had struggled (challenging the last crazy crags) to attain summits to whose height we rose daily, unmindful of the privilege. ·From this exalted eminence we surveyed the earth—an earth grown suddenly remote and insignificant, so vast and overpowering was the dominion of the sky.

The war below us was a spectacle. We aided and abetted it, admiring the tenacity of men who fought in verminous filth to take the next trench thirty yards away. But such objectives could not thrill us, who, when we raised our eyes, could see objective after objective receding, fifty, sixty, seventy miles beyond. Indeed, the fearful thing about the war became its horrible futility, the mountainous waste of life and wealth to stake a mile or two of earth. There was so much beyond. Viewed with detachment, it had all the elements of grotesque comedy—a prodigious and complex effort, cunningly contrived, and carried out with deadly seriousness, in order to achieve just nothing at all. It was Heath Robinson raised to the nth power—a fantastic caricature of common sense. But the humour was grim, fit only for gods to laugh at, since to the participants it was a sickening death-struggle, in which both sides would evidently be exhausted, both defeated, and both eager, when they had licked their wounds, to fly at each other's throats again.

Of all this we were daily spectators, creatures of another element, lending ourselves to things beneath us, and the actual physical aspect of this relation educed in me (since the Western Front was my University and I must needs graduate with some self-taught degree) an attitude to life itself.

The fixity with which men pursued immediate trivialities alarmed and disgusted me. The magnitude of the effort spent on daily futilities was too awful to be faced; it was a sort of St Vitus dance, bound to end in exhaustion. The mentality of the post-war years was no different from that of the war itself—an obsession to take the next objective, whether you wanted it or not, whether you were any better off when you got it or not, whether you had any idea of where to go next or not. It gave men the illusion they were getting somewhere, doing something, when, in reality, they were floundering deeper and deeper into chaos. Civilization, I vaguely realized then—and subsequent observation has confirmed the view—could not progress that way. It must have a greater guiding principle to survive. To treat it as a carcase off which each man tears as much as he can for himself, is to stand convicted a brute, fit for nothing better than a jungle existence, which is a death-struggle, leading nowhither. I did not believe that was the human destiny, for Man individually was sane and reasonable, only collectively was he a fool.

We needed effort, not greater in quantity, but other in quality; a different point of view, a new perspective, a more constant aim, co-ordinating and co-relating circumstances and conditions for the general good. Men with such faculties existed; but they were scarcely listened to, for the conditions under which they would undertake to pilot us to safety demanded heavy sacrifice and drastic change—both utterly abhorrent to those who could not see the danger they were in.

*

The zero hour of the Somme offensive drew nearer. The troops, sent down for a long rest before it, had learnt with us the new co-operative methods of contact patrol, and had now returned to the lines, ready for the attack. The guns were all in position, and most of the squadron spent all their time ranging them. I happened to be the exception, for I was put on to photography.

The whole section of our front, from Thiepval, down past Boisselle, round the Fricourt salient, and on to Montauban, was to be photographed every day, in order that Headquarters might have accurate information of the effects of the bombardment. This aimed at destroying all the enemy first- and second-line trenches, and so making the attack easy for the infantry.

In this it was only partially successful, for the Germans had constructed concrete redoubts and defences that remained to a large extent intact, even after the terrific bombardment. Fricourt, which stood on a sharp rise, was in reality an impregnable concrete fort, bristling with machine guns. It was only evacuated when the advance, more successful on either side of it, pinched it off, and forced those in Fricourt itself to retire.

At leisure we had photographed the line before the bombardment started. But during this last week the weather was poor. On two days, low clouds and rain prevented us getting any photos at all. The 3rd and 15th Corps, for whom we were working, got in a panic. It was essential to know the effect of the shelling. Photos were to be got at all costs.

We went out in the afternoon. The clouds forced us down to two thousand feet. A terrific bombardment was in progress. The enemy lines, as far as we could see, were under a white drifting cloud of bursting high explosive. The shell-bursts were continuous, not only on the lines themselves, but on the support trenches and communications behind.

At two thousand feet we were in the path of the gun trajectories, and as the shells passed, above or below us, the wind eddies made by their motion flung the machine up and down, as if in a gale. Each bump meant that a passing shell had missed the machine by four or five feet. The gunners had orders not to fire when a machine was passing their sights, but in the fury of the bombardment much was forgotten—or perhaps the fact that we were not hit proves the orders were carried out. If so, they ran it pretty fine.

Grimly I kept the machine on its course above the trenches, waiting, tense and numb, for a shell to get us, while Sergeant Hall (who got a D.C.M. and a commission for his work that week) worked the old camera handle, changed the plates, sighted, made his exposures. I envied him having something to do. I could only hold the machine as steady as possible and pray for it to be over. At last, after an hour, I felt a tap on my shoulder. Gratefully I turned for home.

Just above us the heavy cloud-banks looked like the bellies of a school of whales huddled together in the dusk. Beyond, a faintly luminous strip of yellow marked the sunset. Below, the gloomy earth glittered under the continual scintillation of gun fire. Right round the salient down to the Somme, where the mists backed up the ghostly effect, was this sequined veil of greenish flashes, quivering. Thousands of guns were spitting high explosive, and the invisible projectiles were screaming past us on every side. Though they were our own guns, their muzzles were towards us, and suddenly I knew it was at us they were firing. The malevolent fury of the whole bombardment was concentrated on us! Of course it was ridiculous; but for about a minute I was in the grip of nightmare terror. The machine lurched and rolled. It was us they were after! It was us!

In another minute we were through the danger zone; but the vivid memory haunted me back to the aerodrome. Even there we could hear the thud and rumble of the guns, even back in England they were hearing it. For seven nights and days it went on. After dark, we used to come out and watch. Continual summer lightning, flickering and dancing in the eastern sky. Voluminous and austere bursts of thunder rolling by on the night wind. The others used to laugh: " The old Hun's fairly going through it." But I could not forget its blind fury, and pitied the men who for a week lived under that rain. I suppose I was many times nearer death than on that particular evening; but for me it remains, none the less, the most fearful moment of the war.

*

A mile or two behind the front, on both sides of the lines, floated the kite balloons. They hung in the sky like pensive and somewhat inebriated tad-poles, while observers in the baskets beneath ranged batteries by telephone. They thus fulfilled the same function as aircraft in artillery patrols; but, being stationary, were more accurate, within their limits of vision, than a moving machine. They were run up on a steel cable from a winch mounted on a lorry, and at a sign of danger or foul weather could be quickly hauled down.

A string of these observation posts stretched along the salient on the German side, and before the push it was decided that Jerry's eyes must be put out. It was not an easy matter, for their winches were powerful, and at the first sign of danger hauled down the balloons before they could be attacked. Moreover, their position was carefully ranged by their own anti-aircraft batteries, so that any machine attacking them would be flying into an Archie trap. Besides this, they were reputed to have *Flammen-werfer*—flame-throwers—on the ground round the balloons, ready to make it hot for the intruder.

In some cases balloons were used as decoys. When an enemy machine was seen approaching, all the balloons would be hauled down except one.

This one would have no observers in it, but, instead, a charge of high explosive in the basket. This could be fired from the ground. The hero who dived on the balloon would be welcomed by Archie, flame-throwers, and the bursting balloon itself. Such were the rumours, quite sufficient to make the job of balloon-strafing no joy-ride.

There were two methods of attack: one with special tracer ammunition, the bullet containing phosphorus, which would set the gas in the envelope on fire; the other by means of rockets. These were mounted in tubes wired on to the outer wing-struts, pointing forward in the line of flight, four rockets on each side of the machine, eight in all. They were ugly-looking things, with heavy iron-barbed heads to tear open the balloon fabric as they entered and then explode and set off the balloon. All the rockets were wired up electrically to a button in the cockpit. The pilot dived at the balloon, ranged it with tracer ammunition, and then touched off his rockets.

Six Nieuport scouts stood out on our aerodrome, from which the balloon-strafe was to begin. They left the ground on a perfect afternoon when all the German balloons were up hard at work spotting for their batteries; but evidently the men on the winches had sharp eyes, or else they had got wind of the attack, for the balloons bobbed down so quickly that not one of our machines got near them. Instead, they were very badly Archied and returned crestfallen.

The next day was cloudy, and an inexperienced young French pilot in the Allied sector south of us went up on the same job. He got lost above the clouds, and when he came out, saw a balloon immediately beneath him. He dived, fired his rockets and pulled clear. The balloon went up in flames, the observers jumped clear in their parachutes, the pilot looped in his delight. Unfortunately it turned out to be a French balloon! The details never reached the squadron; but the flaming balloon made a beautiful splash of colour in the evening sky, and when we heard that it was not a bold marauding Hun, but just a hilarious Froggie, we had another round of drinks. It seemed an excellent joke at the time, though perhaps the observers who had to jump for it were not splitting their sides with laughter as they floated down in the parachutes.

*

Just about that time a BE 2c landed on the aerodrome one afternoon. It did not taxi up to the sheds, but remained on the far side of the field, engine ticking over. This peculiar behaviour was all the more noticeable because nobody went over to the machine. Usually the arrival of a stranger meant a welcome from the pilots lounging about the sheds. Evidently something was afoot. Then from behind the sheds a civilian appeared. Dressed in a tattered old mac and cap, he walked out to the machine and climbed into the empty passenger's seat. Curiouser and curiouser! For to fly a civilian in those days was absolutely forbidden. The machine turned and took off, to disappear high up towards the lines.

It was only that evening I learned the mysterious 2c was picking up a spy and had flown him over the lines, landed him at a prearranged place in Hun-

land, and returned safely. At that time I thought
more of the pilot's job of getting his machine down
and away again on the enemy side of the line than
I did of the spy who, of all men, took the greatest
hazard in the service of his country. I always
wondered who the man was and what happened to
him. Of course we never heard another word.
Did he get out safely, or was he put up against a
wall and shot, disowned by the country he worked
for? That sort of courage made the rest of us look
cowards.

*

On the eve of the offensive the General Officer
Commanding, "Boom" Trenchard, with his A.D.C.,
visited the squadron. Sitting on his shooting-
stick, he called us all up round him, gave us a bird's-
eye view of the whole attack, and in his pleasant
masterful way congratulated us all on our work.
It had contributed, he said, more than we knew
to the success of the preliminary bombardment.
Artillery observation, photography, reconnaissance,
all received their commendation. "Boom" in-
fused men's enthusiasm without effort by a certain
greatness of heart that made him not so much our
superior in rank as in personality. When he left
we were all sure that victory was certain, that the
line would be broken, the cavalry put through,
and the Allies sweep on to Berlin.

*

July the 1st, the zero day of the Somme offensive,
dawned misty and still. Before it was light I was

down in the sheds looking over my machine—an extra precaution, for I had been over it minutely the evening before. I was detailed for the first patrol, and soon we got the machine out and ran it up.

We were to watch the opening of the attack, co-ordinate the infantry flares (the job we had been rehearsing for months), and stay out over the lines for two and a half hours. Before we left, a second machine would overlap us, stay out its two and a half hours, and so continuous patrols would run throughout the day.

We climbed away on that cloudless summer morning towards the lines. There was a soft white haze over the ground that the sun's heat would quickly disperse. Soon we were in sight of the salient, and the devastating effect of the week's bombardment could be seen. Square miles of country were ripped and blasted to a pock-marked desolation. Trenches had been obliterated, flattened out, and still, as we watched, the gun fire continued, in a crescendo of intensity. Even in the air, at four thousand feet, above the roar of the engine, the drumming of firing and bursting shells throbbed in our ears.

" Keep clear of La Boisselle " were my orders. There was a small but heavily fortified salient there. It was to be blown up. Two huge mines, the largest ever laid, were to lift it sky-high at the moment the attack was launched. Weeks before, I had taken the officer in charge of the tunnelling up over the spot, and had heard stories of how the men worked down there in the darkness with pick and shovel, stopping at intervals to listen whether enemy miners were tunnelling under their galleries. But all was well, the mines were complete, wired, the troops had been retired clear of them, and the officer in charge was waiting, hand on switch, to set them off. Once they were fired, the infantry were to sweep through Boisselle and on up the Bapaume road to Pozières, their first day's objective.

Now the hurricane bombardment started. Half an hour to go! The whole salient, from Beaumont-Hamel down to the marshes of the Somme, covered to a depth of several hundred yards with the coverlet of white wool—smoking shell bursts! It was the greatest bombardment of the war, the greatest in the history of the world. The clock hands crept on, the thrumming of the shells took on a higher note. It was now a continuous vibration, as if Wotan, in some paroxysm of rage, were using the hollow world as a drum and under his beat the crust of it was shaking. Nothing could live under that rain of splintering steel. A whole nation was behind it. The earth had been harnessed, the coal and ore mined, the flaming metal run; the workshops had shaped it with care and precision; our womenkind had made fuses, prepared deadly explosives; our engineers had designed machines to fire the product with a maximum of effect; and finally, here, all these vast credits of labour and capital were being blown to smithereens. It was the most effective way of destroying wealth that man had yet devised; but as a means of extermination (roughly one man for every hundred shells), it was primitive and inefficient.

Now the watch in the cockpit, synchronized before leaving the ground, showed a minute to the hour. We were over Thiepval and turned south to watch the mines. As we sailed down above it all, came the final moment. Zero!

At Boisselle the earth heaved and flashed, a tremendous and magnificent column rose up into the sky. There was an ear-splitting roar, drowning all the guns, flinging the machine sideways in the repercussing air. The earthy column rose, higher and higher to almost four thousand feet. There it hung, or seemed to hang, for a moment in the air, like the silhouette of some great cypress tree, then fell away in a widening cone of dust and debris. A moment later came the second mine. Again the roar, the upflung machine, the strange gaunt silhouette invading the sky. Then the dust cleared and we saw the two white eyes of the craters. The barrage had lifted to the second-line trenches, the infantry were over the top, the attack had begun.

*

My logbook for July 1st contains the following entries:

" From our point of view an entire failure. Not a single ground sheet of Battalion or Brigade Headquarters was seen. Only two flares were lit on the whole of both Corps fronts."

And again on the afternoon patrol that same day:

" Again a complete failure. No flares or any ground signals seen. Nothing whatever to report to the Corps. Only reports sent in were of movements on roads, limbers, ammunition, etc. (other people's jobs) behind Pozières moving up to Contalmaison. Many active enemy batteries seen and though all information was wirelessed to ' M,' our batteries did not reply on the co-ordinates given. There must be colossal lack of organization somewhere. Our patrol was n.b.g."

I was bitterly disappointed. For months we had been preparing, hoping and believing that at last the Air could do something valuable and definite for the wretched men who were carrying forward the line, and in effect it was a complete washout, with no co-operation from the very men we were there to help.

The truth was that at many points the attack had not gone according to plan. The great mines at Boisselle had not blown up the redoubt; they had burst short in No-Man's-Land, leaving the impregnable machine-gun emplacements of the enemy intact. When the barrage lifted, the Huns came up from their dugouts and manned those guns, effectively holding up the advance. We heard afterwards that our infantry had actually gone down the old mine-shafts, dug their way out of the apex (the base) of the crater, and then swarmed up its sides to occupy the lip. Boisselle, which was to have fallen in the first half-hour, did not fall for some days.

*

Next morning we started a practice which was to become a habit during the next few months—going down low enough to see the men in the trenches with accuracy, and getting our reports this way.

We circled above the trenches at a thousand feet, saw the infantry crossing the old No-Man's-Land above Fricourt, saw many Hun dead round the mine-craters, saw the communication trenches running from Mametz to Montauban full of troops, noted it all on scraps of paper, put them in a message-bag, and came back, swooping low to drop it on the brigade headquarters ground sheet, then up and back again for more information.

Now we could see to what extent the great offensive had succeeded. There did seem to be a definite advance all along the front of the 15th and 3rd Corps, except at Boisselle and Fricourt; but there was evident disorder, hesitation, and delay, due probably to the enemy resistance at these two points, which spoiled the outline of the offensive. Still, it was early to be depressed. Perhaps the objectives aimed at for the second and third days of the offensive would be realized and the initial hold-ups compensated for. Actually, I think, the set-back on the first day was decisive. The main object—to break the line, put the cavalry through, and finish the long drudgery of trench warfare—failed by reason of the early delays, from which the push never recovered.

After doing all we could to report on the state of the line, we wandered farther over to see what the Hun was doing behind it. Was he bringing up supplies or reinforcements? On the main road from Bapaume to Pozières, five miles beyond the line, we saw two horse-drawn limbers. They were coming up at the gallop, bringing ammunition to their batteries, their six horses stretching out, the riders crouching low over their necks, the wagon rolling and swaying along the awful road.

We dived. At a thousand feet Pip opened fire with the Lewis gun. Whether he killed or wounded the leading horse of the first limber I shall never know. Perhaps it was just panic; but the horse crumpled up, and the others, with their tremendous momentum, overran him, and the whole lot piled up in the ditch, a frenzied tangle of kicking horses, wagons, and men. The second limber, following close behind the first, swerved, but could not avoid its leader; its wagons overturned, wheels spinning, and split. Shells rolled over the road. We returned elated. We had helped to win the war.

★

We wanted to drop a bomb. It was not strictly our business, and our machines were not fitted with bomb racks; but there were bombs in the store, and we felt that they should be dropped.

We lay on the aerodrome in the sunny grass with the map before us.

" First," I said, " on what shall we drop a bomb ? "

" There is a house beyond Pozières," said Pip. " It is not demolished. It might be a dump. It probably could do with a bomb." (He is dead now; but I remember how he looked at me sideways, finger on map, and smiled.)

" We must calculate the height and speed, and allow for the wind."

He rolled over on his back and, arms behind head, blinked in the July sunshine.

" Do you know how bombs work ? " he said.

" No; but I s'pose we can find out. There ought to be a fuse with a pin to pull out, or something."

We considered it carefully. It was the third day of the Somme battle, and anything that could be done ought to be done. Besides, a bomb!—it might do any amount of damage. . . .

We will fly this way. . . . Four thousand feet. . . . Seventy miles an hour. . . . Measure it carefully. . . . Allow for the wind. . . . We'll drop it from there.

We went to the Major.

" We want to drop a bomb," we said.

" All right," he said. " Where? " And we told him.

That afternoon we set out. The Sergeant stood by nursing the bomb. He lifted it up and placed it gingerly on Pip's knees. It was a twenty-pound bomb, and Pip held it in his arms like a baby.

" It can't go off, I suppose, can it, Sergeant? " he inquired mildly.

" Not till you pull out the pin, sir," replied the Sergeant. "But mind how you chuck it overboard, sir. See it doesn't touch anything."

He thought we were mad. (On reflection, we certainly were.) We climbed up to the lines. When we got over the spot, I turned and nodded. Pip pulled out the pin and dumped the baby overboard. We circled and watched it falling. Then we lost sight of it and looked at the house. It was still there. Then—a flash and a cloud of dust about a hundred yards away. We returned home, strangely elated.

" Did you hit it? " said the Major.

" No."

" I didn't think you would." He was reflective. " Still, you dropped it. That's something."

For days on patrol we used to look for the crater it had made. It seemed a friendly crater. Then we forgot it; but we never bothered to drop another bomb.

★

Next day we were up at 3 A.M. and took the air at four. Dawn over the trenches, everything misty and still above, with the prospect of heat to come; even the war seemed to pause, taking a deep, cool morning breath before plunging into action. We were out to find the exact position at Boisselle, for even now, on the fourth day of the offensive, the Corps Intelligence did not seem clear on the point. We sailed over the mines and called for flares with our Klaxon. After a minute one solitary flare spurted up, crimson, from the lip of the crater. It looked forlorn, that solitary little beacon, in the immense pitted miles of earth around. We came down to five hundred feet and sailed over it, trying to distinguish the crouching khaki figures, huddled in their improvised trenches in the khaki-coloured earth. It was not easy. We crossed the crater going north, wheeled south again to come back over it, when suddenly there was a crash, and the whole machine shook, as if at the next moment it would wrench itself to pieces.

I thought we had been hit by a passing shell. In a flash I pulled back the throttle and switched off. The vibration lessened; but we still shook fearfully. Now! Where to land? Five hundred feet over the front line, the earth an expanse of contiguous shell-holes! We should certainly crash, perhaps catch fire, right on the line! Such thoughts raced through my head as I looked frantically for some spot less battered than the rest. There was a place! Right underneath me! I dived at it, and the speed of the machine rose to a hundred miles an, hour. Of course we could never hope to stay in that one green patch. We should overshoot, crash in the trenches beyond; but at five hundred feet there is no time to change your mind. You select your spot for better or worse and stick to it. So we dived.

" What's the matter? " shouted Pip from behind me.

" Cylinder blown off, I think," I shouted. (Actually it was a connecting-rod which had crystallized and snapped in half.)

" Undo your belt! " I yelled. I didn't want him to be pinioned under the machine when it caught fire, if it did catch fire.

By now we were down to a hundred feet, and the contours of the earth below took on detailed shape. I saw—God be praised!—that the green patch that had caught my eye was the side of a steep hill. There was no wind. I swung the machine sideways and pulled her round to head up the slope. She zoomed grandly up the hillside. The speed lessened. Now we were just over the ground, swooping uphill, like a seagull on a steep Devon plough. Back and back I pulled the stick. The hill rose up before me, and at last she stalled, perched like a bird on the only patch of the hill free of shell-craters, hopped three yards, and stopped—intact!

With a gasp of amazement and relief—for no one could have hoped to have got down in such a place undamaged—we jumped out of the machine. It was Pip's twenty-first birthday. Suddenly I remembered it. " Many happy returns ! " I said.

We stood looking at the machine—for nothing, perhaps, is quite so awkward and useless as an aeroplane that can't fly. Evidently we should have to get a new engine put in. Equally evidently it would be quite impossible to fly the machine out of this tenement patch of turf. It would have to be dismantled. As if the thought had entered other heads than our own, at that moment came the Wheeeeee . . . . wheeee . . . . whee—ow . . . whe—ow . . . . whow . . whow . whow . . . Zonk ! " of a German shell. They were evidently going to dismantle it for us. The shell fell wide. We dived for a trench beyond, and waited. Two more shells came over. Then silence. They had given it up. Well . . . we'd better get back to the aerodrome and have some brekker. It was five o'clock.

From the air we could have found our way home from any part of the line ; but the earth was a strange country. We set off along the duckboarding at the bottom of a deep communication trench, unable to see over the top. We turned left at a junction, right at another. They were all deserted. We were lost. So we climbed out of the trench and walked down towards a neighbouring copse, where we could hear in the distance the sound of orders and the rattle of accoutrements. A battalion of infantry was waiting there to go up into the line. An officer, who had seen us come down, directed us back on the road to Albert.

We stood a moment chatting with him. The imminence of action seemed to leave him unperturbed. His men sat round resting in attitudes of dejection or repose, dun figures bowed under the heavy strappings of their kits, hats pushed back, cigarettes hanging from their lips. They sat about on the fallen tree trunks, on overturned wagons, on dud shells, silent and resigned in that blasted wood under the glory of the summer morning. Then the thunder of the guns began, south at the Somme, and rose and rose as the nearer batteries took it up. It was like jungle drums beating the rhythm of tremendous news, rising, falling, echoing, repeating, till the whole air was shaking with the imminent event. The officer looked at his watch. The men rose and shook themselves into order.

" Good luck ! "

" Good luck ! We 'll keep a watch out for you on patrol ! "

We turned away up the hill towards Albert, he through the gully of the wood up towards the line.

We trudged along in our heavy sheepskin thigh-boots, long leather coats, mufflers, and helmets— unsuitable walking kit for a breathless sunny morning. At last we emerged out on to a sort of road, badly shell-holed, almost impassable for wheeled traffic. We marked it on our map, for, somehow or other, the men were going to have to get a tender along it, dismantle the Parasol, and tow it back to the aerodrome. It was going to be tricky. Once out of the hollow we were glad enough to pause and take our bearings.

How different it all looked from the ground ! We could see the contours of the trenches, could realize why this point had been easy to carry in the attack, how that one was well-nigh impregnable ;

but more than this, we could inspect at close quarters the fury of the bombardment. It was a desolation, unimaginable from the air. The trees by the roadside were riven and splintered, their branches blown hither and thither, and the cracked stumps stuck up uselessly into the air, flanking the road, forlorn, like a byway to hell. The farms were a mass of debris, the garden walls heaps of rubble, the cemeteries had their crosses and their wire wreaths blown horribly askew. Every five square yards held a crater. The earth had no longer its smooth familiar face. It was diseased, pocked, rancid, stinking of death in the morning sun.

Yet (Oh, the catch at the heart!), among the devastated cottages, the tumbled, twisted trees, the desecrated cemeteries, opening, candid, to the blue heaven, the poppies were growing! Clumps of crimson poppies, thrusting out from the lips of craters, straggling in drifts between the hummocks, undaunted by the desolation, heedless of human fury and stupidity, Flanders poppies, basking in the sun!

As we stood gazing, a lark rose up from among them and mounted, shrilling over the diapason of the guns. We listened, watching, and then, I remember, trudged slowly on down the road without a word. That morning seems stranger than most to me now, for Pip is dead, twenty years dead, and I can still hear the lark over the guns, the flop and shuffle of our rubber-soled flying-boots on the dusty road; I can remember, set it down, that here on this page it may remain a moment longer than his brief mortality. For what? To make an epitaph, a little literary tombstone, for a young forgotten man.

For months we worked together daily on patrol. His life was in my hands a hundred times, and once, at least, mine was in his. He was the darling of the Flight, for he had a sort of gentle, smiling warmth about him that we loved. Besides, from the old rattling piano, out of tune, with a note gone here and there, he would coax sweet music—songs of the day, scraps of old tunes, Chopin studies, the *Liebestraum*, *Marche Militaire*. Youth and the sentiment attaching to those days obscure my judgment; but I believe that he had talent. Well, that does not matter now, and it did not matter then. He had enough for us, to make us sit quietly in the evening, there in that dingy room where the oil lamp hung on a string thick with flies, and listen.

In September I went on leave; Pip carried on with another pilot. One morning, on the dawn patrol, they, flying low in the arc of our own gun fire, intercepted a passing shell. The machine and both the boys were blown to bits.

*

Bodie was the Gadget King. He couldn't leave his machine alone. The carpenters and riggers were always making him something—a rack for his Very lights; a box for sandwiches; a special gun mounting; extra cases for spare drums; a new sort of wind-screen; special seat-cushions, and so on. He was a sort of modern White Knight. The classic conversation of this Bold Adventurer was typical of him:

" THE WHITE KNIGHT. Yes, it's a very good beehive. One of the best of its kind, but not a single bee has come near it yet, and the other thing is a mouse-trap. I suppose the mice keep the bees out or the bees keep the mice out. I don't know which.

" ALICE. I was wondering what the mouse-trap was for. It isn't very likely there'd be any mice on a horse's back.

" THE WHITE KNIGHT. Not very likely, perhaps, but if they *do* come, I don't choose to have them running about."

So it was with Bodie. He chose to be prepared for every eventuality. At one period of the Somme offensive he used to go up solo because he had equipped his machine with so many Lewis guns that it was incapable of lifting a passenger as well. He had one firing forward over the top of the propeller. Another was fixed behind him, shooting upwards over his tail, in case any one should be so rash as to attack him from the rear. A third fired downwards under his tail—presumably, in the words of the White Knight, " to guard against the bites of sharks." None of these guns had any sights, and indeed it would have been almost impossible to hit anything with them. But evidently Bodie, in some strange nightmare, had seen himself surrounded by enemy aircraft, and imagined that by pulling the plug of all three guns at once he might manage to " brown " half a dozen.

The gun craze lasted about a week, and then the Squadron Commander gently but firmly told Bodie that his aeroplane was not a Christmas tree and that he really must get down to work! The guns were dismantled, and Bodie was forced to exercise his ingenuity again.

Now it so happened that an infantry battalion had come down from the lines to rest, and was quartered in the village. One of the sergeants had a case of rifle grenades. These were small bombs with a long stalk which slipped down into the rifle barrel. You fired the rifle and the bullet forced the stalk, with the bomb on the end of it, out of the barrel, and theoretically it burst on hitting the enemy trenches. His remarks about them were very much to the point :

" These 'ere bloody bombs are no bloody good ! Either they bloody well burst before you can shoot them off, or they don't bloody well burst at all ! " And he added further technical information about burst rifle barrels and wounded men.

This was an opportunity after Bodie's heart. He swapped a pair of flying-gloves (which the sergeant thought might keep him warm in the front line) for the case of rifle grenades and had it brought down to the hangar, where its explosive possibilities made it much respected by all the air mechanics ! Not so by Bodie. A case of bombs which could be induced to go off had the sort of lure a mouse-trap must have to one of those experienced mice who know how it works ! He proceeded to cast about for a method of utilizing this consignment of bombs for the discomfiture of the enemy.

Having hit on a plan, he sent for the carpenters and riggers and instructed them to make two small racks of three-ply wood with five holes in each, just large enough to hold the body of the grenade. In the Morane Parasol the observer's seat was immediately behind the pilot, and just behind and below it again was a small cupboard which held the wireless set. The two bomb racks were screwed on to the outside of the fuselage, one on either side, level with the wireless. The stalks of the grenades were unscrewed and replaced by pieces of tape which, by a complicated system of pulleys and guides, were led through and attached to a hook in the pilot's seat. Unfasten them, and the weight of the grenades would pull away the tapes and they would fall. Simple! But the rifle grenade was quite harmless until the fuse-pin in the head was removed, after which nothing could stop it going off in about three seconds. So Bodie devised a further system of pieces of string to withdraw the pins. In the cockpit, when all was complete, there were therefore ten pieces of string to release the fuses, and ten pieces of tape to release the grenades.

This piece of super-gadgetry completed, Bodie could hardly contain himself for delight. He invited every one to inspect the ingenuity of his contrivance, and decided to sally forth that very afternoon and drop these ten grenades on the Kaiser himself (for there was a rumour he was up at the line). Failing the All Highest, he was going to " bloody well drop them on the first thing he saw," and when a machine came back and reported Hun reinforcements moving out of Bapaume, some ten miles behind the lines, nothing could restrain him from departing immediately to blow them up.

" You see," he remarked naïvely, " they will never expect me to drop anything on them."

His accomplice in this dastardly scheme was a certain good-looking youth with wavy hair and a beautiful moustache. He was an observer and, strangely enough, did not seem very much concerned at the idea of flying over Germany with this Heath Robinson paraphernalia.

The machine was wheeled out, the grenades placed in position, the tapes adjusted, and at last all was ready. As they were about to leave, Bodie nearly upset the whole expedition by catching his foot in the gear as he climbed into the cockpit.

" Look out! Look out! " yelled a mechanic. " He's gone and pulled the pins out! "

Bodie remained suspended, with one leg in the air, like an ecstatic puppy at his first lamp-post, saying in rather a quavering voice, " It's all right, it's all right! "

When three seconds had elapsed and the aeroplane had not turned into a sort of Brock's benefit, they swung up the engine and were heartily glad to see the machine disappear " This side up with care " in the distance.

It was a beautiful evening, and nearly all of us were sitting about on some baulks of timber near the sheds smoking, talking, and waiting for the last of the afternoon patrol to return. At last, in the distance, a machine was seen staggering in a sort of drunken roll towards the aerodrome.

" Christ Almighty! " said the men who first saw it. " What the hell's happened to her? " As the machine came nearer it was seen that the fabric on one side of the fuselage had been ripped off and was flapping wildly in the wind. Needless to say, it was Bodie returning from his gallant attempt to Win the War.

When he landed there was a general stampede to the machine. The first thing noticeable was the good-looking face of the observer, who had, in this incredibly short space of time, grown a beard, consisting of small pieces of red vulcanite which were sticking into all parts of his chin and cheeks. He climbed out of the machine, using the sort of language which will remain for ever unprintable, and a cheer went up when it was seen that his posterior had been the recipient of the disintegrated components of the wireless set! Condensers and transformers, one end well embedded in his anatomy, waved jovially in the air. His breeches were torn, his coat in ribbons. He was badly shaken, trembling and laughing.

"What happened? What happened?" And, when the first convulsions of merriment had died down:

"One of those bloody bombs," he said, cautiously rubbing his backside, "went off."

So much was obvious. The fuselage was a wreck. One of the longerons had been blown right through. Two or three struts and a dozen wires had been snapped. By a miracle the controls had remained intact. Bodie climbed out of the machine. He surveyed the wreckage with an expression of pained surprise.

"It's a pity about that," he remarked. And then he told the story. He had flown over to Bapaume and failed to find the enemy reinforcements. However, he spotted a number of Huns in a trench and came down to do his deadly work.

"I'm going to drop them," he shouted. "Look out!" And the observer did!

Bodie withdrew the strings, converting ten harmless grenades into ten extremely dangerous ones, and a second later released the tapes. They all fell clear (incidentally doing no damage whatever where they fell) except one, which got caught, and hung there dangling on its tape. A second later it burst.

It was two days before the machine was serviceable again. In the interval Bodie was busy planning a more complicated apparatus to drop double the quantity of grenades. But one of the Flight-Sergeants, either on receipt of instructions or else from motives of self-preservation (he might have had to go up with Bodie himself), privily took the case of grenades out of the sheds one night and had it dropped in the river near by.

Bodie never quite got over its disappearance, and used to wander about muttering vague imprecations about sabotage in the Royal Flying Corps.

*

As I turned to come back from the lines one evening, I saw to the north of Thiepval a long creeping wraith of yellow mist. I stared for a moment before I realized: Gas! Then, instinctively, although I was a mile above the earth, I pulled back the stick to climb higher, away from the horror.

In the light westerly wind it slid slowly down the German trenches, creeping pantherlike over the scarred earth, curling down into dugouts, coiling and uncoiling at the wind's whim. Men were dying there, under me, from a whiff of it: not dying quickly, nor even maimed or shattered, but dying whole, retching and vomiting blood and guts; and those who lived would be wrecks with seared, poisoned lungs, rotten for life.

I stared at the yellow drift, hypnotized. I can see it at this moment as clearly as I could that day, for it remains with me as the most pregnant memory of the war. It was, in fact, the symbol of our enlightened twentieth century : science, in the pursuit of knowledge, being exploited by a world without standards or scruples, spiritually bankrupt.

To-day all treaties, conventions, leagues, all words of honour, contracts, obligations are evidently worth nothing once the lust for power has infected a nation. Within twenty years of these days of which I write, every country, under a veneer of self-righteous nationalism, is preparing, with increased ingenuity and deadlier weapons, a greater Armageddon—all the while protesting their love of peace. People who cannot learn from their mistakes are damned—" the state of them who love death more than life." What have we learned from ours? We are, collectively, the most evil and destructive of human creatures. We back up our greeds and jealousies with religion and patriotism. Our Christian priests bless the launching of battleships, our youth is urged to die gloriously " for King and Country." We even write on the tomb of our Unknown Warrior that he died " for God "! What a piece of impudent and blasphemous nonsense to write in the House of Him whose greatest saying was : " This is my commandment, that ye love one another."

The next war will see that yellow drift not stealing down into front-line dugouts, but along London streets. My breed, the pilots, whose war has been more chivalrous and clean handed than any other, will be ordered to do violence to the civilian population. We shall drop the gas bombs and poison the reservoirs. We shall kill the women and children. Of course the thing is insane; but then if the world submits to the rule of homicidal maniacs, it deserves to be destroyed.

For, intellectually, the problem is not insoluble, though it is vast and has been rushed on us in under a hundred years, that is practically instantaneously. Science is the first cause; but scientists wash their hands of it, saying they are bound to advance knowledge, but cannot control the uses men put it to. But if there is to be any safety in the world, dangerous inventions will have to be protected as carefully as dangerous poisons. To nearly every modern problem there is an intellectual answer; but that, unfortunately, is not enough, for we have passions as well as minds, and they are more difficult to educate.

We are aware, for instance, that the incredibly rapid development of communications has telescoped space and time. We know that prosperity is interdependent, that currencies are linked, that commerce is international. But only a few (mainly business men whose pockets are affected) take all this for granted. They demand, as a matter of common sense, that international relations should have international control. For the rest it is an ideal, not an urgent practical necessity. The general public remains isolationist, patriotic, aware (like Nurse Cavell) that patriotism is not enough, but aghast at the problem of co-ordinating and controlling the life of the planet.

So vital a division puts everything in flux. Nobody knows where to pin their faith, so they believe nothing. Moral and social standards are confused.

Disillusion, introspection, defeatism are the lot of all those who can only live by the yardstick of black and white. The fear of feeling the ground slipping from under their feet drives whole nations back into mediaeval despotism. They will submit to anything sooner than face this social relativity where nothing is straight, nothing constant, nothing sure. But emulating the ostrich, though it may bring relief for a space, does not solve the problem. It leads straight back to self-immolation on the altar of outworn patriotism, that is to barbarism.

Thus the rational solution, as yet unsupported by the emotional drive which would make it a common faith, a cardinal necessity not to be denied, drifts in the doldrums, while the hysterical crew wring their hands and pray for a fair wind, instead of manning the boats and rowing the ship out to the Trades.

And all this arises because the ideal remains apparently unattainable, nebulous; it has not crystallized into a single urge. Yet this is clear and simple: World state, world currency, world language. It will demand new disciplines, new allegiances, new ideals. Probably two or three more world wars will be necessary to break down the innate hostility to such changes; but that is the way it must go. The days will come when the nations, sick of fighting themselves to a standstill, will claim the protection of the International Guard as we claim the right to a policeman. It is a question only of degree. Peace and security are civic virtues: those who disturb them must be quickly dealt with, and if their offence is serious enough, put out of the way.

It is a fight between intellect and appetite, between the international idea and armaments. The latter will probably win the first two or three rounds ; but, if civilization is to survive, the idea must win in the end. Meanwhile, if a few million people have to die violent deaths, that cannot be helped. Nature is exceedingly wasteful.

★

The initial tension that preceded the offensive relaxed and became a routine duty as day after day the pressure on the enemy was sustained. My daily morning and afternoon patrols to keep contact with the front line, or photograph some strategic point, would be of no interest except to a student of military history. That work has already been done with wider knowledge of all the factors involved by men more able to do it than a Second-Lieutenant in the R.F.C.

As I look through my logbook, I find detailed references to trenches, map co-ordinations, hostile batteries ; but not one of those patrols remains clearly in my mind. I choose a few entries, less obscure than the rest, to show the laconic attitude of the time :

7th July /16. *Morning*. Second phase of the attack. Idea to sweep North in 15th Corps area and force Boisselle defence to break. Terrific bombardment. Attack had not fairly begun when we left. Flares seen well through Boisselle, smoke attack from North. Clouds down to 800 feet.

7th July /16. *Afternoon*. My most valuable piece of work to date. Attack had proceeded at

Quadrangle trench; but there was a party in Quadrangle Support whose identity was unknown. Came down to 800 feet to see. Several Huns bent down showing their grey coats and helmets. Corps acted on our information and put up a two hour heavy bombardment. Quadrangle was attacked and carried later in the evening.

8th July /16. I am inclined to think that the push, as a whole, is a failure. Machine guns are the secret.

10th July /16. Dawn patrol. This is the most impressive time of day to be out. The light has barely come and gun flashes twinkle all over the country in little points of blue flame. From time to time rockets soar up into the grey dawn. Flares glow like fires in the trenches and far over in Hunland the white plume of a train.

12th July /16. In the middle of the morning Huns were reported to be approaching in large numbers towards Pozières. Rushed off to have a look. Of course there was nothing to be seen as far as Bapaume. We spotted a couple of Archie batteries and came back. Helped to relieve the monotony of the day. To-night we hear that twelve Hun battalions are being rushed down to support the Third Line. The Second Line is to be relinquished and the Third held. Therefore we expect to work four machines with the cavalry and destroy the Third Line at any cost. We shall see what we shall see!

13th July /16. Cavalry are to be put through on the Third Line between Bazentin-le-Grand and Longueval. Fine if it comes off—otherwise, good-bye cavalry! Here's luck, anyway!

14th July /16. Cavalry massing at High Wood. Lots of Hostile Batteries. Advance proceeds.

16th July /16. Our fellows almost entirely occupy High Wood. Called for flares with Klaxon. Splendid co-operation! We came lower, and Hun gave away his position by opening machine-gun fire on us. Located parties of bombers from Pozières to High Wood. Hun put up Very lights and turned machine guns on us again. We cleared up the whole position. Job earned congratulations of General, Colonel, and Major.

19th July /16. There was an attack at dawn on High Wood. It seems to have been successful. I personally saw two Battalion ground sheets this side of the wood and flares beyond it. Men could be seen waving handkerchiefs on rifles. Damn fine the Tommy is! The war generally seems to be hanging fire. What about the general attack? Will it go through? Always to-morrow. . . . To-day four De Havillands met eleven Fokkers. They downed four and the rest ran.

22nd July /16. Heavy bombardment proceeds. When we get through, well and good! But these heavily-wired lines, dugouts, and machine guns are the very devil. They are almost impossible to knock out, and they say the fellows are chained to their guns. I doubt it. There is talk of holding on to what we have here and pushing somewhere else. This bit is done for.

24th July /16. Dined with General. Seems a cheery card—as Generals go!

1st August /16. Gorgeous day! Went up to test new Klaxon for General. In the evening went out, ostensibly to fire at ground target, but really to have a look round the lines. Saw a lot of new trenches and sketched them in. Saw Huns attack De Havillands above us. Climbed to join in ; but got there too late. Ran into a swarm of FE's and 2c's bombing. Followed them over and watched bombs falling. Find I have been twice mentioned in despatches for work on Quadrangle trench and contact patrol on the 16th—that must have been the trench reconnaissance at 300 feet. Very hot, consequently long range artillery spotting and photography difficult, owing to haze. Have never felt so confident of British Air Supremacy as I did to-night when I saw that Squadron of FE's and 2c's going over. Most impressive !

4th August /16. Went out on photography. Archie was so good that I actually felt the puff of hot air when one of the damn things burst. Pretty good shooting !

*

It was considered advisable for pilots to go up to the lines from time to time and make personal contact with the batteries for whom they did artillery observation. Also it was important for us to have some idea of the conditions of ground warfare, which, to me at least, never ceased to be terrifying.

So, one day when the weather was bad for flying, a small party of us set out in a tender for the front. The roads had been repaired, though they were still terrible, and we were forced to abandon the tender near the old front line before Fricourt. We set out on foot towards Caterpillar Wood to visit a nine-inch howitzer battery.

On our way past Fricourt we stopped to examine

its defences. We were amazed at their complete-
ness. No wonder the place had not fallen! There
was a whole series of dugouts, forty or fifty feet
underground, approached by stairways on the reverse slope of the hill. It was said that the Hun
had installed a complete field hospital here, right
on the front line, invulnerable in the heaviest bombardment. Certainly the place was big enough to
shelter hundreds of men in complete security.
Everywhere around lay debris—tangles of barbed
wire, piles of ammunition, wooden boxes, torn
tunics, overcoats—all the leavings of a retreating
army. As we stood on the German front line and
looked to right and left along the arms of the
salient, it seemed as if the Hun had always secured
the higher ground. Fricourt itself occupied a commanding position. We began to understand the
tremendous obstacles the offensive had had to face.
In future we should be less surprised when the men
did not always arrive at their objectives on time.

We wandered on past Mametz, up the valley,
staring curiously at everything we saw. There was
little troop movement up and down the track.
Batteries were perched below the crest of the rise.
A few scavenger gangs were working. There was
no shelling. In one place two dead horses, horribly
swollen, lay on their backs, their stiff legs sticking
up in the air. Farther on, three Tommies were
lying by the roadside, heads on their packs, water-
proof sheets drawn up, quietly sleeping.

We reached the battery and made the acquaint-
ance of the Major, the wireless operator, and some
of the men. They were quite snugly settled into the
little valley, living in dugouts made of large semi-

tubular steel caissons, corrugated and shell-proof. These, standing on a low rampart, made a domed room within, and the sandbagged roof was invisible from the air. They were divided into sections, the entrances, a narrow opening just wide enough for one man to pass, between them.

I was sitting outside on the parapet beside one of these entrances talking with the battery commander, who sat on the other. He pulled out his watch.

" Four o'clock," he said. " Time for the afternoon strafe to start."

And, sure enough, a moment later, shrapnel began to come over. The first shell, with its ominous crescendo, burst some hundreds of yards up the valley.

" They usually traverse the valley for half an hour, but never seem to hit anything. It's rather amusing." He sat on where he was, quietly smoking. I was not used to this sort of war. I felt that reasonable caution would have indicated a withdrawal to the dugout. But if the Major found it amusing, I supposed I ought to find it so too. So I sat on. Another shell came over : nearer. The Major did not budge.

" I suppose you can tell more or less where they're going to fall?" I inquired, simulating a calm I did not feel.

" Yes, pretty well. You get to know the note. Now, this one . . ." he was listening for the next arrival, " will probably . . . Look out ! " We bolted simultaneously for the narrow doorway. There we collided and stuck fast, neither of us able to get in or out, and the shell screaming up to burst.

With a prodigious effort the Major heaved himself clear, and stepped back into the open. " After you," he said.

The shell burst fifty yards short. At our leisure we went below and had tea. Candle-light and rancid tinned butter ; but the tea was good. About six, we set off home again.

The freshly dug cemeteries, made in the hurry of the advance, had been blown up by German shelling, and stank as we passed. We went down the same road, past the dead horses, past the three slumbering Tommies. I wondered how they could sleep so deep, there, in the open, with the men and guns passing, until I paused to look more closely, saw the horrible bluebottles crawling—and knew.

*

We were out taking photos. A perfect summer evening made the work go quickly. Archie was poor, the front quiet, it seemed a pity to go home. Far above, I spotted a Hun two-seater, its white planes, almost transparent against the sky, showing up the black crosses clearly.

" Let's go up and have a fight," I shouted to Pip. He nodded enthusiastically and we climbed.

It took a long time to get up there ; but we took care to keep under the Hun's tail, for we badly wanted to surprise him. Pip got the gun all set, and surprise him we did, opening in a long burst from under his tail. Without a second's hesitation he turned sharply and dived for home. It was too easy ! All you had to do was stalk them, get under them, and scare them out of the sky.

Cock-a-hoop we wandered about, searching for another quarry. Soon we saw a second two-seater. It wasn't so far above us ; but we stalked it as before. Pip opened fire. The Hun turned sharply and came down on our tail. It was our turn to be surprised.

I have already explained that the gear which enabled a machine gun to be fired through a propeller was non-existent (on Allied aircraft) in the summer of 1916. But the enemy were ahead of us. That they had it was proved by the way this Hun dived and opened fire on us in a long rattling burst. It was awkward. We hadn't counted on any opposition. We had only a single-drum Lewis gun, handled by the observer from the rear cockpit. So to fight we had to run away. Also we were only carrying a couple of drums of ammunition (100 rounds), and the first of these we had used on the other Hun. The second was soon expended on this one. It didn't seem to deter him. Now we were quite unarmed, so we dived away and he followed, pooping at us.

Of course we had no business to be taking on Huns like this. It was our own fault. And now we were going to be shot down. I tipped the machine up on one wing, diving steeply, engine full on. The Parasol was not built for this sort of flying, and I knew it. The next moment the wings would drop off. I cut off the engine and dived steeper, turning in a close spiral. By now the Hun could not get his sights on us (for the Parasol dropped like a brick), so, having secured a moral victory (and damn nearly a material one), he sheered off. I pulled the machine out gently, opened up, and we headed for home, feeling a bit sheepish. I was worried about the machine. The right-hand plane seemed loose. It shook in a peculiar way. Throttled right down, we came back at stalling speed, nursing her on to the ground.

Once down, we examined the machine. There were hundreds of holes through the planes, of which about fifty formed a group, almost severing the mainspar, about six feet to the right of my head. No wonder the wing had felt sloppy coming home! That Hun must have held his machine wonderfully steady to put a close group through the spar like that. Said Pip: " I think he was sighting on your head, and his sights were a fraction out. He could never have kept his gun steady on a point in the plane."

" Maybe it was your head."

" Maybe. It's a lovely group anyway."

★

A week's leave! The ship steamed out of Boulogne crowded with officers and men. The escorting destroyers picked her up on her twenty-knot dash for Folkestone. England again! Unchanged, unscarred, meadow, orchard, and oast-house, dreaming still in the warm August twilight. We clattered through at sixty, and crowded to the windows, nearing London. The taxis, driving on the left, put the wind up me after six months of the French rule of the road. Then the luxury of a steaming hot bath, dinner off a white cloth, and after, the night train to Exeter.

In the perfect early morning I chartered a Ford and drove off up the valley of the Exe, bound for

North Devon. There was a wonderful haze over the trees beside the river. I remember I could feel my heart great under my ribs, swollen with the beauty, the peace of it all. This was another world. I had forgotten, my eyes attuned to the wide rolling landscape of northern France, that roads twisted and wandered through wood and coppice, that each turn brought a new vista, that there were moors and streams and thatched roofs where blue smoke curled upward on the still air.

I was to visit and live in other countries. Strange peoples, far lands, each with their art and architecture, their custom, philosophy and life. Very fine and exciting they were to me then, young and curious about the face of the world and the people that lived on it. And many times have I been carried away by the unexpected beauties of the foreign scene. But, finally, a man comes home. For nowhere else, I think, does the beech grow just so, noble and straight, crowning the rounded hill. And nowhere else do the deer go, secret under the bracken, while the watcher notes their track by the gently swaying fronds. The partridge covey lifts with a clatter of surprise over the hawthorn hedge, the morning mushroom snaps under probing fingers in the dewy grass, and there are long twilights before the lamps glow in the windows of the immemorial farms. To each his own allegiance. One forgets till one returns ; then comes the warm assurance— nothing excels our green and secret land.

So the old Ford came grinding up the steep lane. There, before the whitewashed cottage, stood my father. Life had never worked out quite as he hoped, so, like a wise man, he had retired into seclusion to

try and get things straight. We embraced, a little
shyly (we still do), as if such demonstrations of affection weren't quite the thing between grown men.
Jock, the large Airedale, galloped about, then lay
with his forepaws in the Love-in-a-Mist that edged
the lawn. The Siamese cat cried pitifully from the
orchard apple tree. The sun lay on the little valley.
Below I could hear, at the Mill, the sound of a saw.
We sat on the grass and talked. There was, divinely,
nothing whatever to do. All that day we talked;
I of my preoccupations, the jargon of aircraft and
fighting, he (when he had patiently heard me
out) of his lifelong studies, religion, philosophy,
Nietzsche, Bergson, the things of the spirit. My
nervous chatter was soon stilled, for the eternal
quests of Man, seeking to see himself in relation
to the Universe, seemed somehow safe and sane,
however inconclusive, beside my perilous madness.
He was thinking in terms of life and I of death,
and the nobility of the eternal search shamed my
narrow vision.

Next day we purloined some petrol, hired an
ancient motor-car, and trundled over to Clovelly
(Oh, the raspberries and cream!) and Heddons
Mouth, where we bathed and watched the buzzards
circling high over the narrow valley. And all the
time there was, or so it now seems, this steady
quiet flow of thought on abstract problems, marvellously healing because so different, thrusting all
the folly of the time back into its place, making me
feel, strangely, that I was dedicated not to death
but to some future life; should live, not to destroy,
but to add my iota to the wisdom and beauty of the
world to come.

Running his fingers through his white hair, continually sucking at and relighting his ancient pipe, my father walked and talked, eyes fixed on some visionary world, seeing not things before him but an empyrean of thought in which he gambolled happily, while I finned along in his wake. He has not, I am glad to say, improved with advancing years. Throw him an idea, like a herring to a sea-lion, and immediately, with a bark of joy, he will leap from the high rock of his threescore years, catch it in the air, and plunge into that ocean into which all philosophers have plunged since time began, and to which, mercifully, there seems to be no further shore.

" Socialism's a pretty theory ; but it won't work, this equality business. People aren't equal: even when you grind the lot down to the lowest common denominator, they pop up. It's only the first-fruits of this mass education and universal suffrage, this feeling that the labourer's as good as his master, and the master as good as the Prime Minister. It'll pass when the novelty passes—in a few hundred years. No, we're all part of the corporate state, and the state, like the body, must have special functionaries to do the special jobs. You don't expect your thumb to see the time, nor your elbow to hear the clock strike. You leave that to your eyes and ears—specifically developed to the work. The thumb and elbow obey the senses and don't argue. The mind governs. The senses perceive the outer world that it may govern well. The limbs labour to achieve necessary tasks. There's no equality in that. It's a diversity of effort for the common good. But nowadays the toes all think they can govern as well as the mind. And they think they've an equal right to. Result, chaos. No, Socialism is an unnatural state of affairs. Of course, I agree that you must look after your toes, see they have a sufficiency of nourishment and warmth. If you starve or freeze them, they'll rebel and cause you pain; but give them enough for their simple needs and leave it at that. Educate them to their function, and keep them at their function. Don't teach everybody the same things. Don't pretend they've equal rights and equal opportunities : they haven't. We must get rid of the idea that society's a skyscraper with the king on the roof. The potato flower isn't more important than the potato because it's a foot higher up ! It's just part of the organism. Superiority of position must give a man power, but should not give him wealth. It is the confusion of the two, the reaping of the privileges of power in wealth, that leads to revolutions. Witness Marx. Now, Marx . . ."

And so it went on. And so now, twenty years later, it still goes on, praise be. Long may it continue !

Too soon I was back in town again, spending my bank balance in riotous living. To belong to the R.F.C. in those days was to be singled out among the rest of the khaki-clad world by reason of the striking double-breasted tunic, the Wings, the little forage cap set over one ear, but more than this by the glamour surrounding the " birdmen." Flying was still something of a miracle. We who practised it were thought very brave, very daring, very gallant : we belonged to a world apart. In certain respects it was true, and though I do not think we traded on this adulation, we could not but be conscious of it.

The R.F.C. attracted the adventurous spirits, the devil-may-care young bloods of England, the fast livers, the furious drivers—men who were not happy unless they were taking risks. This invested the Corps with a certain style (not always admirable): we had the sense of being the last word in warfare, the advance guard of wars to come, and felt, I suppose, that we could afford to be a little extravagant. Certainly our pay gave us the opportunity to be so in one sense. It was good because our work was skilled and hazardous. But, looking back on it now, I feel we had many compensations.

Under the most arduous conditions we were never under fire for more than six hours a day. When we returned to the aerodrome our war was over. We had a bed, a bath, a mess with good food, and peace until the next patrol. Also, since we were well equipped with transport, we could get about to neighbouring squadrons and big towns, enjoying ourselves and forgetting temporarily the risks of the morrow. Though we lived therefore always in the " stretch or sag of nerves," we were never under any bodily fatigue, never filthy, verminous, or exposed to the long disgusting drudgery of trench warfare.

Courage takes various forms. With us it lay more in audacity than in tenacity. We admire in others the qualities lacking in ourselves, so the Infantry admired our nerve while we admired their phlegm. Speaking personally, I think I should have gone out of my mind under a heavy trench bombardment. My instinct in emergency has always been to do something—attack or run away. To sit and wait to be blown to pieces requires characteristics I have not got, so I can never honour enough the plodding men who bore the burden of the war, who gave us victory (for what it proved to be worth) because they stuck it.

So on my return to town, true to type and the tradition of the R.F.C., I plunged into a frenzied rush of meaningless " pleasure," which because of the sense that it might never be repeated, took on a glamour out of all proportion to its worth. Indeed to-day I cannot remember a single incident, nor face, nor word, in all that week, nothing beyond the vague feeling that somehow or other, with someone or other, I had a " jolly good time."

I reported to the pool and was sent down to Farnborough to ferry a machine back to France. They gave me a BE 12—a single-seater BE 2c, built for long reconnaissance, with a 140-h.p. R.A.F. engine, which rattled and clattered, full out or throttled down, like a can of old nails. It was a day of cloudless blue and summer haze. I went up to ten thousand to say good-bye to England. One never knew. . . . At the coast already I could see the beckoning pattern of the Flanders fields ; below, the toy ships were ploughing the Channel; behind, London under a murk, the Thames estuary, Kent, the southern coast as far as the Isle of Wight. Dover pier, with little dots of people on it, threads of white foam marking the surf, white cliffs guarding the Weald. Slowly it fell away behind me. My eyes were set for St Omer, from that height seemingly only a stone's-throw from the coast. I reported there, saw Patrick, and pushed

on south to the new depot (No. 2 A.D.) at Candas.
A tender picked me up, and I was back for dinner in
the Mess. It had all gone so quickly, I hardly
seemed to have been away.

*

The next day I plunged back into the old routine.
A sort of recklessness, bred of my short rest, came
over me. Besides, I had a new observer, Hoppy
Cleaver. Hoppy was a gallant, good-looking
young bloke, with a slight stammer and a sort of
jerky audacity which, coupled with a sense of
humour, made him laughed at and liked by the
squadron, which did not, at first, take him seriously.
He was fresh to this part of the war, and out to get
his M.C. (which he received, and richly deserved, a
fortnight later). Together we planned our new
private offensive. Its slogan was : fly lower.

We went out twice a day, averaging about four
hours over the lines. Whatever we did, photos,
trench reconnaissance, artillery observation, we
made it our business to deliver the goods. We
patrolled usually below the thousand-foot mark, and,
now that the attack was steadying up, we began to
receive unwelcome attention from machine-gun fire
on the ground. We retaliated, never leaving the
lines without emptying all our ammunition into the
trenches where the Huns looked thickest. When
this happened, they used to fire white lights and a
moment later Archie would open at us. But he was
inaccurate at low altitudes and didn't bother us much.

On the 3rd of September a local attack was
launched on Ginchy. It was a well-organized show.

The barrage lifted to schedule, the Tommies lit their flares, we dropped our messages on head-quarters every half-hour. Our patrol covered the luncheon hour, so we fed in the air off chocolate and whisky in milk. A machine-gun bullet came up through the floor of the cockpit, missed my ankle by half an inch. " A miss "—I recorded in my logbook—" is as good as a mile."

But the character of the war was changing. The great offensive was almost through, though there was still one great attack to come. But the Hun was everywhere consolidating his positions, and pay-ing much more attention to us than hitherto. In the early part of the year we had wandered about over the lines, unmolested ; but now we took bets on the number of bullet holes the machine would gather on patrol. Twenty or thirty was the aver-age. The riggers were constantly patching the planes and fuselage. And yet, somehow or other, they always (or almost always) seemed to miss the vital points.

*

Half a dozen of us were sitting having tea in the orchard behind the sheds, when a machine was heard. Soon it came in to land, passing overhead. We looked up at it casually. It was Hoppy, out with another pilot (for my machine was dud) return-ing from patrol. Suddenly the camp table, on which the tea was set, flew up into the air, described a pretty parabola above the grass, and landed ten yards farther down the slope—a debris of broken china and spilt jam. We all jumped up, very annoyed.

" That silly little bastard, coming down without
winding in his aerial ! "—for the meteoric flight of
the tea-table was caused by the lead weight attached
to the end of the aerial catching it as it swept past
at sixty miles an hour. The peace of the orchard
was gone, tea entirely ruined. " Besides which,"
added the Major, " the damn thing only missed my
head by six inches."

We all rushed out to tell young Hoppy what we
thought of him. We found him sitting on the edge
of his cockpit, talking away excitedly with his pilot.
He was in his usual high spirits, dismissed the tea-
table with a snigger, and pointed to the fuselage.

I have said already that the Morane was tricky
to fly. You never took any liberties with it. As
for stunting it, spinning, or anything like that,
nobody but a lunatic would have dreamed of such
a thing.

Hoppy had lured his pilot to attack some Huns
after their patrol was over. In his excitement at
seeing enemy aircraft and going in to fight them,
he had forgotten to wind in his aerial. The Huns
gave a very good account of themselves, and the
pilot was forced to do something pretty drastic to
out-manœuvre them. By mistake (for he certainly
wouldn't have done it on purpose) he put the
machine into a spin, during which the aerial wound
itself several times round the fuselage. Somehow
or other the pilot managed to get the bus out, and
terrified out of his life, not at the Huns, but at the
strain he had put on his machine, legged it for
home. Of course the aerial could not be wound in.
Hence the conjuring trick with the tea-table.

All the same, the Major was really upset. The

next night Squadron Orders contained very definite instructions to pilots and observers : " Before engaging enemy aircraft or returning to the aerodrome, particular care must be taken to rewind aerials to avoid danger to or disorganization of ground staff."

★

For some time there had been rumours of yet another general offensive on the Somme front. There was persistent talk of some new weapon, but details were secret, and it was only twenty-four hours before the attack I heard the magic word—Tanks.

Hoppy and I were detailed for the first contact patrol with the Tanks. It was launched on the 15th of September at 6.30 A.M.

A systematic heavy bombardment had been carried out, morning and evening, for a week prior to the attack, so that on the morning itself the Hun should not imagine anything was brewing. But at 6.17 an intense hurricane bombardment was put over from Thiepval to Delville Wood.

When we climbed up to the lines, we found the whole front seemingly covered with a layer of dirty cotton-wool — the smoking shell-bursts. Across this were dark lanes, drawn as it might be by a child's stubby finger in dirty snow. Here no shells were falling. Through these lanes lumbered the Tanks in file, four to each lane. By 6.20 they had reached the front line and the barrage began to roll back as they advanced, the infantry with them. We could see them sitting across the trenches and enfilading the enemy with their four-

142

pounders. By eight o'clock the complete network of trenches known as Switch Line and Flers Line was taken.

Some of the Tanks were put out of action. Some took fire, some suffered direct hits from enemy shell-fire; but later many were still to be seen, refuelling in Flers, the red petrol tins visible on their brown backs. In my logbook appears the following entry:

" The Gueudecourt Line should have fallen by 10 A.M.; but this failed. It will be attacked to-morrow at dawn. We are at present digging a new front line. Little is known of what happened on our flanks; but it is pretty certain the cavalry are not through as they intended. Perhaps to-morrow. Always to-morrow! A partial success; but from programme a failure. I shall never forget the way the Tanks waltzed through Flers. There was a little white terrier, a mascot I suppose, following one of the Tanks. Apparently the little chap was not hit, for we saw him running round barking at his Tank on the afternoon patrol."

The next day we were out at dawn again:

" A further attack on the third line failed. We were flying very low. No Huns were visible in the trenches and the line very quiet. A heavy bank of cloud came up at twelve hundred, and when we climbed up through it we saw, above us, an FE 2b attacked by three Huns. We thought he was hit, for he spun vertically for a thousand feet—a sicken-ing sight, round and round and round—then, to our surprise, he flattened out and glided home. We cheered him as he passed. Then a Hun attacked us. We only heard machine-gun fire, and thought it came from the ground. He missed us, and Hoppy, who just spotted him as he went by, gave him a drum for luck. He disappeared east. We came down through the clouds again. We had left the line quiet. Now it was an inferno. A violent barrage from us and one equally violent from the Hun. The machine rocked continuously in the eddies.

" I knew it was not going too well because the Hun had time to turn his guns on us. Two more bullets came up through the floor between the stick and my feet. One went out over my left shoulder, and a splinter of wood knocked the stick out of my hand. Of course it fell forward on the tank with a crack and we went into a nose-dive—damn nearly flung old Hoppy out! However, I grabbed it and steadied her up. The other shot went through the oil tank, gushed oil all over me, on through the back-plate, *missing* the engine (extraordinary luck and probably saved our lives), and finally out through the propeller, through which it tore a nasty hole. We were right over Gueudecourt at the time. We struggled in to the advance landing-ground at Carnoy. Hoppy dashed off to report. I patched the tank and trundled on home.

" I shall remember for ever the Horse Artillery coming up into action behind Flers, on a road that was mostly shell-holes, under a hail of shrapnel. A team of six roan chargers, sweeping up at full gallop, dumping ammunition by the guns and, with hardly a pause, galloping back again, the outriders crouching low over the necks of their plunging beasts with their flying manes and terrorstruck eyes! There isn't much picturesque or visibly heroic to be seen in this war when you're in the air—but that was ! "

That afternoon we went out again. The attack was still going on as we left, and the light was failing. As we landed, a crowd came up and surrounded the machine. They lifted Hoppy and carried him shoulder-high into the Mess. His M.C. had come through.

★

Six months' continuous flying low over the trenches had affected my eyes. I had long ago given up goggles because they fogged in the oil fumes from the engine. Besides, leaning out of the cockpit to scan the ground carefully—for you dared not make a mistake as to the identity of the men in the trenches when the guns bombarded the place on the strength of your report—was almost impossible with goggles on. Now it was getting colder ; acute conjunctivitis set in. I had to stop flying, and went home for another fortnight's sick leave. Secretly I hoped for a longer rest ; for I was utterly tired of it all. But, after a fortnight, with eyes cured, I returned to the squadron.

★

The tender bumped and bounced along the Amiens–Albert road. Dark. Guns moving. The oil lamps hardly lit the mud in the gutters. In the village, no lights. I dumped my kit in my billet and walked down to the Mess. The gramophone was wheezing, " I'll see you to-night, dear, and your eyes will be bright, dear." Two chaps were playing vingty, drinking port. The gramophone stopped. The lamp was smoking. They hardly greeted me. I was eighteen, conceited, unpopular.

" Had a good leave ? "

" Fine, thanks."

I ordered some coffee. The place smelled of stale smoke. The chairs wobbled. The tablecloth was stained and dingy. The wire that held the lamp was thick with dead flies.

" Orderly ! "

" Sir ? "

" Whisky ! "

" Sir."

" Where's Rudd ? " I asked. Only four chaps here. Where were the others ?

" Killed. Archie. This morning. Orderly ! "

" Sir ? "

" Cigarettes."

" Sir."

" Both of them ? " I couldn't believe it somehow.

" Suppose so. Machine took fire. Couldn't recover the bodies."

The boy who spoke was only eighteen too. A good pilot. Brave. Rudd had been his room-mate. God, how quiet the Mess was !

" And Hoppy ? "

" Wounded : gone home."

" And Pip and Kidd ? " I was almost frightened to ask.

" Done in last night. Direct hit. One of our own shells. Battery rang up to apologize. New pilots coming."

Kidd, with the funny quirky laugh ! Pip, who had seen the poppies with me. I turned instinctively to the piano. After dinner he was always there. Never again those yellow keys under those gentle hands. . . . It was so still. Surely they were near. The door would open, and . . .

"By the way, congrats on your Military Cross!"

Echoes. Congrats! Congratulations. Five ghosts in the room. Five friends. Congrats!

"Thanks," I said.

★

Now a sort of desperation was in the air. The battle had failed. The summer was over. The best men had gone. Well, you had to carry on. Harvey Kelly, the Major, had gone too, and I didn't like the new man. I went off to the lines and wandered round at any old height, two hundred, three hundred feet, asking for trouble. My good luck must be over. Why should I remain when those chaps were gone? It seemed unfair. What I needed was a direct hit. That would wind up the show in style.

They gave me a new machine, faster, prettier, more comfortable than the other, the latest thing, and mine the first in the squadron. But even that didn't cheer me. I could only write epitaphs for the old one: "This was my last trip on old 5133. I had her when I arrived at the squadron and I've flown her ever since. Two or three half-axles and one Vee-piece were the only things ever replaced. She always flew well. She never let me down. On her I got an M.C. and did the best work I shall ever do in this war. She's held jolly gallant men in the back seat. The best one is dead. I flew her over to be broken up. She looked a bit decrepit standing

147

there beside the new one—all spit and polish. But she's seen me through—so far. She might have lasted me out. God, how sick I am of this war!"

★

Magnificent days of blue and crystal, when to be in the air made everything worth while, were over. Damp hangars, muddy roads, cold quarters, clouds and rain—these were to be our lot from now on.

One dreary grey morning I went up alone on patrol. The clouds were at two hundred feet, but they might break farther east over the lines. I rose into the cloud-bank—a featureless obscurity, a white dark, as you might say—and started climbing.

A pilot flies by his horizon. He keeps his machine on an even keel, or indeed in any position, by reference to it. Take away the horizon and he doesn't know where he is. This is the reason for gyroscopic controls, false horizon indicators, and all the modern gadgets (to say nothing of beam wireless) which enable a man to fly " blind," and a commercial pilot to bring his thirty-eight passengers on to Croydon aerodrome in a pea-soup fog without too much anxiety. But in 1916 a chap had an air-speed indicator and a lateral bubble (which was supposed to tell him if he was on an even keel), and the rest was the luck of the game and his native " nouse."

In a cloud there is no horizon, nothing above, below, in front, behind, but thick white mist. It's apt to make you panic after a while, and many a man has fallen out of the clouds in a spin through losing his head and, without knowing it, standing his machine on its ear. Usually low cloud-banks

148

aren't so very deep, so if you go carefully and watch
the controls closely you get up through them all right;
but on this particular morning there seemed to be
no top to them. I climbed and climbed, looking up
all the time, hoping to see that thinning of the mist
and the halo of the sun above which means you're
almost through. But it wasn't until I reached two
thousand feet that I saw the welcome sheen of gold
overhead. It thinned. Mist wraiths drew back
and showed blue. They curled away. I was out.

But what in heaven had happened to this cloud-
bank? It wasn't level. It was tilted as steeply as
the side of a house. The machine was all right—
airspeed constant, bubble central—and yet here were
the clouds defying all natural laws! I suppose it
took me a second to realize that *I* was tilted, bubble
or no bubble, that I had been flying for the best
part of fifteen minutes at an angle of thirty degrees
to the horizon—*and had never noticed it!* If I had
tried to fly this way on purpose, it would have
seemed impossible, at the best most unpleasant.
The machine would have shuddered and slipped.
I should have been in a dither after half a minute.
If you'd told me any one could fly like it quite
happily for ten minutes, I should just have laughed.
It shows what a little ignorance can do.

I put the machine level and gazed around in
wonder. Here it was still summer. Below, life was
dying back into the earth. Gold plumes fluttering
from the poplars. The mournful voice of the
October wind. But here! As far as the eye could
reach, to the four horizons, a level plain of radiant
whiteness, sparkling in the sun. The light seemed
not to come from a single source, but to pervade

and permeate every atom of air—a dazzling, perfect, empty basin of blue.

A hundred miles, north, south, east, west. Thirty thousand square miles of unbroken cloud-plains! No traveller in the desert, no pioneer to the poles had ever seen such an expanse of sand or snow. Only the lonely threshers of the sky, hidden from the earth, had gazed on it. Only we who went up into the high places under the shadow of wings!

I sailed on for a time, alone in the wonderful skies, as happy as I have ever been or ever shall be, I suppose, in this life, looking lazily for some rift in the white floor; but there was none. It was complete, unbroken, absolute. I was about to turn west again when I saw, in the distance, a cloud floating above the floor, small, no bigger than a man's hand; but even as I looked, it seemed to grow. It swelled, budded, massed, and I realized I was watching the very birth of a cloud—the cumulus cloud that chiefly makes the glory of the sky, the castles, battlements, cathedrals of the heavens. What laws had governed its birth at that moment, at that place, amid the long savannahs of the blue? Heaven, that bore it, knew. Still it was there, creating a growing loveliness out of nothing! A marriage of light and water, fostered by the sun, nourished by the sky!

I turned towards it, fascinated. It grew rapidly. Soon it was vast, towering, magnificent, its edges sharp, seemingly solid, though constantly swelling and changing. And it was alive with light. Radiant white, satin soft, and again gold, rose-tinted, shadowed and graded into blue and mauve shadows—an orient pearl in the oyster shell of heaven! And all the time I knew that I had but to come close enough for all the illusion to be gone, the solidity and beauty to dissolve, the edges to fray and dull, and that within it would be the same grey mist that you may meet on any moor in England.

Wisdom said: Keep distance and admire. Curiosity asked: How much closer without losing the illusion? I edged nearer. I was utterly alone in the sky, yet suddenly, against the wall of the cloud, I saw another machine. It was so close that instinctively, as an instantaneous reaction to the threat of collision, I yanked the stick and reeled away, my heart in my mouth. A second later, I looked round and laughed. There was nothing there! It was my own shadow I had seen, the silhouette of the machine on the white cheek of the cloud. I came back to observe the strange and rare phenomenon. There on the cloud was my shadow, dark, clean-cut; but more than the shadow, for around it was a bright halo of light, and outside that a perfect circular rainbow, and outside that again another rainbow, fainter, reversed.

From the ground the rainbow is an arch spanning the visible heaven. From the next hill-top, so it seems, one would be high enough to solve the riddle of where it ends. But here it was small, bright, compact, a perfect circle, and at the centre the shadow of the Parasol, like the stamped image on a golden coin.

I shut off, turned east, and came down. The white floor, several thousand feet below, rose up towards me, turned at last from a pavement of pearl to just a plain bank of fog. I plunged into it. I might be going back from paradise to purgatory, so grey and cold and comfortless it was. And as I sank through it, listening to the singing of the wires, I was thinking how some day men might no longer hug the earth, but dwell in heaven, draw power and sustenance from the skies, whirl at their will among the stars, and only seek the ground as men go down to the dark mysteries of the sea-floor, glad to return, sun-worshippers, up to the stainless heaven.

The melancholy landscape of stubble fields and bare trees appeared. I picked up a road, got my bearings, and swept off home at a hundred feet.

" Did you see anything? " said another pilot, strolling up to the machine.

" Nothing. It's completely dud."

*

Roberts had got a D.C.M. as a sergeant pilot, been wounded, given a commission, and now specialized in artillery observation. He was a quiet phlegmatic fellow, went about his work in an unobtrusive way, and about this time spent most of his time ranging heavy calibre guns on distant objectives. To do this he used to go well over into Hunland unescorted. Earlier in the year there had been so few hostile aircraft that this was reasonably safe. Now the Hun was getting frisky : it was looking for trouble. Roberts found it.

He had been out ranging a twelve-inch gun, and coming home was attacked by an enemy scout at eight thousand feet. His observer did what he could ; but in the first burst the Hun put a bullet through the rudder controls of the Morane. The machine immediately went into a spin.

Roberts was a crack pilot, and if human skill could have got that machine out, he would have done it. His elevators and ailerons were still intact, and by shutting off his engine he almost managed to avert disaster—but not quite. He could not stop the machine spinning; but he could stop it going into a vertical diving spin. He tried every combination of elevator and bank. No good. The machine went on slowly spinning, round and round and round, all the way down from eight thousand feet to the ground. It took about five minutes. He and his observer were sitting there, waiting for death, for that time.

The machine fell just this side of the lines. They say a man in the trenches heard shouts, as it might have been for help, come from the machine just before it struck the ground and smashed to a pile of wreckage.

The observer was killed, for the fuselage broke in half; but Roberts escaped. He was badly smashed up, but breathing. They got him on to a stretcher and sent him down to hospital. He had been out all through the Somme battle without leave, his nerves were right on the edge, and we heard, with what truth I never knew, that this fearful experience put him out of his mind. As far as we were concerned he was gone—the dead or wounded never came back to us—and in the swiftly changing pattern of the days we lost him.

*

Only a fortnight later my eye trouble returned. The General put me up for a week. The comfort of his château and his charming hospitality were very welcome after the racket of the daily patrols. Then I was posted to Home Establishment, and climbed into the train at Amiens with a wonderful feeling of relief. While I had been on the job, screwed up to the pitch of nervous control it demanded, all had been well. In fact, the only effect of a long spell at the front seemed to be to make me more reckless and contemptuous of the danger. But now that tension had been relaxed, I realized how shaky and good-for-nothing I was. Eight months overseas, four months of the Somme battle, three hundred and fifty hours in the air, and still alive! Pilots, in 1916, were lasting, on an average, for three weeks. To-day it seems incredible that I came through; but at that time I did not calculate the odds, for, as I have said, I had an absolute and unshakable belief in my invulnerability. I can give no reason for this. It was quite groundless; but then all faith is groundless. It is a divine example of the illogicality of the human soul, backing itself with arrogant humility against the laws of Chance or Fate. When it triumphs we affirm that the hand of God was upon us, when it fails it has at least sustained us; and others who continue to believe dismiss its failure, saying those it abandoned did not possess it in sufficient measure. So, in either event, it is vindicated and flourishes. " Si Dieu n'existait pas, il faudrait l'inventer.'

III

TESTING

To be posted to Home Establishment meant either going on instruction or joining Home Defence.

I always regarded instruction as a come-down, a confession that the pilot was finished, no use at the front, and condemned to flip young aspirants round and round the aerodrome day after day on obsolete types of machines. Of course it was unreasonable, for competent instructors were most valuable to the rapidly expanding Force. Although their qualities were not necessarily those of successful active service pilots, they were equally important. A good instructor was, and still is, a pretty rare bird. It needs some guts to turn a machine over to a half-fledged pupil in the air and let him get into difficulties and find his way out of them. Instruction demands, besides, an ability to communicate oneself to another person (the secret of all good teaching), and not so simple as it sounds. Add to this great patience, the quality of inspiring confidence, and an extremely steady flying ability in the man himself, and it will be obvious that nobody need look down his nose at an instructor. All this I know now; then, the idea of flying an uninteresting machine condemned the thing out of hand, for flying itself, handling the latest and fastest types, trick flying, exhibitionism if you like, was all I cared about. Unconsciously quoting Shaw (with whom I was then unfamiliar), I thought, " Those who can, do; those who can't, teach," and prayed that I might not be posted to a Training Squadron.

On the other hand, Home Defence seemed equally uninviting. In the winter of 1916-17 the Gotha had not made its appearance. London had only been raided and bombed by occasional Zeppelins. To defend the city against them a few detached flights of BE 2c's had been placed at strategic points north and south of the Thames estuary. Zepps flew so slowly that even 2c's could get up to them before they got away! But what a job! To stand by waiting, night after night, for the possible chance of a raid; to have nothing to do all day but fly a 2c for pleasure! Those who have struggled thus far will have read something about the 2c and what I thought of it. No, Home Defence was, if anything, more uninviting than Training.

I should have to go where I was told, of course; but these were the private horns of my dilemma. Therefore imagine my excitement and relief when I found I had been posted to the Testing Squadron. I didn't know such a squadron existed. I didn't know exactly what it existed for. But the very word " testing " was enough! The luck was still holding. I packed and entrained for Upavon.

*

With the exception of the Royal Aircraft Factory at Farnborough, which was a Government organization, the manufacture of aircraft was then, as now, a private business. Handley Page, De Havilland, Sopwith, Vickers, Armstrong Whitworth, these firms (and others) were all vying with each other in producing aircraft for the various requirements of the Flying Corps. All new machines were handed over to the Testing Squadron, to be put through their paces and reported upon. On the strength of this report, orders for successful types were placed.

So in the sheds were to be found a miscellaneous collection of all kinds of aircraft, from heavy double-engine bombers to the smallest fighting-scouts. Many of them got no farther than the Testing Squadron. Some ought never to have got that far. The design of aircraft was a very much more fluky business then than it is to-day. Although war was a tremendous stimulus, aerodynamical data was almost non-existent. Every new machine was an experiment, obsolete in the eyes of the designer before it was completed, so feverishly and rapidly did knowledge progress. But even in 1917 the major designers were beginning to stamp their work with sufficient individuality for the trained eye to decide on sight from which factory a new machine had been turned out. Sopwiths, for instance, had beautiful lines, far in advance of others; but always looked a shade light to stand up to war conditions. De Havillands were sturdier but less prepossessing; while Vickers seemed to have a blunt disregard for anything approaching streamline. From the smaller firms came the freaks, dangerous little scouts, modelled on existing types with retrograde "improvements"; sloppy old cows, designed to carry torpedoes or large bombs, that wallowed through the air at incredibly slow speeds; triplanes and quadruplanes, but (it is interesting to note in view of the present-day trend) practically no monoplanes: all these machines were received (not always welcomed) by the squadron, flown, tested thoroughly, reported on to the Air Ministry, and returned to their makers.

It was, of course, a paradise for the enthusiastic pilot to whom flying itself was a continual delight. I was avid of all air experience; the way each different machine answered the controls, took off, turned, stunted, glided, landed, all this never ceased to fascinate. A nice arrangement of instruments in the cockpit, the comfort of the pilot's seat, the handiness of the controls, or the reverse of all these things, were matters for eulogistic praise or damning criticism. It was grand to fly a well-thought-out machine, infuriating to test one where some important control or indicator had been inefficiently placed.

Machines were tested for their rates of climb, light and loaded, for their speeds at ground level and at various heights, for absolute ceiling (as high as the machine would go), and, in the case of scouts, for manœuvrability and safety in diving. To stand a scout on its nose and dive it straight at the ground, engine full on, is a somewhat hair-raising experience; but such a need arises in aerial combat. I have seen pilots dive the wings off their machines fighting over the lines; but under such circumstances one could never tell whether the break-up was due to constructional weakness or to the fact that some vital wire or spar socket had been shot away during the fight. Nowadays it would be possible (though somewhat costly) to dive a machine until it reached its breaking-point, if any, and for the pilot to jump clear in his parachute. But in those days pilots' parachutes did not exist, so we did not carry our tests quite that far. When the revolutions got abnormally high and the vibration of the wires or wings looked dangerous, we noted the speed, and gingerly eased the machine upwards; for at such speeds the controls were very sensitive, and to yank a machine out of a dive, changing its direction suddenly, would have put enough strain on the wings for them to snap off and fold back at the roots.

Engaged on work of this kind, in which I was as happy as the day was long, I spent all the winter, first at Upavon and then at Martlesham Heath. After the front, it was a quiet and uneventful life (except, as far as I remember, for one gorgeous binge when the squadron divided and had a pitched battle with fire-extinguishers), and by March I was rested and ready for transfer to a new scout squadron going overseas.

*

But, at Martlesham, I realized a long-cherished ambition—to fly scouts. My attempt with the Bristol Bullet at St Omer in the spring of the previous year had been disastrous. Since then no opportunity had come along; but one day the Sopwith Triplane arrived at Martlesham for tests.

Of all machines, the Triplane remains in my memory as the best—for the actual pleasure of flying—that I ever took up. It was so beautifully

balanced, so well-mannered, so feather-light on
the stick, and so comfortable and warm. It had
what was then a novel feature, an adjustable tail
plane to trim the machine fore and aft. Set correctly,
with the throttle about three-quarters open, the
Tripe would loop, hands off, indefinitely. Not for
this, but for its docility, the lack of all effort needed
to fly it, and yet its instantaneous response to the
lightest touch, it remains my favourite. Other
machines were faster, stronger, had better climb
or vision; but none was so friendly as the Tripe.
After it I never wanted to fly anything but a scout
again, and on active service I never did.

Flying alone! Nothing gives such a sense of
mastery over mechanism, mastery indeed over
space, time, and life itself, as this. Most men
covet the power of putting the world, their world,
into perspective, of seeing themselves in relation to
it, of achieving some sort of harmony with their
environment. It involves mastery, for that alone
gives detachment, and only from detachment
comes harmony—a sense of values. Never, it
seems, has the world had so poor a sense of values
as to-day. So, if the muddle-headed idiocy of men
angers and intimidates you—for though fools
running about with loaded revolvers may only
make you angry, their potential power for damage
cannot but be frightening—if the daily mani-
festations of an approaching cataclysm, which
mutter and shake on the four horizons, make you
despair, I recommend a trip to ten thousand feet
to recover your sense of values—and your sense of
humour.

From such a height how insignificant the works

of men's hands appear! How everything they do seems to disfigure the face of the earth; but when they have done their worst, what a lot of it is left! This curious and intricate agglomeration of little pink boxes is a city. It looks rather like an open sore in the green flesh of the earth; but not, after all, such a very large one. Left for a few hundred years it will heal up and the world be none the worse. In contrast, how satisfying and permanent are the shapes of the woods and the pattern of the tilled and fallow fields. These are the first and last things, and will persist in the face of all conquest or defeat while any men endure. That minute cluster of weathered roofs set in the fold of the valley is a village. It looks right, as if it had grown there; it cannot be far wrong. Beyond, how ample are the courses of the rivers and the contours of the coasts! With what grace and spontaneity is the world laid out! Man-made order and precision, square, circle, or straight line, is an offence among this greater harmony, where nothing seems planned, yet all falls home just so. In truth it cannot last, this mechanical geometrical civilization of ours, for the simple and final reason that it does not *look* right. It offends the aesthetic sense, and that, of all men's senses, is the most deeply rooted and changeless. So, let it go. After all, if we take a perspective in time comparable to the one we have taken in height, how mushroom-like is our scientific epoch. Two hundred years ago it was not thought of. Now it rages, like a cholera epidemic. Soon, having taken its toll, it will die out, leaving us inoculated or immune. That we are doomed to live in this feverish age, rushing hither and thither, crying Lo, here! or Lo, there! like madmen in a darkened room, is our misfortune; but momentarily withdrawn from it all, sailing godlike above its clamour, comes a curious certainty: it does not matter, it will not last; the world is very foolish, but it is very young.

IV

AERIAL FIGHTING

JUST before my nineteenth birthday I was posted to London Colney to join No. 56 Squadron, which was then forming to go overseas. The squadron was to be equipped with the SE 5, the last word in fighting-scouts, turned out by the Royal Aircraft Factory. It was fitted with a 140-h.p. Hispano Suiza engine and two guns: one Vickers, synchronized, and firing through the propeller by means of the new Constantinesco gear; and one Lewis gun, clamped on to the top plane and firing over the propeller. To change drums, the Lewis could be pulled down on a quadrant mounting, and in this position it could, if necessary, be fired straight upwards. The machine (for 1917) was quite fast. It would do about a hundred and twenty on the level and climb ten thousand feet in twelve minutes. It could be looped and rolled and dived vertically without breaking up. Altogether it was a first-class fighting-scout (probably the most successful designed during the war), and was relied upon to re-establish the Allied air supremacy lost during the winter.

The success of a squadron depends enormously on the personality of the Commanding Officer. Major Bloomfield, O.C. 56, was determined to allow nothing to come between him and making

163

his the crack fighting squadron in the R.F.C. His geniality did not prevent him being very sharp-eyed and nimble-witted. Efficiency was his watchword.

In appearance he was shortish and slightly built. He wore leggings, and invariably carried a short leather-covered cane, with which he directed everything, reminding one irresistibly of a dapper little ringmaster. Tremendously energetic and keen, he was always to be seen hurrying here and there, giving close personal supervision to every detail of the squadron's work—activity and organization personified. He had all his pilots out for a run before breakfast, kept them busy round the sheds all day, and turned them loose in town at night. They had to be tip-top aviators and bring down Huns. Nothing else mattered.

This atmosphere of eager preparation was a change after the quiet isolation of Martlesham. When I arrived only one SE 5 had been delivered; but every day during the next fortnight before we left for France experienced pilots were rushed over to Farnborough to bring back others, till, on the 5th April, the establishment of twelve was complete.

But the SE 5, as delivered from Farnborough, was fitted with a cumbersome celluloid wind-screen covering the breach of the Vickers gun, with an aperture for the Aldis telescopic sight above. The " greenhouse "—as we called it—greatly interfered with forward visibility, and in the event of a crash its sharp edges would have been dangerous to the pilot's face and arms. As soon as the Major saw that the fighting efficiency of his pilots was going to be impaired, he moved heaven and earth to get these greenhouses removed. If the Factory did not see eye

to eye with him about it, very well ; *he* would make
the alterations. So for a week after reaching France he
put the whole squadron out of action while a sensible
design of wind-screen was fitted to every machine.

A first-class fighting mechanism needs a first-
class personnel to render it effective, so the Major
ransacked all the training centres in England to get
the pick of the pilots. His Flight-Commanders
were men with previous fighting experience, headed
by Captain Ball, D.S.O., and all the rest of us had
been most carefully selected. But even the machines
and the personnel were not enough. To keep fighting pilots on their toes there must be an A1 morale.
For this there was nothing like music : the squadron
must have its own band. The Major got scouts out
round the depots, and whenever a saxophone player
or a violinist turned up, he swapped one of his own
men of equal rating for the man who was a musician
as well. A sergeant who had been a theatre orchestra
conductor was put in charge, and later, in France,
whenever things were not quite as bright as they
might be, out came the squadron band.

At last everything was ready. The machines had
all been tuned up, the men entrained for overseas,
the kits packed and sent off, and only the pilots were
left with a pair of pyjamas, a toothbrush, and a
towel to cram into the pockets of their flying-coats
when they left for France on the morrow.

★

Another last night in England ! Rooms had
been taken in the little hotel at Radlett near by.
That evening we all sat down to a cheery dinner

and went early to bed, strictly sober! It was our ambition to do what no squadron had previously done, namely, arrive at our aerodrome overseas without losing a single machine by the way. (Usually squadrons left quite a few machines scattered along their route with dud engines or broken undercarriages.)

Eleven o'clock next morning, the 7th of April 1917, saw us all in our cockpits, warming up our engines. On the tarmac stood a small group of parents and friends, two pretty girls picked up in the hotel the night before, and a few other pilots and officers under training at the aerodrome. Captain Foot, the squadron leader, a crazy and gallant pilot (who was killed several years after the war, civilian flying), had smashed himself up in a car the night before. Consequently, because of my many trips across the Channel and my knowledge of the French aerodrome we were going to, the honour of leading the squadron overseas fell to me.

Proudly I fixed the leader's streamers to my rudder, and on the Major's signal led the way out across the aerodrome, followed by all the others in single file, turned into wind and took off. Waving to our friends below as we soared above them, we climbed into formation, and headed for St Omer, via Chingford, Romford, Gravesend, Maidstone, Folkestone and Calais.

The weather conditions were good, the pilots were all nursing their engines and keeping fine formation. We made St Omer in an hour and forty minutes, lunched in the town, took off again, and by four o'clock the whole squadron had landed safely at Vertgaland. A record!

The next days were spent in getting the Mess and sleeping quarters comfortable and making alterations to the wind-screens. After this, some time elapsed before the first Offensive Patrol. Young pilots new to France needed to be on tours round the area over which they were to operate, to get the hang of the country and put in time on the new machines. Besides this, there were guns to test, sights to adjust, and personal gadgets to fit. It was over a fortnight before the Major judged us ready to go into action.

*

On the first Offensive Patrol, with two others, we attacked five German scouts: four bright red and one green. I chose one and dived, got him in the sights, and pressed the trigger of the Vickers. Not a shot! I continued in the dive, trusting to the Lewis gun to do the trick: it fired two shots and jammed! Damnation! I zoomed away, trying frantically to clear the Vickers jam. Nothing would shift it, so I pulled the Lewis down its sliding quadrant to clear it and reload. The spade grip of the gun knocked down the hinged wind-screen, and the blast of a 100 m.p.h. wind nearly blew my head off. This was a pretty state to be in surrounded by five enemy scouts! I was a sitter for any Hun, so I turned west and climbed away, working all the time to get my screen up and clear the Lewis jam. At last I managed it; but then, try as I would, I could not force the gun up the quadrant back into place on the top plane. The slide was twisted. I came home fed up, my gun pointing straight up into heaven. Nevertheless, that day the squadron got four Huns : a good start. Ball accounted for two of them.

*

In 1917 co-operative tactics in single-seater fighting were rudimentary. A combat was a personal matter. In a fight no pilot has time to watch others ; he is too occupied in attempting to down his own man or in avoiding an enemy intent on downing him. Tactics apart, the vital question is that of performance. A machine with better speed and climbing power must always have the advantage. During the next ten days Offensive Patrols were carried out daily, and, unfortunately, it soon became clear that, good as the SE5 was, it was still not equal to the enemy. Scrapping at high altitudes, fifteen to eighteen thousand feet, the Huns had a marked superiority in performance. This naturally tended to make us cautious, since we knew that, once we came down to their level, we should not be able to get above them again. Height, apart from its moral superiority, means added speed for the one above, who in his dive and zoom away has gravity on his side. Since machine guns in a scout are fixed, firing forward in the line of flight, it follows that the pilot aims the whole machine at his adversary. If that adversary is above him, he will be forced to pull his machine up on its tail to get him in the sights. That means loss of speed, manœuvrability and, if carried to an extreme, a stall, and wandering about at stalling speed is asking for trouble when there are enemy guns about. This inferiority of performance was an initial difficulty.

Later, when the SE 5 got a larger motor, things looked up.

Single combat, a duel with another machine, was, performance apart, a question of good flying. Two machines so engaged would circle, each trying to turn inside the other and so bring his guns into play. Ability to sustain such tight vertical turns is the crucial test of a fighting pilot. Once the balance of the controls is lost, the machine will slip, lose height, and the enemy will rush in. Then, by all the rules of the game, you are a dead man.

But when a number of machines had closed and were engaged in a " dog-fight," it was more a question of catch as catch can. A pilot would go down on the tail of a Hun, hoping to get him in the first burst; but he would not be wise to stay there, for another Hun would almost certainly be on *his* tail hoping to get him in the same way. Such fights were really a series of rushes, with momentary pauses to select the next opportunity—to catch the enemy at a disadvantage, or separated from his friends.

But, apart from fighting, when twenty or thirty scouts were engaged, there was always a grave risk of collision. Machines would hurtle by, intent on their private battles, missing each other by feet. So such fighting demanded iron nerves, lightning reactions, snap decisions, a cool head, and eyes like a bluebottle, for it all took place at high speed and was three dimensional.

At this sort of sharpshooting some pilots excelled others; but in all air fighting (and indeed in every branch of aerial warfare) there is an essential in which it differs from the war on the ground: its absolute coldbloodedness. You cannot lose your temper with an aeroplane. You cannot " see red," as a man in a bayonet fight. You certainly cannot resort to " Dutch " courage. Any of these may fog your judgment—and that spells death.

Often at high altitudes we flew in air well below freezing point. Then the need to clear a jam or change a drum meant putting an arm out into an icy 100 m.p.h. wind. If you happened to have bad circulation (as I had), it left the hand numb, and since you could not stamp your feet, swing your arms, or indeed move at all, the numbness would spread to the other hand and sometimes to the feet as well. In this condition we often went into a scrap with the odds against us—they usually were against us, for it was our job to be " offensive " and go over into enemy country looking for trouble— coldbloodedly in the literal sense; but none the less we had to summon every faculty of judgment and skill to down our man, or, at the worst, to come out of it alive ourselves. So, like duelling, air fighting required a set steely courage, drained of all emotion, fined down to a tense and deadly effort of will. The Angel of Death is less callous, aloof, and implacable than a fighting pilot when he dives.

*

There were, of course, emergency methods, such as standing the machine on its tail and holding it there just long enough to get one good burst into the enemy above you; but nobody would fight that way if he could help it, though, actually, an SE 5 pilot could do the same thing by pulling his top gun down the quadrant. He could then fire it vertically upward while still flying level.

This was how Beery Bowman once got away from an ugly situation. He had been scrapping a couple of Huns well over the other side of the lines. He managed to crash one of them, but in so doing exhausted the ammunition of his Vickers gun: his Lewis was jammed. The other Hun pursued him and forced him right down on to the "carpet"— about a hundred feet from the ground. There was nothing to do but to beat it home. The Hun, out to avenge the death of his friend, and having the advantage of speed and height over Beery, chivvied him back to the lines, diving after him, bursting his gun, zooming straight up again, hanging there for a moment in a stall, and falling to dive again. He repeated this several times (he must have been a rotten shot) while Beery, with extraordinary coolness and presence of mind, pulled down his Lewis gun and managed to clear the jam. The next time the Hun zoomed, Beery throttled right down and pulled back to stalling speed. The result was that when the Hun fell out of his zoom, Beery was not ahead of him as before, but beneath him. As the Hun dropped into his dive Beery opened fire with his Lewis gun, raking the body above him with a long burst. The Hun turned over on his back, dived, and struck the ground, bursting into flames. Beery laconically continued his way home. He was awarded the D.S.O.

With the exception of Ball, most crack fighters did not get their Huns in dog-fights. They preferred safer means. They would spend hours synchronizing their guns and telescopic sights so that they could do accurate shooting at, say, two or three hundred yards. They would then set out on patrol, alone, spot their quarry (in such cases usually a two-seater doing reconnaissance or photography), and carefully manœuvre for position, taking great pains to remain where they could not be seen, *i.e.* below and behind the tail of the enemy. From here, even if the Hun observer did spot them, he could not bring his gun to bear without the risk of shooting away his own tail plane or rudder. The stalker would not hurry after his quarry, but keep a wary eye to see he was not about to be attacked himself. He would gradually draw nearer, always in the blind spot, sight his guns very carefully, and then one long deadly burst would do the trick.

Such tactics as those were employed by Captain McCudden, V.C., D.S.O., and also by the French ace, Guynemeyer. Both of them, of course, were superb if they got into a dog-fight; but it was in such fighting that they were both ultimately killed.

★

Typical logbook entries:

"5/5/17. Offensive patrol: twelve thousand feet. Hoidge, Melville and self on voluntary patrol. Bad Archie over Douai. Lost Melville in cloud and afterwards attacked five red scouts. Sheered off when seven others came to their assistance. Two against twelve 'no bon.' We climbed west and they east, afterwards attacked them again, being joined by five Tripehounds, making the odds seven to twelve. Think I did in one, and Hoidge also did in one. Both granted by Wing."

" 7/5/17. Ran into three scouts east of Cambrai. Brought one down. Meintjies dived, but his gun jammed, so I carried on and finished him. Next fired on two-seater this side lines, but could not climb up to him. Went up to Lens, saw a two-seater over Douai, dived and the others followed. Fixed him up. Afterwards this confirmed by an FE 2d, who saw him burst into flames. Tackled three two-seaters who beat it east and came home. Good day!"

★

The squadron was doing well in Huns. Ball came back every day with a bag of one or more. Besides his SE 5 he had a Nieuport scout, the machine in which he had done so well the previous year. He had a roving commission, and, with two machines, was four hours a day in the air. Of the great fighting pilots his tactics were the least cunning. Absolutely fearless, the odds made no difference to him. He would always attack, single out his man, and close. On several occasions he almost rammed the enemy, and often came back with his machine shot to pieces.

One morning, before the rest of us had gone out on patrol, we saw him coming in rather clumsily to land. He was not a stunt pilot, but flew very safely and accurately, so that, watching him, we could not understand his awkward floating landing. But when he taxied up to the sheds we saw his elevators were flapping loose—controls had been completely shot away! He had flown back from the lines and made his landing entirely by winding his adjustable tail up and down! It was incredible he had not crashed. His oil tank had been riddled, and his face and the whole nose of the machine were running with black castor oil. He was so angry at being shot up like this that he walked straight to the sheds, wiped the oil off his shoulders and face with a rag, ordered out his Nieuport, and within two hours was back with yet another Hun to his credit!

Ball was a quiet, simple little man. His one relaxation was the violin, and his favourite after-dinner amusement to light a red magnesium flare outside his hut and walk round it in his pyjamas, fiddling! He was meticulous in the care of his machines, guns, and in the examination of his ammunition. He never flew for amusement. The only trips he took, apart from offensive patrols, were the minimum requisite to test his engines or fire at the ground target sighting his guns. He never boasted or criticized, but his example was tremendous.

*

The squadron sets out eleven strong on the evening patrol. Eleven chocolate-coloured, lean, noisy bullets, lifting, swaying, turning, rising into formation—two fours and a three—circling and climbing away steadily towards the lines. They are off to deal with Richthofen and his circus of Red Albatrosses.

The May evening is heavy with threatening masses of cumulus cloud, majestic skyscapes, solid-looking as snow mountains, fraught with caves and valleys, rifts and ravines—strange and secret pathways in the chartless continents of the sky. Below, the land becomes an ordnance map, dim green and yellow, and across it go the Lines, drawn anyhow, as a child might scrawl with a double pencil. The grim dividing Lines! From the air robbed of all significance.

Steadily the body of scouts rises higher and higher, threading its way between the cloud precipices. Sometimes, below, the streets of a village, the corner of a wood, a few dark figures moving, glides into view like a slide into a lantern and then is hidden again.

But the fighting pilot's eyes are not on the ground, but roving endlessly through the lower and higher reaches of the sky, peering anxiously through fur-goggles to spot those black slow-moving specks against land or cloud which mean full throttle, tense muscles, held breath, and the headlong plunge with screaming wires—a Hun in the sights, and the tracers flashing.

A red light curls up from the leader's cockpit and falls away. Action! He alters direction slightly, and the patrol, shifting throttle and rudder, keep close like a pack of hounds on the scent. He has seen, and they see soon, six scouts three thousand feet below. Black crosses! It seems interminable till the eleven come within diving distance. The pilots nurse their engines, hard-minded and set, test their guns and watch their indicators. At last the leader sways sideways, as a signal that each should take his man, and suddenly drops.

Machines fall scattering, the earth races up, the enemy patrol, startled, wheels and breaks. Each his man! The chocolate thunderbolts take sights, steady their screaming planes, and fire. A burst, fifty rounds—it is over. They have overshot, and the enemy, hit or missed, is lost for the moment. The pilot steadies his stampeding mount, pulls her out with a firm hand, twisting his head right and left, trying to follow his man, to sight another, to back up a friend in danger, to note another in flames.

But the squadron plunging into action had not seen, far off, approaching from the east, the rescue flight of Red Albatrosses patrolling above the body of machines on which they had dived, to guard their tails and second them in the battle. These, seeing the maze of wheeling machines, plunge down to join them. The British scouts, engaging and disengaging like flies circling at midday in a summer room, soon find the newcomers upon them. Then, as if attracted by some mysterious power, as vultures will draw to a corpse in the desert, other bodies of machines swoop down from the peaks of the cloud mountains. More enemy scouts, and, by good fortune, a flight of Naval Triplanes.

But, nevertheless, the enemy, double in number, greater in power and fighting with skill and courage, gradually overpower the British, whose machines scatter, driven down beneath the scarlet German fighters.

It would be impossible to describe the action of such a battle. A pilot, in the second between his own engagements, might see a Hun diving vertically, an SE 5 on his tail, on the tail of the SE another Hun, and above him again another British scout. These four, plunging headlong at two hundred miles an hour, guns crackling, tracers streaming, suddenly break up. The lowest Hun plunges flaming to his death, if death has not taken him already. His victor seems to stagger, suddenly pulls out in a great leap, as a trout leaps on the end of a line, and then, turning over on his belly, swoops and spins in a dizzy falling spiral with the earth to end it. The third German zooms veering, and the last of that meteoric quartet follows bursting. . . . But such a glimpse, lasting perhaps ten seconds, is broken by the sharp rattle of another attack. Two machines approach head-on at breakneck speed, firing at each other, tracers whistling through each other's planes, each slipping sideways on his rudder to trick the other's gun fire. Who will hold longest? Two hundred yards, a hundred, fifty, and then, neither hit, with one accord they fling their machines sideways, bank and circle, each striving to bring his gun on to the other's tail, each glaring through goggle eyes, calculating, straining, wheeling, grim, bent only on death or dying.

But, from above, this strange tormented circling is seen by another Hun. He drops. His gun speaks. The British machine, distracted by the sudden unseen enemy, pulls up, takes a burst through the engine, tank and body, and falls bottom uppermost down through the clouds and the deep unending desolation of the twilight sky.

The game of noughts and crosses, starting at fifteen thousand feet above the clouds, drops in altitude engagement by engagement. Friends and foes are scattered. A last SE, pressed by two Huns, plunges and wheels, gun-jammed, like a snipe over marshes, darts lower, finds refuge in the ground mist, and disappears.

Now lowering clouds darken the evening. Below, flashes of gun fire stab the veil of the gathering dusk. The fight is over! The battlefield shows no sign. In the pellucid sky, serene cloud mountains mass and move unceasingly. Here where guns rattled and death plucked the spirits of the valiant, this thing is now as if it had never been! The sky is busy with night, passive, superb, unheeding.

*

Of the eleven scouts that went out that evening, the 7th of May, only five of us returned to the aerodrome.

The Mess was very quiet that night. The Adjutant remained in his office, hoping against hope to have news of the six missing pilots, and, later, news did come through that two had been forced down, shot in the engine, and that two others had been wounded.

But Ball never returned. I believe I was the last to see him in his red-nosed SE going east at eight thousand feet. He flew straight into the white face of an enormous cloud. I followed. But when I came out on the other side, he was nowhere to be seen. All next day a feeling of depression hung over the squadron. We mooned about the sheds, still hoping for news. The day after that hope was given up. I flew his Nieuport back to the Aircraft Depot.

It was decided to go over to Douai and drop message-bags containing requests, written in German, for news of his fate. We crossed the lines at thirteen thousand feet. Douai was renowned for its anti-aircraft. They were not to know the squadron was in mourning, and made it hot for us. The flying splinters ripped the planes. Over the town the message-bags were dropped, and the formation returned without encountering a single enemy machine.

★

> " If you want to find the Sergeant-Major,
>   We know where he is ! We know where he is !
>   If you want to find the Sergeant-Major, we know where he is !
>   He's lying on the canteen floor.
>   We've seen him, we've seen him,
>   Lying on the canteen floor we've seen him,
>   Lying on the canteen floor.
>   Oh ! Oh ! Oh ! Oh !
>   Covered all over with tissue paper, tissue paper,
>   Marmalade and jam ! "

A sing-song was being held in a large barn of some farm buildings near by. Anything to raise the morale. The band played brassy music, and the men sang the old songs. " There's a long, long trail," " Way down upon the Swanee River," " Pack up your troubles." A corporal disguised himself as a Lancashire comedian. A batman tenor gave " Pale hands I loved." Then I sang the Stevenson " Requiem."

> " Under the wide and starry sky,
>   Dig the grave and let me lie.
>   Glad did I live and gladly die,
>   And I laid me down with a will.
>
>   These be the words you grave for me :
>   Here he lies where he longed to be ;
>   Home is the sailor, home from sea,
>   And the hunter home from the hill."

179

The men applauded huskily: they understood.
Then the band struck up " Tipperary " and soon
had them shouting again.

★

Some time later, news was received that Ball,
posted as missing, had been killed, and it was not
until a month later that his V.C. was announced as
a supplement to the *London Gazette* on the 8th of
June:

" HIS MAJESTY THE KING has been graciously
pleased to approve of the award of the Victoria
Cross to the Undermentioned Officer.

"Lieut. (temp. Captain) Albert Ball, D.S.O.,
M.C., late Notts. and Derby Regt. and R.F.C.

" For most conspicuous and consistent bravery
from the 25th April to the 6th May, 1917, during
which period Captain Ball took part in twenty-
six combats in the air, and destroyed eleven
hostile aeroplanes, drove two down out of control,
and forced several others to land.

" In these combats Captain Ball, flying alone,
on one occasion fought six hostile machines,
twice he fought five and once four. When landing two other British aeroplanes he attacked an
enemy formation of eight. On each of these
occasions he brought down at least one enemy.

" Several times his aeroplane was badly
damaged, once so seriously that but for the most
delicate handling his machine would have collapsed, as nearly all the control wires had been
shot away.

" On returning with a damaged machine he

had always to be restrained from immediately going out on another.

" In all, Captain Ball has destroyed forty-three German aeroplanes and one balloon, and has always displayed most exceptional courage, determination and skill."

*

Rumours of the new SE 5 with a 200-h.p. engine had been prevalent for some weeks, and at last the machine arrived. I was detailed to take it up on test. I found it faster, and it climbed so well that, since it was a beautiful evening, I decided to find its ceiling.

At ten thousand feet the view was immense, England quartered on its northern perimeter. Oh, to be home again! Just to be over England, even if one could not land on it! After all, why not? I turned north. At twenty-two thousand feet, Kent was below me. Somewhere down there my countrymen were walking, talking, going about their daily business in the peaceful lanes of England. The faintest drift of blue smoke from the chimneys of some country house! There would be the scent of a wood-fire down there, far, far, far below!

The wing-tips of the planes, ten feet away, suddenly caught my eye, and for a second the amazing adventure of flight overwhelmed me. Nothing between me and oblivion but a pair of light linen-covered wings and the roar of a 200-h.p. engine! There was the fabric, bellying slightly in the suction above the plane, the streamlined wires, taut and quivering, holding the wing structure together, the three-ply body, the array of instruments, and the slight tremor of the whole aeroplane. It was a triumph of human intelligence and skill—almost a miracle. I felt a desire to touch these things, to convince myself of their reality. On the ground they seemed strong and actual enough, but here, suspended on an apparent nothing, it was hard to believe that flying was not a fantastic dream out of which I should presently awake.

From the ground I should be well-nigh invisible. Only the trained observer with powerful glasses would see the minute white gnat five miles up in the profound sky. Only in absolute silence would the faint sound of my engine be audible. They would not know of this brief visit of a homesick man to his native country. To them I was "somewhere in France." I looked long at the island below me, then shut off the engine, and in one long, unbroken glide swept back to France.

I came over St Omer at about five thousand feet and saw a back-staggered scout circling the aerodrome. I turned to have a look. When I came close, I saw it was one of the new Sopwith Dolphins. I plunged down on to its tail as a challenge for a scrap. This new SE I was flying would be more than a match for anything in the sky.

The reader will not take it amiss if I say that by this time I was a fairly competent pilot. I could do every stunt then invented with ease and style. I admitted none to be my superior in the handling of an aeroplane. So I confess I dived on the Dolphin with the intention of showing him just how an aeroplane should be flown in a fight, sitting on his tail for a bit, and then, when it was quite obvious I had killed him ten times over, coming up alongside, waving him a gracious good-bye and proceeding to my aerodrome.

But it didn't work out a bit like that. The Dolphin had a better performance than I realized. He was up in a climbing turn and on my tail in a flash. I half rolled out of the way, he was still there. I sat in a tight climbing spiral, he sat in a tighter one. I tried to climb above him, he climbed faster. Every dodge I had ever learnt I tried on him; but he just sat there on my tail, for all the world as if I had been towing him behind me. Who was the fellow anyway? What was it coming to when the test pilots at Aircraft Depots could put it over a crack pilot of 56? This would have to be looked into. The Dolphin shut off and dropped on to the carpet. I followed. We jumped out of our machines. I seemed to recognize the spare figure crossing towards me. He lifted his goggles. It was Patrick!

" Well, Lewis," he said, as we shook hands, laughing, " still learning to fly? "

*

One jolly June morning the peace of London Town was disturbed by the unexpected arrival of about twenty German bombers, who laid their explosive eggs in various parts of that comfortable metropolis. They did not actually do very extensive damage; but their appearance was quite enough to scare the civilian population very thoroughly, and raise an outcry. Barbarians! Dastards! Bombing open towns! Waging war against defenceless women and children! The daily hymn of hate rose to a frightened scream. England was, as usual, un-prepared. The arrangements made for home defence were quite inadequate. True, a few old 2c's had staggered into the air to attack, but they could not climb up anywhere high enough. They might be all right for Zepps; but against Gothas they were a joke—worse than useless! The complete German squadron returned home triumphant.

Agitation in the press! Scandalous neglect of the defence of dear old England! Questions in the House! Panic among the politicians! Lloyd George acting quickly! Result: a crack squadron to be recalled for the defence of London immediately, and twelve elated pilots of 56 Squadron packing a week's kit into our cockpits. God bless the good old Gotha!

*

Actually that raid was a very stout effort. And nobody in his right mind would deny that the Germans were perfectly right to bomb the capital of the British Empire. Their objectives were Woolwich, Whitehall, the Houses of Parliament—the very nerve-centres of the whole organism. The Allies would have bombed Berlin without hesitation if they had happened to have machines good enough to get there. But they hadn't. So they made capital out of their inferiority by propaganda. (And dropped a hundred bombs on towns behind the enemy lines for every one dropped on London.)

In the years which were to follow the Armistice, many conventions and conferences were held whose aim was to ensure future peace. But men like

MacDonald, who strove to limit armaments, to reduce navies and make Peace Pacts, all conspired to pass over the air. Conference succeeded conference; but reading the results you might have imagined that aeroplanes had never been invented. This glaring omission continued, and it was not until twelve years later that the first sign of a need to control air power began to appear.

But when the world did wake up to the dangers of the air, it woke with a shudder of horror. No wonder. Frontiers were gone. Security was gone. No man could hope for peace or prosperity under the threat of a violent death. The days of wars were over: massacre had taken their place, wholesale massacre of the community in which children would retch their lives away, women would be blinded, and men powerless to protect or succour. The end of civilization was in sight.

Yet, faced with annihilation, what did the world do? Those far from the immediate focus of danger washed their hands of the problem, or used the preoccupation of their rivals as a good opportunity to grab what they could. Others, nearer at hand, talked piously, earnestly (and interminably) of Collective Security, and used the time so gained to pile up armaments behind their backs. The voice of the people was never heard; the dictators, the press, the armament rings had muzzled all opposition. Greed and Power disposed of the human destiny, while mankind cowered like a rabbit hypnotized by a snake.

In our own country, one of the few where freedom of speech and some civilized instincts remained, governments fought a losing game against others who broke pledges, treaties, or any code of human decency whenever it suited them. Though the days of nationalism and isolationism were manifestly over, we were forced into an armaments race in the vain hope that it might afford us some protection. Vain hope because, in the air, equality of armaments gave no protection. An army could stop an army, a fleet a fleet; but a thousand aeroplanes could not stop a thousand enemy aeroplanes. Wire netting would not keep flies out. *Both would get through to their objectives.* The effect of increasing air armaments was simply to multiply the horrors that would be loosed on the civil populations. And they would not even have the satisfaction of seeing their own men avenge the raiders by taking at least the life of the enemy pilot, for there need be no men in those machines, they can be controlled by wireless: their destruction will mean nothing: they will go on coming day and night.

To-day the voice of no one man, or no one country, can save Europe (and after the whole civilized world) from imminent destruction. If we cannot collectively rise above our narrow nationalism, the vast credits of wealth, wisdom and art produced by Western civilization will be wiped out. If we really want peace and security, we must pool our resources, disarm, and set up an international air police force, federally controlled. That force must be as incorruptible, free from bias and self-interest, and devoted to law and order as our civil police are to-day. There is no other way.

★

How mercifully free from all such forebodings we were that summer day in 1917! It was a

morning of stainless beauty with promise in the
sky. The squadron arrived at Bekesbourne without incident, vastly elated. Machines were put
away, and the men, who had been rushed home,
took charge of them. Needless to say, all the
musicians were among them. The defence of
London was quite a secondary affair. The things
of real importance were squadron dances. To
fight Hun bombers over London would have been
a picnic for us after a month of gruelling Offensive
Patrols. Good old Jerry! Good old Lloyd George!

A large marquee was run up as a Mess. The
Major scrounged some planking, and very soon
there was a regular Savoy dancing floor. Visits
were paid to Canterbury to enrol the fair sex.
Those lightning two or three day acquaintanceships
began to ripen.

The weather continued cloudless and perfect for
bombing London, but, whether the Hun had advice
of the squadron's return or not, he evidently felt he
was unlikely to get away with another daylight raid.
Anyway there were no signs of him. The squadron
stood by, gloriously idle. It was a grand war.

*

Arrived the night of the dance. The marquee
was gaily decorated and candle-lit. Through the
open end was a background of summer night.
Tables were glittering with china and silver brought
out from Canterbury. The Mess cooks had excelled themselves. Bubbly wine popped happily.
The squadron was living up to its reputation for
cheeriness and hilarity. The girls had been roped
in from heaven knows where, and before dinner,

standing in their evening cloaks in the long grass at the edge of the aerodrome, Henderson and I gave them an exhibition of stunt flying. After dinner, a little music. One or two pilots sang, another played the fiddle. Then, of course, the band. The party flourished all night, and when the last guest departed, the east was already flushing with dawn.

★

" Why go to bed? " said Rhys-Davids. Why indeed? Arm-in-arm, we trailed off through the dripping grass. We were tired and silent. One of us would frame a thought, a phrase, a comment, and the other would grunt, nod, or laugh. Not what is said enriches the heart. A phrase may remain embedded in the mind like dagger or diamond; but memory is a subtler synthesis—a tone of voice, a turn of the head, a pause, a blade of grass that the feet brush aside, a glance, the first lark arising, stillness, some aspect of the skies. . . . This is the argosy of friends.

We skirted the aerodrome and came to the edge of the hill that looked away over the quiet trimness of the Kentish fields, two dark silhouettes, one, slight and tall, the other, short and thick-set, close together in the first glory of the morning.

" God! It's good to be alive! " I said.

" We may be dead in a month." He was gazing at the sunrise, darkly.

" In a week! To-morrow! " I laughed. The cold hand had not touched me on the shoulder.

" Yes! " He came out of his reverie and stretched, smiling. " Ah! It's good to be young! To have friends! "

188

We turned and smiled into each other's eyes.

" What about turning in ? "

" Righto ! " He took my arm again.

We sauntered back, threw ourselves on our beds to sleep, fully dressed, giving orders we were only to be called in the event of a raid. This being denied, we slept peacefully till lunch.

*

Ten days passed. The Hun had not come. On the last night before returning overseas I got leave to go to town. Friends welcomed me at their flat in the Temple. We were to dance. In my bath I remembered that one of the girls was supposed to lack evening shoes. Naked, I walked to the phone and told some shop to send shoes, all sizes, all designs, up to the flat. Then I returned to soap and lather in the welcome water. The bell rang. Boxes were being dumped on the landing. Fifteen, twenty boxes of white cardboard. What was the shop ? Who was the buyer ? Credit ? An officer on leave—that was enough. When I had dressed I turned them out on to the floor, mentally made my choice. A ring. She came.

" Have some shoes," I said.

I had never seen her before. My host and hostess had found her. A relation. A friend. Companion for a night's leave.

" Shoes," I said. " Choose ! "

" But I bought some. Look ! "

I looked. It was annoying. I wanted to give her the shoes. Her feet, very good feet ; excellent feet— and the shoes too ; excellent shoes. . . . I laughed.

"Well, these had better go back to the shop, then." They disappeared as magically as they had come.

★

Officers in uniform were not allowed to dance in public, and what was the good of taking a girl out to dinner if you could not dance? Happily there existed, known only to the fortunate, a studio in Kensington which ought for ever to go down in grateful memory to a multitude of officers on leave. For in that studio were held the most perfect small dances. Hospitality glowed in the smile of the hostess. There was, in the words of a topical song of the time, "Welcome on the mat."

The door was small and unimposing, almost at the bottom of a little cul-de-sac. It would be opened by a fine white-bearded Chelsea Pensioner in a long red coat. At the top of the narrow stairs was a big studio with another little wooden staircase to a gallery above, where a tiny bedroom was curtained off. Down two steps from the studio, through an archway, was another small room for refreshments. On the wall above the drinks hung a framed notice—

WORK LIKE
HELEN B. MERRY.

which mystified all those who did not read it aloud —but set an accurate seal on the spirit of the time. And it was here we went to dance.

★

Why do two strangers suddenly find themselves irresistibly drawn to one another? Why do the same two, the attraction spent, stand amazed that there should have been anything between them? Only some arrangement of cells, some bio-chemical affinity, can explain it, can marvellously create this something out of nothing. " Love," we call it— a pretty name—but the force is the urge of Life itself, as abstract, as ruthless, as unsentimental, as inexorable as Death, which is its counterpart.

And now, with Death so eager, should not Life be eager too? Good-bye to courtships and convention! Away with ritual! All that belongs to the spacious days, to the spring and summer time. Now Life is in winter, and just as the cut-down plant will send up weakly shoots and blossoms long after flowering time—a reflex of its urgent will to live—so men and women under the dread of an eternal winter snatch wildly at the flimsiest promise of life. Men and women do not " love " in war. They desire, they demand, they take. The conventions, the morals, the obligations go. It is not pretty, the war-time psychology, and its attitude is violently repudiated, by those who are past the age when life is rising in them. By those most under its spell it passes unperceived, hidden by glamorous words—patriotism, heroism, sacrifice, and glory! Life is a past-master at throwing such dust in the eyes of mankind that men and women should obey its curt commands and find the best possible reasons for doing so. " What does it matter " ? says Life. " Let them create. I must go on."

*

The studio was crowded, the band thrummed,

the couples moved blindly in the vacancy of the dance. . . .

"Poor butterfly in the shadows waiting . . ."

The girls, close to their men, hummed the catchy, sentimental refrain.   White hands resting on khaki shoulders, bent heads, eyes closed, they floated out on the seas of rhythm, dreaming.   On the steep stairs going up to the balcony the young people sat, a cascade of silks and khaki, overflowing on the floor below, drifting across to the doorway where two more Chelsea Pensioners stood guard.   Chatter and laughter came from the little lounge where the drinks and sandwiches were.   Applause!   The dance over.   Pause.   And then the young negro with the crinkly hair sang quietly in a hushed studio :

"As long as the Congo
Flows to the sea,
As long as the leaves grow
On the bamboo tree,
My love and devotion
Shall be deep as the ocean.
Won't you take a notion
For love of me ? "

★

At the back of the balcony a little door led out on to the roof.   We slipped through.   At the top of a few sooty steps, a platform, a crow's-nest, looking out over the sea of roofs, dark sharp-crested waves, above which a pale moon fought her way up through the heavy pall of London air.   A pair of cats improvised two-part harmony in the shadow of a chimneystack. Just ordinary sooty roofs ; but, that night, so romantic ! The music welled up from below like sound from a sea-cave :

> " And when I told them how beautiful you are,
> They didn't believe me. They didn't believe me."

We did not speak. No vows, no promises, no plans. Only this moment, our moment : the moon on her hair, the slow rhythm of her breathing, the trusting lips. . . . At last she slipped gently from my arms.

" And so to-morrow . . .? " She plied the question vaguely. To-morrow? Was there such a thing? The future would slip into the past ; the present, alas, must die like music in the very moment of creation. Yet it might remain, a soft echo at the cross-roads of our memory, and when we listened it would still be there, faintly ringing, deeper down the vista, but for ever perfect, undefiled.

" And so to-morrow . . .? "

" I shall be gone."

" But not for ever? " She was in my arms again.

" Say not for ever. . . ."

" Not for ever."

And then, suddenly shaken by the fear that it might indeed be so, that with a thousand thousand others I might go before my time where all hope ends, I began to say over those magic words, the sum of all farewell :

> " Remember me when I am gone away,
> Gone far away into the silent land ;
> When you can no more hold me by the hand,
> Nor I, half turn to go, yet turning stay.

Remember me when no more day by day
You tell me of our future that you planned ;
Only remember me ; you understand
It will be late to counsel then or pray.
Yet, if you should forget me . . ."

And then, bursting up from below :

"Another little drink, another little drink,
Another little drink wouldn't do us any harm."

The cheery blatant chorus, dancing, clapping,
yelling, finished in a stampede of merriment, while
we two on the roof stood silent, waiting till the world
should have shouted itself by, till the almost-silence
should come like a slow tide and separate us from
the rest again. . . .

"Yet, if you should forget me for a while
And afterwards remember, do not grieve :
For if the darkness and corruption leave
Some vestige of the thoughts that once I had,
Better by far you should forget and smile
Than that you should remember and be sad." [1]

At last we turned our backs on the moon and
started to come down.
" One more dance."
" Yes.   Then I must go."
" You've missed your train."
" Wasn't it worth it . . .? "—curve of her arm
reaching to the door-latch, line of her back, grace of
the upturned, smiling head . . .
" Darling . . ."   I raised her hand, turned it
to kiss into the palm.   " I shall take a taxi, all the
way to Canterbury."
" Won't it cost the earth? "
" Who cares? "

[1] Christina Rossetti.

She was close again, low laughing in my ear, the supple back yielding, the lips parted—

> "Any old night is a wonderful night,
> If you're there with a wonderful girl."

" Come on," I cried. " This is a good one ! "

★

The old two-cylinder Renault which, from a sense of war-time economy, seemed to run on one cylinder most of the time, chugged and bucked its way down the Mile End Road. The seats were hard and slippery, and the cab too small for me either to lie on the floor or loll on the seat. It was a sort of purgatory; but I was oblivious of everything, dreaming of this new shining bond.

At last dawn came up, ghostly over the hopfields, and seven o'clock found me paying the taxi-driver eight pounds at the Bekesbourne. sheds. The machines were standing out, engines running. The sun was up, the day glorious, cloud-free. We took off, wheeled, formed flights, and turned south. Two hours later we were lunching, back in the Mess at Estrée Blanche.

★

A Wing of French machines had been sent up from the south to operate in the Dunkerque area. In order to familiarize the French pilots with all types of Allied aircraft operating in the sector (so that they might not enthusiastically shoot down their friends by mistake), a machine from every British squadron was sent over for the French pilots to see. I was detailed to take over an SE. About half a dozen different types of British machines stood on the aerodrome when I arrived, and the pilots were doing their best to make friends with our Allies in broken French.

The crack squadron in the French Wing was the " Storks," so called because each carried on his fuselage the stencil of this bird with neck out-stretched and down-drooping wings (now the mascot of Hispano cars). The squadron flew " Spads," a neat low-winged biplane, and its leader was the famous French ace, Guynemeyer. He was a slight, pale, consumptive-looking boy with black curly hair and a timid manner. He had three machines: a standard Spad, a high-compression Spad, and a larger special machine made by the same firm with a 200-h.p. Hispano engine (similar to the one fitted to the SE). But this machine was unique in having a four-pound Pom-Pom firing through the hollow propeller boss. Guynemeyer sighted it with an auxiliary machine gun firing tracer ammunition, and, having sighted it, released his " cannon " as he called it. I believe it was the only fighting scout to be fitted with a gun firing explosive shells during the war.

A race was held between the two special Spads and the SE 5. Their speeds were almost identical, but the high-compression Spad climbed quicker. After the race was over, Guynemeyer and I held a demonstration combat over the aerodrome. Again I was badly worsted. Guynemeyer was all over me. In his hands the Spad was a marvel of flexibility. In the first minute I should have been shot down a dozen times. Nothing I could do would shift that

grim-looking French scout off my tail. Guynemeyer sat there, at about thirty yards' range, perfectly master of the situation. (In self-justification,
I feel I must add that both the Sopwith Dolphin
and the Spad were more manœuvrable than the SE 5.
So that, given equal flying ability, they would win.
Given still greater skill, the SE 5 was right out of
it.) At last we came down, landed, shook hands,
and went into the Mess to drink sweet wine and
eat sugar cakes. Only a week later Guynemeyer
was shot down and killed.

*

Of all patrols the early morning one was the
most hazardous, because the sun, rising in the
east, blinded us, and the Hun, attacking with this
armour of light about him, was invisible even when
the tracers from his machine gun were spinning
through our wings.

A few days later I was out on this dawn patrol.
It was a cloudless, perfect morning with a sun
like a white eye, glaring, overpowering; a blinding
arrogant sun dominating the alien heaven. I was
in the rearguard position, sailing a hundred feet
above the rest of the patrol to guard their tails. But
the sky seemed a dazzling crystalline void. Three
miles below, the scarred earth witnessed the existence
of war; but the air was innocent, clear as a draught
of spring water.

Then, far over from the east, a patrol of three red
Huns ventured out to sniff the war. We saw
them and dropped like hawks; but whether they
were fledglings prospecting or decoys to lure us

into enemy country, they did not wait to engage, but turned and ducked for the Vaterland.

I dived with the others, testing my guns. The Vickers jammed, and I had to take off my glove to clear it. It was very cold at eleven thousand feet early in the morning. My hand went numb. I blew through it, banged it on my thigh, and crouched into the cockpit to keep warmer, still trying to clear the jam. Seeing the Huns dive away, I did not follow the patrol right down, but remained a thousand feet above, hoping to get my gun right while they re-formed and climbed up to me again. Thus, inadvertently, I became a straggler—alone in the sky—but what matter when the heavens were so utterly empty of danger? Then, faintly, I heard the intermittent chatter of a machine gun. I looked round. Nothing. No sign of a fight, no one in the sky—but the chatter became a jabber and then a stuttering menace—the sun ambush was down on me. I tried vainly to look up, but the glare shrivelled my eyes to sightlessness. But tracers were whistling through the planes, and suddenly a white-hot rod was flicked along the round of my back. I jammed over stick and rudder and went flashing into a spin, then shut off the engine and collected myself to look up. It was one of the latest Pfaltz scouts: the SE was no match for that machine.

Evidently my sudden spin bluffed him. Seeing the machine apparently out of control, he thought he had got me, and did not follow. Instead he pulled out, and sat watching me plunge earthwards; but when, having dropped a thousand feet down to the patrol below me, I stopped shamming dead, he plunged after me. Now, with the rest of the patrol, we should certainly have got him; but this hornet's nest was not to his liking, he pulled away sharply and, thanks to his superior climb, rose high out of our reach, going east.

My back burned terribly. I tried to feel it. Was it bleeding? My shirt seemed sticky. I worked my shoulder tentatively. It ached, that was all. Nothing serious, probably; still, I had better get back to the aerodrome and see. I climbed gingerly out of the machine. The body was well shot up, a longeron had two big holes in it, one elevator wire was cut; but the duplicate controls had saved me.

I called in a friend and undressed. A long red furrow had seared my back. A six-inch graze. No more. But for the cold I should have been sitting upright, and then that bullet, instead of glancing by, would have torn its way down through the shoulder and embedded itself in the heart. A miss is as good as a mile! The wound was dressed. The Major came in.

" Hullo! " he said. " You've got a cushy one! Splendid! You'll be able to put up a wound stripe now! "

To him a wound stripe was as good as a decoration. Two days later I left for home.

V

HOME DEFENCE

AFTER a fortnight's leave I was made a Flight-Commander and posted to No. 44 Squadron, stationed at Hainault Farm, just out beyond Ilford in Essex. The squadron was quartered in a large farmhouse by the aerodrome. It was not particularly comfortable; but as Hainault was within three-quarters of an hour of the West End, pilots spent most of their nights in town.

We were equipped with Sopwith Camels, the latest single-seater scout, fitted with a 110-h.p. Clerget engine and two Vickers guns. The machine was new to me, so for the first few days after my arrival at Hainault I spent a good deal of time in the air getting used to it. In the SE 5 the long stationary engine, the tanks, and the pilot's cockpit behind them meant that the load was spread over more than half the length of the body. It was this that made the machine impossible to turn sharply, and unwieldy in aerial combat. The Camel, whose engine was a flat rotary, and whose tanks and pilot were all packed close together, had its weight concentrated, and was thus far lighter and handier in the air. (The best trick flying during the war was put up on Camels by pilots such as Armstrong or Banks.) The machine was not particularly fast on the level, but it climbed well and could best any other scout in a fight. Like all Sopwith productions, it was a bit on the light side; but for actual flying, next to the Triplane it took first place with me.

★

The squadron's duty was Home Defence. This had grown rapidly since the big daylight raid that had called 56 back to Bekesbourne so hurriedly a few months before. It was now a Brigade of squadrons equipped with the latest aircraft. London was not to be caught napping again.

There was an elaborate system of communication to give warning of approaching raiders. This was said to have its farthest outpost somewhere in Holland and to be backed up by patrol ships in the North Sea and Lightships in the Thames estuary. Any of these watchers could communicate direct with Home Defence Headquarters, at the Horse Guards. From here, in Whitehall, direct telephone lines radiated to every squadron. Thus it was possible for machines to be in the air within two minutes of the first warning of a raid. They would be up to intercept the Huns before they even reached the coast.

The first line of defence was composed of several squadrons patrolling on beats north and south, approximately over Southend. If the raiders eluded the most distant watchers this first line might fail to catch the enemy on its way in; but would, in any case, be waiting for them on their way back.

Between this outer ring and the inner ring of London Defence was an area reserved to anti-aircraft guns. Their job was to put up a barrage, through which the enemy could not penetrate. Within this area again rose a ring of Kite Balloons, anchored at some height and distance from one another, in the pious hope that some unfortunate Hun might fly into their cables. (We all regarded this as ludicrous.) Lastly, within the Kite Balloon ring was the inner ring of air defence, girdling London's eastern perimeter from Epping in the north to Kenley in the south.

Each squadron had a telephone operator constantly on duty. When raid warnings came through, he pressed a Morse key close to hand sounding three large Klaxon horns set up on the roof of the men's quarters and the officers' Mess. The men swarmed into the sheds and rushed out the machines, the pilots struggled into their kit and warmed up their engines. If the raid warning was followed by the action signal, machines were off the ground within a minute.

At this time, beyond one or two desultory Zeppelin raids, London had not been attacked by night. The organization was designed to repel large daylight raids. When night raids began, tactics had to be altered. Instead of being able to launch every machine against the raiders, the difficulty was to find them at all. It was futile to loose a hundred machines into the air at night haphazard. So a system of patrols was worked out.

These were at ten, eleven, and twelve thousand feet. Each pilot had his allotted beat, and had strict orders (and good reason) not to leave it for fear of colliding with another machine. His duty was to remain patrolling for two hours, keeping a sharp look-out for Huns, and then come down. By this time, if the raid were still in progress, a second machine would have taken his place. So the relays could continue indefinitely.

When the August harvest moon loomed up over the flats of Essex one evening about ten o'clock, just after dark, a raid warning came through. Nobody expected it. Most of the pilots were in town. We were thoroughly unprepared. At that time scout aeroplanes were considered tricky enough to land in the day-time, nobody thought of flying them at night. Moreover, most of the pilots had no experience of night flying. None of the machines was fitted with instrument lights, so to go up in the dark meant flying the machine by feel, ignorant of speed, engine revs, and of the vital question of oil pressure. If this gave out, a thing which happened quite frequently, a rotary engine would seize up in a few minutes, and the pilot might be forced down anywhere.

However, two intrepid spirits crashed off into the warm moonlight, trusting their luck. These were the first night flights made by scout aircraft during the war. They remained up for two hours, failed to locate the raiders, who dropped their eggs and returned home unscathed. The next morning a feverish activity pervaded the squadron. Tenders rushed off to Aircraft Depots and returned with instrument-lighting installations which were hurriedly fitted in the machines. All pilots were instructed to make practice night landings, and in twenty-four hours the Home Defence squadrons ceased to be looked upon as anything but night fighters.

★

Although I was now an experienced pilot with hundreds of hours' flying to my credit, I had never yet been up at night. My first night flight was almost like going back to the days of first solo.

In those days night landings were effected by illuminating the aerodrome with flares. These consisted simply of two-gallon petrol tins with the tops cut off, half filled with cotton waste and soaked with paraffin. They were placed in an " L," the long arm pointing into the wind and the short arm marking the limit past which the machine should not run after landing. The long arm had four flares, and the pilot endeavoured to judge his landing so that his wheels touched at the first flare, thus bringing him to rest about the third, when he could turn and taxi into the sheds.

After dark the following evening I had my machine wheeled out, ran up the engine, and taxied out along the line of flares. The night was clear, but the low-lying country threatened ground mist. The rising moon did not shed enough light to give much confidence. It all looked very black indeed, and I had the impression that to take off into this would be the same as flying into a cloud, a topless black cloud out of which I could never climb into clear skies above, and out of which I should only stumble back to earth by luck. I paused for a moment before opening up, tested my controls and, with that feeling of fatalism which so many pilots must know, pushed open the throttle. If I was going to be killed, I was going to be killed, why worry? If I was going to get away with it, why worry either? Avanti! The machine gathered way and lifted serenely from the ground.

A second later I was reassured. This was no dark cloud, no impalpable void of blackness; but a lovely dim landscape lit only by the rising moon, with a shining ribbon of water, the Thames estuary, on the southern horizon. I was surprised at the amount of detail visible by night. Every roof made a soft mirror for the moon. Railway lines glistened, and even roads were lighter lines among the dark network of hedges dividing the fields. Expecting to be keyed up to the highest degree of nervous tension, I relaxed at once. I had entered a new enchanted world. As I climbed higher the detail of the ground grew less distinct, the horizons wider, and the long drifts of cloud out of which the moon had risen, stately and calm, gave an exquisite aspect to the August sky. The earth seemed soft, luxuriant, taking the moonlight like a cloak of moleskin. Below, the golden flares on the aerodrome shone like a brooch. Soon I could see the flares of other aerodromes marking the ring of the squadrons which guarded the city. London itself was a dark, crouching monster within. The sky signs which threw a dome of glowing copper above her were no more. Two solitary searchlights, one to the north and one to the south, raised thin silver pencils, wheeling and pausing, uncertain seekers in the depths of emptiness, and again a feeling of amazement gripped me, that I, alone, in a frail contrivance, should have been given such keys to the paths of heaven, should have found my way to this undreamed-of paradise of night: more marvellous, more serene, than any earthly landscape under the garish blatancy of day.

I could have sailed on for ever towards the moon

which seemed within the compass of the nearer clouds. And indeed I did wander vaguely towards it, until I found the broad reaches of the river below me. Here and there a tiny pin-point of light marked the existence of human beings upon an earth which seemed otherwise reserved to trees and waters and the moon. A passing train, like a golden snake with a long white ostrich feather plume, wound sinuously into the smoke-shrouded obscurity of London. The black silhouette of a steamer passed out to sea. I looked back to the lights of the aerodrome, five golden pin-points shining from the earth, shut off my engine and glided quietly down through the magic of the moon-lit sky. Now I began to forget the placid world above and concentrate only on bringing myself safely to earth. I watched the slowly falling alti-meter, manœuvred myself into the right position for landing, working my way down in gradual " S " turns towards the flares below, where I could see the mechanics standing in the glare, listening to my engine and watching for my return. At five hundred feet I fired a Very light. The red ball curled away like a rocket in the darkness. A second later an answering red light curled up from the ground. All clear! Now I was alert, every faculty keyed up to get down safely on this, my first night landing. At fifty feet I was coming straight towards the line of flares. Suddenly they blurred. The first flare, a moment ago plainly visible ahead, disappeared to a glimmer in a bank of white mist. Instantaneously I calculated : ground mist! Careful! Land close to the lights. Don't bother about the earth. I flicked my rudder to swing nearer the line of flares, opened up my engine, held it off with the button switch so that if I miscalculated I could immediately correct with a burst of power. The first flare loomed up and flashed past in white drifting vapour. I must be ten feet off the ground. I held the stick back, letting the machine sink a little, and then, as the second flare loomed up, buzzed my engine twice. An instant later the wheels and tail touched together, and the steady rumble told its tale of a perfect landing.

★

Memories of the past are like jewellery left lying forgotten in a cupboard. The dust covers it, tarnishes the settings, dims the stones, and when we turn to look at it again, only a few gleams shine out from a pattern that was once so vivid. All these days I know had their incident, their humour, their tragedy; now most of it is lost. Only a few brilliants remain to mark the outline of the months: perhaps even in these I am deceived.

So it may have been a week or a month later that I received a letter from a friend in 56 Squadron telling of the death of Arthur Rhys-Davids. It read as follows:

" Soon after we crossed the lines we spotted two enemy two-seaters below us and started to dive on them. Rhys-Davids forged ahead, closely followed by the others, the two Huns running for home all out. Meanwhile the rest of us spotted five enemy scouts coming down on us from above, so we stayed up and scrapped them to prevent them going down on the others. After about five minutes we drove them off and re-formed formation. Every one was there except Rhys-Davids, who was never seen again. He was last seen chasing the Hun two-seaters, and was perfectly all right and going strong. We expected all day to hear that he had forced landed this side of the lines as he was well within gliding distance at the time of the scrap. He had, as you know, just got a bar to his D.S.O., and at the time of his death had over thirty Huns to his credit."

So Arthur had gone too. We had been great friends, not obvious inseparables, but joined securely by a deeper tie of understanding and being understood. Sometimes, returning from patrol, we would break off and chase each other round about the clouds, zooming their summits, plunging down their white precipitous flanks, darting like fishes through their shadowy crevasses and their secret caves : such pleasure lay in this that never did we seem more intimate than when we traced five-mile hyperbolas across the evening sky. And then to land, grin at each other, stroll into the Mess arm-in-arm, still mentally aloft, away up there, remembering the clouds, find me more true perfection ! Sometimes we used to walk at night down to the stream in the valley that flowed under the poplars. He would quote some line of half-forgotten poetry. I would take it up. Then a long pause, looking at the shadowy landscape, listening to the water, our cigarettes glowing fitfully. Or perhaps, turning to music, each of us would hear in the quietly hummed tune an orchestra behind it, sounding in our heads. At such times the war was quite forgotten. Was this quiet contemplative boy the hero of half a hundred fights? I could not reconcile the strange division, till one day, when I had praised him, he shrugged his shoulders: It was our job, he said, we ought to try to do it well, but when peace came, we would do better. When peace came! I hope the gunner of that Hun two-seater shot him clean, bullet to heart, and that his plane, on fire, fell like a meteor through the sky he loved. Since he had to end, I hope he ended so. But, oh, the waste! The loss!

*

Pilots stood by for night raids in relays, so they were able to take it in turns to go to town. It was about 11.30. The Savoy was crowded after the theatre. Looking down the steps from the foyer to the restaurant, hundreds of people could be seen at supper. On the little platform at one side a curly-haired half-caste was singing to the banjos:

> " He may be old, but he's got young ideas,
>   And he's a devil in his way . . ."

I walked slowly down the steps to look for friends in the crowd. The little man was still singing lustily:

> " Now astronomy's a thing he doesn't know about,
>   But he's always at the stage door when the stars come out.
>   He may be old, but he's got young ideas,
>   And there are hundreds living like him to-day."

The empty music throbbed, the band took up the second chorus, the waiters hurried, the people chattered, the smoke rose like a mist over the tables. . . . Crrrrump! The whole building shook.

If every one had been suddenly struck dead the silence could not have been more absolute. The band broke off in the middle of a bar. One little Dago dropped his banjo and bolted up the steps. Bombs! Bombs! Then a terrific shattering roar just outside the restaurant. The whole crowd stood up and rushed, panic-stricken, up the steps to the foyer. A woman fainted. Another leaned against the wall, sobbing. Pause. Every one waited, breathless, for the next bomb. Silence. Nothing happened. The machines had passed over. People began to whisper. A man laughed, and then—like a flood—a wave of forced hilarity swept over every one. Some went out to try and make their way home; but the streets were deserted, no taxis in sight. Others went quietly back and resumed their suppers. A few brave spirits went out to see where the bombs had fallen. The first had just missed Cleopatra's Needle. Fragments had pierced the paws and side of the bronze lion; the second had torn its way through four floors at the corner of 2 Savoy Hill, thirty feet from the hotel! So much for Home Defence. The bombers would always get through.

*

I had friends living down by the river. Sometimes I used to walk back to the station along the Embankment. On calm overcast nights the searchlights would be practising. Suddenly, in the dark heavens, a shaft of light would appear, throwing a bright disc on the under surface of the clouds; then another would open, joining in to throw its

beam on the same spot; a third would join the
second, and soon the whole firmament would be
standing on pillars of light: pillars that suddenly
moved and swept in broad arcs across the sky, that
chased each other, hesitated, dipped, hid themselves, and then shone out in a new place. The
circular image of the light would move deftly and
hurriedly like a white mouse over the floor of the
sky, other white mice would follow it, catch it,
stand round it and then hurry off again on some
new quest.

Strangely quiet and deserted were the streets.
Petrol restrictions had reduced motor traffic almost
to zero. Street lights were no more than glowing
pin-points along the shadowy chasms between the
houses. Darkened London seemed like a dim
underwater world, and the searchlights thin, sinuous
weeds reaching up to the surface. On the floor of
this deep sea, pedestrians hurried by quickly, in
the shadow of walls, glancing apprehensively at
the sky. Would they come to-night? London
seemed breathless, in the tense expectancy of
disaster, and the lights were the only bold things,
majestically wheeling.

*

The Mess President, on a visit to Stratford, had
purchased a keg of old ale. When he got back with
the spoils in a tender, it was just on lunch-time, so
we all turned out to roll the barrel into the Mess.
The ale was broached and gushed out dark, mellow,
and extremely intoxicating. The entire squadron
voted it necessary to drink the Mess President's

211

health with two glasses apiece—and then one more for luck. Lunch became hilarious and finally rowdy. We were certainly not sober; but we were certainly not drunk: we were merely in excellent spirits. Then some one shouted " Let's go up for a flip!" This most original suggestion met with a chorus of approval. There was a stampede to the sheds, the machines were turned out, and then a brilliant idea struck me : " Let's have an aerial follow-my-leader." Genius! We voted that Armstrong should head the snake, and took off—in all directions. My Flight-Sergeant told me afterwards it was a hair-raising sight. Machines staggered into the air at stalling speed, missed each other by inches, turned vertically within a foot of the ground, invited every kind of accident; but somehow nothing happened, and at last we managed to get into line—a long snake of eighteen machines. Having achieved this unique and beautiful formation, we came careering back over the aerodrome about ten feet up and set off contour-chasing all over Essex.

Of course we were crazy, but that was the Mess President's fault. However, after half an hour's hedge-hopping and barn-skipping, the effects of the ale began to wear off, so that when Armstrong saw some duck over the Thames marshes and gave chase, the rest of us couldn't be bothered to follow him, and one by one we all came back and landed—one ginger-haired hero excepted.

On the tarmac we found the General Officer Commanding Home Defence and his A.D.C. talking to the Squadron Commander. Some question of gun-testing targets or wind indicators took them out over the muddy aerodrome. It was here that Sandy spotted them.

Whether he was anxious to show off his beautiful climbing turns, whether he resented people walking over the aerodrome where he wanted to land, or whether it was just Stratford ale and good spirits, heaven knows; but down he came like a hawk. The G.O.C. Home Defence was at first amused, screwing his monocle tighter into his eye; but soon he became alarmed, and finally sat, panic-stricken, in the mud while the undercarriage of the Camel shrieked by about a foot above his head and the slipstream from the prop blew his beautiful brass hat off. Now if you are a General, accustomed to the respect and deference of your subordinate officers, it is a little difficult to know how to deal with such a situation when sitting in the mud with a 2nd Lieutenant and a Major on either side of you! This General replaced his hat and, making some quite unprintable remarks about the pilot, resumed his dignity. The three walked on.

But Sandy was not satisfied with this ignominious defeat of what (I presume) he thought to be three Tommies wandering about the aerodrome, so he gave them the other barrel, as it were, and dived again. The result was precisely the same, except that the General managed to hold his hat on! By this time the seat of his trousers was sopping, his dignity had been outraged, and he was altogether a very angry General. It is a terrifying experience to be dived on by an aeroplane, particularly when the pilot is cutting it so fine; besides, there is always the chance he may miscalculate by a split second and cut off the heads of his target with the undercarriage. So the General was annoyed and intimidated. Sandy, zooming up to about five hundred feet, half rolled on to his back, laughing like hell.

" I'll teach those ruddy A.M.'s to go snooping about the aerodrome when I want to land," he said to himself, and fell out of his half-loop into a third more gorgeous pounce. His objectives were still sitting angrily in the mud. This time he shaved them even closer than before, so that the General thought his hour had come and lay flat on his back, cursing!

Meanwhile the rest of us were standing in groups on the tarmac, first on one leg, then on the other, divided between wild hilarity at the ridiculous figure cut by the General, and a fear of what would happen to that perfect idiot, Sandy, when he came down. Once the machine was safely on the ground with the engine off, the General retraced his steps, recovering indignation and composure at every stride. By the time he got back to the sheds all the pilots had mysteriously drifted away. The unfortunate Sandy was sent for to the Major's office, and when we heard he had been deprived of his Sam Browne and put in irons for three days, the squadron was not in the least surprised.

His comment on returning to the Mess was—

" Well, I bloody well put the wind up him, anyway ! "

*

A few days later the moon had set and the dark velvety nights began. There was a certain relaxation in the squadron. We did not believe the Hun would attempt to make raids on moonless nights. We were mistaken. Two days later, warning came through, the action signal followed quickly, and within a minute of the hooter I was off the ground climbing up to patrol height.

In the starlight the earth was almost featureless, a black opaque expanse against the blue-black translucent sky. The flares on the aerodrome dropped below as I circled, climbing steadily to get on my beat. Other pin-points of light shone from neighbouring aerodromes and witnessed that they too were in action. To the east, far down the Thames estuary, two searchlights roved the heavens, impatiently hunting for that white flash in their beams—the wings of an enemy machine. Evidently the invaders were just crossing the coast. Flashes of anti-aircraft bursts could be seen winking for a second like yellow low-hung stars. London was dark and silent, not a searchlight showing, but presently, as if at some order, a number of them opened up together. Their long stiff tentacles began combing the night sky.

Archie began to get busy. The Gothas were evidently passing through that belt of country between the outer and inner ring of Home Defence, and were running the gauntlet of the barrage.

I was now all eyes, peering through the night trying to spot the black silhouette of an enemy, but it was futile; like trying to see a fly in a dark room. Soon the barrage grew heavier: thirty or forty batteries on both banks of the river were speaking; pin-points of greenish-gold on the ground, and, after about fifteen seconds, a smoky yellow flash a bit below me in the sky. The gunners were as blind as I; but they at least had the advantage of being able to hear the Gotha's engines. I wished I could hear those engines, but the roar of my own made such a thing impossible.

Now the anti-aircraft batteries in London proper were beginning to open up, and suddenly a big flash—Crrrrrump!—down in the city told that the Hun was dropping his eggs. The searchlights were wheeling and flickering excitedly like the antennae of monstrous butterflies, but they failed to locate the raiders.

More bombs! Smouldering heavy flashes down by the river. Suddenly I realized that the only person I cared about was down there somewhere in that blackness among those gun flashes, behind that grille of light beams, and that perhaps one of those bombs might fall on her. For the first and only time in the war, I saw red. I wrenched over the stick, and went in, through the gun fire, right off my patrol beat, to get into the centre of things where those bombs were falling. I was, for about two minutes, mad with rage, mad with the impotent rage of a blind man who knows his enemy is near and cannot find him. I circled over London, while Archie, thinking I was a Hun, took pot shots at me. But I could find no Gothas, so I wheeled sharply and swung off down to the river, thumb on the triggers of the guns, grinding my teeth. How ludicrous it sounds! A single madman, alone, up there in the darkness, bent on vengeance for one among those millions who cowered in the roots of the lights below! But it was all useless: I could find nothing, so I wheeled north again, back on to my beat. The A.A. fire grew less.

My anger wore itself out. If she had been killed, well, there it was. Some one had to be killed by falling bombs. If she had escaped, so much the better. Anyway, I could do nothing about it. Now I was tired. For two hours I had been at strain, peering into darkness, screwed up for an emergency. It had not come. Mental alertness could not last at that pitch. Petrol was running low. I was cold, and seeing, far below, the welcome " L " of the flares, shut off, and came down.

" Any one have any luck? " I asked my sergeant rigger.

" No, sir, no one ain't seen nothin'. But, judgin' by the row, them Huns must have been goin' through it good and proper."

*

A good-looking Norwegian, who somehow or other had joined the R.F.C., was the host in one of the many parties we used to hold in town on our off-nights. The procedure was invariably the same. The two opposite stage boxes for *Some* or *Bric-à-brac* were filled with those invited to the party. Most of the girls in the show were known to us personally, and a sort of cheerful badinage would soon be struck up between the boxes and the stage. On more hilarious evenings conversations between the boxes across the theatre had been known to be held, but this was not encouraged ! After the show there would be a guard of honour at the stage door, and a procession of taxis would set forth to one of the big hotels, where, in a private room, supper would be served. Some one would haul out a portable gramophone, and dancing would begin.

How decorous those evenings were! I do not remember the least suggestion of impropriety or even excessive rowdiness. Wild parties I suppose there were. The R.F.C. had a hectic reputation. But I, personally, never attended one where a Bishop could have taken exception to our behaviour. By two o'clock it was over, and the procession of taxis would again set forth, spreading out to the various parts of London. Then the pilots, having made a rendezvous, would meet again and motor down to Hainault.

On one such night I picked up Bill at the Savoy. We climbed into the old Singer two-seater that he ran. It was about three o'clock in the morning and pouring with rain. We were both very tired. Half-way to Stratford the bus conked out, and we sat there under the hood with the rain drumming on the canvas, quietly swearing. At length Bill got out and poured a spare can of juice into the tank. He swung it, but it would not start. We took it in turns, swinging and panting, and panting and swinging, in a drenching downpour. No good. At length we gave it up, got back into the car, closed the doors, turned up our collars and went to sleep.

We woke at six next morning horribly stiff and damp and done in. The rain was still pouring down, the sky was grey and heavy as lead.

"We must push it," said Bill, "to the nearest garage." So we took off the side brake and pushed.

The car was heavy, and the road slightly uphill.
We paused exhausted opposite a Police Station.
Bill went in and found a large constable asleep on
a wooden bench.

"Hi, Sergeant!" he said. "I want you."

The constable rolled into a sitting position and
rubbed his eyes.

"Yes, sir," he said.

The three of us pushed the car another mile and
ran it into a garage, knocking up the proprietor.
Then I dropped back into the seat and immediately
went to sleep again. When I woke the sun was
shining and the car coming up the long lane towards
the aerodrome. Bill was driving, fresh and composed.

"What was the matter with her?" I said, feeling
guilty about my sleep.

"I poured in two gallons of paraffin!" said Bill.

*

There was something mysterious about Bill. He
seemed to know what was going to happen.

"That Norwegian," he remarked one day.
"He's a spy. He'll go. You'll see."

Sure enough, two days later the Norwegian did go.
After that, Bill wore the air of a successful conjurer.
We shared a room, and as we lay in bed before
going to sleep the next night, Bill confessed to a
connection with the Secret Service. He had been
in charge of espionage work in London for a year.
Also he had been dropped from a machine the other
side of the lines and had succeeded in getting out
through Holland. There was something thrilling

about Secret Service work. I plied him with questions; but he was discretion itself.

Bill was a man of about thirty. He was tall and spare, had a voice with a break in it, a queer and expressive way of using his hands, a great sense of humour, and a funny sort of snigger instead of a laugh. The strain of a year's work in the Secret Service had tired him out, also he hinted that things had got a little warm for him. He was on the enemy list of those who were " Wanted," so for a rest(!) he had taken up flying, and was stationed at Hainault so as to be within easy reach of town if he were needed. We became great friends.

With Armstrong making a third, we used to see how close we *could* fly in formation. Happy in the skill of being able to keep our machines in perfect control, we used to float over the surrounding country, the two pairs of wing-tips either side of the leader's sandwiched in between his mainplanes and tail within four feet of his body. It was foolhardy, of course; a nasty " bump," a little too much engine, and the answer was collision; but taking such risks was, in those days, part of the fun.

*

A new Commanding Officer was appointed to the squadron. He did not like me. I don't know why. My Flight was efficiently organized; but somehow we did not hit it off.

" I think it's time you went overseas again," said he.

" I've not been back three months."

" Still, I think it's time you went overseas."

A week later he took me up to town to the Air Ministry. I was ushered into a Staff-Colonel's office.

" Your Commanding Officer says he thinks you're ready for overseas."

" I haven't been home three months," I answered. " I don't feel ready to go back. I had a heavy time this summer."

" Who were you with? "

" 56. I'm not really a rotary engine pilot, I'm an SE pilot."

" I see."

" I'm perfectly ready to go out again, sir, but I should like a month or two longer at home. It will be my third trip across the water when I do go."

" You say you're a stationary engine pilot. An SE pilot."

" Yes, sir."

" Hm. I think that is a perfectly good reason. Where did you get your M.C.? "

" On the Somme, sir. I was all through the offensive. Contact patrol."

" Hm. I'll post you down to Rochford. There is a Home Defence SE Squadron forming there under Prettyman. Know him? "

" Yes, sir."

" Very well, then. I'll have your transfer sent down to you."

" Thank you, sir." I saluted and left.

The thing had been a plant, and I knew it. The Major wanted to get rid of me to promote a friend. He didn't care where I went as long as I was out of his way.   But to hell with him anyway!   Two days later I was posted to Rochford.

★

Rochford was a magnificent aerodrome, almost a mile square.   No. 61, the Home Defence squadron to which I had been transferred, was quartered on one side of it, while up at the other end were a couple of training squadrons.   Rochford village was about two miles from Southend, and the squadron formed part of the ring of the outer defence of London previously referred to.   61 was equipped with Pups, another lovely Sopwith scout; but its performance and armament were not good enough to deal with Gothas, so the squadron was changing over to SE 5's.

I managed to keep a Pup for joy-riding, and some time after, one cloudless day, I decided to drop down and see my father in the Isle of Wight, where he was now being trained as an anti-aircraft gunner. He had refused a commission, preferring the obscurity of the ranks; and my job, having found the Isle of Wight, the Training School somewhere on it, a field adjacent to land in, was to locate Private Lewis.

I had togged up to do the Old Man proud, and, having put the Pup down in a field, walked into the Mess—it was just on lunch-time—and asked for the O.C. School.   My visit was unannounced, and the O.C. was not accustomed to R.F.C. Captains dropping from the clouds and demanding their Private parents.   However, he took it very well, gave me lunch, and afterwards managed, among the few thousand men he had in training, to locate the one I had come for. Before the amused stare of hundreds of men we met. My Venerable drew himself up and saluted. I returned the salute, trying hard to keep a straight face, and we strolled off together, looking as unconcerned as we could. Most of the afternoon we spent lying under a tree in a field, talking. He was finding the life vastly diverting, and told story after story of the types he was living among. One employed him as letter-writer to his wife : Father used to insert the most blasphemous adjectives before all his terms of endearment, much to his horror. Another refused to treat him as an equal and insisted on making his bed and looking after his kit. A third was teaching him billiards. He always attributed any favours he afterwards received to the effect of my visit, though he continued to resist all attempts to make him an officer. When, at last, he was forced to give in, the Armistice arrived to save him. On that wonderful morning, stationed with his Battery somewhere in the north of London, he leapt upon the bonnet of a motor-bus and rode it all the way to Piccadilly, thereafter retiring with all possible speed to the little white-washed cottage in the folds of the Devon hills.

About five I left for home. It developed into an awful journey. A heavy bank of fog came up and forced me lower and lower, so that at last I gave it up and climbed clear above it to eight thousand, trusting my compass to get me back to Rochford. I hoped that over the east coast it might break, but I was out of luck. As far as I could see in every direction was an unbroken floor, yellowish in the setting sun.

Up here it was all right, a clean dome of blue, full of pale sunlight; but this vast tranquillity did not reassure me. I didn't like the colour of that floor. It was not cloud, it was fog; and how the devil was I going to get down?

I flew on for a couple of hours. Petrol would be getting low. Better to come down while I had something in hand than to be forced down willy-nilly. I shut off and dropped into the fog, watching the altimeter like a cat. Here I should point out (for the benefit of the uninitiated) that an altimeter is really a barometer. To set it at zero before you leave the ground there is a thumb-screw beside the dial. But the ground at Rochford was not necessarily at the same height as the ground I was at this moment dropping towards. I might come out over a hill, say two hundred feet higher than Rochford. My altimeter would still read two hundred feet—but I should hit the ground just the same. Forgetting this has accounted for many an accident. I was not going to be caught if I could help it, but the trouble was that in a fog I should not see the ground until I was right on it. The needle dropped to five hundred feet. I opened the throttle and dropped slowly, buzzing the engine (it was a Mono) on the button switch. If I suddenly saw a hill or a church spire, I should have full power to help me away. Now I forgot the altimeter and kept my eyes on the fog below me, peering through it anxiously for the first signs of the earth. Suddenly, an elm tree right ahead! Engine! I zoomed it, missing the crown by a few feet. It was one of a row, the edge of a field. Well, now I knew more or less where the ground was, anyway. I edged round slowly, looking at the stubble beneath me. How big was the field? Could I get down in it? Were there high trees all round? I peered anxiously. More trees, then a gap. If I could strike that gap, I might be able to get in. I circled away. Now everything was lost in the fog again. I must trust to my sense of direction and get down below the tree level—or I couldn't hope to get into the field. I dropped, flipping the engine anxiously. A tree ahead! I kicked the rudder and slid sideways, putting it on my right. Was there one to the left? Yes; but just room to squeeze through. Telegraph wires? Apparently not. The hedge passed underneath, the stubble was beneath me. She floated on for what seemed an eternity. At last I touched the ground. The opposite hedge loomed up. Should I stop in time? Should I run into it? The heavy stubble dragged at the wheels. The Pup came to rest nosing the hedge. Whew!

I jumped out. After the noisy engine, the sudden silence was profound. The world was holding its breath, suffocating under this dank blanket of vapour. The trees were dripping quietly, monotonously, as if weeping for the death of the world. No signs of human habitation. Not a sound broke the stillness. I pushed through the hedge, found a lane, and followed it to a large house. I rang the bell. "Where am I?" I said.

The sudden apparition of a stranger in flying kit on such an evening must have startled the maid. She fetched her mistress. I was a few miles from Gravesend. So much for the compass course. I thought I was in Essex, I turned out to be in Kent.

Well, what of it? I was down, anyway. Next morning the fog had cleared. The grocer's boy swung my prop, I squeezed out through the gap again, crossed the river, and made the aerodrome on the last drop of petrol in the gravity tank.

★

Our machines were equipped with wing-tip magnesium flares, which could be touched off electrically in case of a forced landing.

"If," I said, "you went up to three thousand and then lit your flares and came down in a spin, wouldn't it look awfully pretty?"

"Probably," they said, thinking me the idiot I was.

It was winter now, dark before dinner. I had my bus wheeled out and rose into the air. At three thousand I touched off the flares, threw a loop and a couple of rolls, and then went into a spin. I dropped a thousand feet before the flares finally burnt out and came down to land. Meanwhile the wind had changed, I landed across it, bounced, wiped off the undercarriage, and turned over. It was a very ignominious ending to the exhibition. I was greeted with loud guffaws.

"Not so good," said the Major. "Drinks all round."

I was on duty that night. Pilots detailed for first patrol, in the event of a raid, had to stand by until dismissed, completely dressed in their flying kit, waiting for the hooter. There was nothing to do but play poker, put on the gramophone, and drink —but not too much, in case you had to take the air.

The Mess was strangely quiet on such nights. The voices of the pilots calling their hands, Kreisler's *Caprice Viennois*, the chink of bets dropping into the saucer on the table, these seemed small noises against the vast stillness of the November evening. One had the feeling of the whole world going slowly to sleep, lapped in waves of silence. Then—suddenly the raucous Klaxons right overhead. Their nerve-shattering blast jolted our hearts into our throats. Instantly everything was confusion.

" Where's my helmet? " " Give me a hand into this." " You've got my gloves." Pilots dashed about, frantic, picking up odd bits of kit, and tumbled through the door of the Mess, pell-mell. There was a sound of many feet as the men doubled up to the sheds. In a minute the engines were running.

On this particular evening my machine was a wreck. I called the Flight-Sergeant.

" I'll take up that new bus." I had just ferried it over from the Park that afternoon. It was O.K ; but the oil pressure was low. (Oil pressure was the bogy with the Hispano. It always needed tinkering to get it right.)

" But we haven't been over it yet, sir," said Sergeant Forrester. He was a very conscientious man, and he didn't like his pilots taking risks.

" Never mind. It's O.K."

" But she hasn't got any instrument lights, sir." Machines were delivered from the Parks without night-flying gear.

" Get me a torch."

He went off, much perturbed, while I got into the machine.

" Switch off. Petrol on. Suck in." Slowly the prop was pulled round, jerking against the compression.

" Contact ! " Click went the double switch. " Contact ! " A sharp pull, and away she went. Once she was warm I opened her out. The revs were a bit low, and the oil pressure twenty instead of the requisite forty-five ; but she seemed steady. It would have to do. Forrester returned with the torch. It had a battery which you slung over your shoulder on a strap. From it flex ran to a bull's-eye which hooked on to the button of your flying kit. He didn't like it at all.

" Don't take her up, sir," he kept saying as he adjusted the torch on my coat. " You 'aven't no call to take chances with a new bus like this, sir. Them ruddy Park fitters, I wouldn't trust them to tune a cookoo clock."

But if the Huns were over, our place was in the air, and I didn't feel like giving the excuse that I'd wiped off the undercarriage of my bus doing a stupid stunt.

" She's O.K., Forrester. Don't worry." He retired, shaking his head, and I took off.

The night was overcast, starless, moonless, the very darkest kind of night, the nearest approach to flying in absolute obscurity. I rose over the dim river and climbed up to patrol height. On either side of the body, the extremities of the exhaust pipes glowed like coals. Blue flames flickered about them. Within the cockpit the gleam of the little torch shone on the instruments. The revs were holding ; but the oil pressure was slowly, very slowly, ebbing away. Still, I could stick up until it fell to about five pounds, then I should have to come down. I wheeled up and down my beat for half an hour, trying to judge where the Huns might be from the anti-aircraft bursts; but, as usual, saw nothing. Then I caught my hand in the flex of the torch and pulled off the wire. The cockpit was plunged in darkness. I tried to get the wire back on the terminal, but couldn't manage it. The bus was new; it wouldn't fly hands off. I tried to hold the stick with my knees; but this didn't work either. Now what was to be done? What was my height? What was my speed? Were the engine revs steady? The oil pressure, I knew, was dropping. It is not pleasant to fly a machine with no instruments on a pitch-black night. One grows super-sensitive to each vibration of the engine, there is a tendency to panic, to imagine the machine is diving, stalling, slipping one way or the other, and the earth looks a very long way below. This fear began to grow on me; but I reassured myself. I knew the SE backwards. I'd flown it for hundreds of hours; but still, there were machines patrolling only five hundred feet above and below me. If I was diving or climbing, mightn't I easily run into them? I began to peer more closely into the darkness. What was that? Was it the light of another machine's exhaust? Turn! Turn quickly. That was a funny shudder as she went round. Now what was happening? The controls didn't seem to answer. The next second she dropped a wing and fell into a spin. I cut off the engine, straightened the controls, pushed the stick forward, and came out into a dive. This was altogether too tricky. Home, John. And be damn careful on the way not to stall. No more spins to-night. I came whistling down at, I suppose, about eighty, touched, tail up, well short of the flares, and ran down them, beyond the end of the " L," and came to rest in darkness. Thank God Rochford was a large aerodrome.

I turned in and went to sleep. There was a knock on the door. It might have been two hours later. I half woke up. " What is it now? "

" There's a Gotha down, sir. Crashed on the edge of the aerodrome, sir. The crew are prisoners in the guardroom, sir."

It was exciting news enough; but I was too sleepy and tired after that patrol. The thing would still be there in the morning. I grunted and went to sleep again.

Thus it happened that I never saw a Gotha, for the thing was not there in the morning.

The story, as I heard it next day, was strange. The Gotha had developed engine trouble, had seen the flares of the aerodrome and come in to land, firing a Very light. We had three colours of lights —red, green, and white. The colour was changed daily, a sort of password. The Gotha, heaven knows how, fired the right colour, was answered from the ground, and came in to land. Unfortunately, not knowing the aerodrome, the pilot miscalculated, hit a tree on the edge of it, and slewed round, crashing on to the golf-course. The mechanics rushed down, thinking it was one of our machines, and found the Hun crew of three, one officer and two. N.C.Os., climbing out of the wreckage. They were taken prisoners. All were quite unhurt. Some officers turned out to inspect the wreckage and remove the bombs, of which there were two hundred-pounders and about twenty babies. They also took out the Very Light pistol and the cartridges. The machine was pretty well smashed up and the tanks had burst, flooding the ground with petrol. The Equipment Officer, who had taken the Very Light pistol, slipped it into the pocket of his mackintosh. As he walked away, he pulled it out to show to one of the others. The trigger had no guard, caught in his pocket flap, and the pistol went off. The white-hot magnesium flare bounced along the ground, reached the petrol, and instantly the whole wreckage was in flames. Next morning, only the charred iron-work of the fuselage, the engines and wires were left.

We were very upset about this, because, at that time, a great controversy raged as to whether the rear gunner in the Gotha had a tunnel to enable him to fire under his tail. I have already explained that the way to attack a two-seater was to sit in the blind spot, below and behind the tail of the machine. But if this blind spot was not blind at all, if the gunner could lie on the floor and cover us as we rose under him to attack, then obviously tactics would have to be altered. As far as I know, this was the only Gotha that came down in England anything like intact. Examination of it would have solved our problem and settled the controversy. If I hadn't been so sleepy, I might have solved it myself. As it was, it remained, and still remains to this day, to me, a mystery.

Next morning, we went in to look at our prisoners. They were very quiet and rather sorry for themselves. I believe, they feared victimization : raiders were not popular with the general public. However, whatever the public thought, we knew they were brave men and had a fellow-feeling for them. So we gave them a good breakfast, and took them round the sheds. Then they were ordered an escort to take them to town. I accompanied them.

We had a reserved first-class compartment, locked, with the blinds down. But somehow the news had got about, and at every station there was an angry crowd. The officer in charge had to keep them off at the point of a revolver, otherwise we should all have been lynched. The Germans were anxious. We endeavoured to reassure them. One cut off the flying badges on his tunic and gave them to me. I suppose he thought they made him a little too conspicuous. At Liverpool Street there was a heavy armed escort, and the wretched men were marched away, through a hostile mob, to the safety of an internment camp.

*

A new Flying Officer had just been appointed to my Flight. He was very young, raw, and thrusting—ham-fisted we used to call these new fellows who hadn't mastered the lightness of touch and deftness of movement which is the sign of a good scout pilot. He could do anything with the SE; but he yanked the machine about as if he was angry with it. It wasn't pretty to watch, and his riggers were always having to go over the machine, so much did he strain it. This wouldn't do. I told him off.

At this time all the squadrons in the Brigade were

preparing to compete in aerial fighting, formation flying, etc. We spent the days practising. I was in charge of squadron formation flying, and when the new man came I thought it would be best to have him close to me, so I put him on my immediate left, with instructions that he was to stick there and fly soberly and quietly, thus he would best do himself and the Flight credit. The formation made a lovely sight in the air. The boys were all up to their work, and the whole squadron turned and wheeled about the sky in perfect style. When it was over I fired a Very light and we came down and landed by Flights. All except the new-comer. He had kept beautiful formation with me. I was very pleased with him. He was there all the time, his wings swaying slightly about ten feet off my tail. Nobody could have done better. The fellow could fly all right. Perhaps I had been a little hard on him.

I was standing on the tarmac, watching the last of the machines down, when the scream of a machine was heard. It was our youngster, to whom the repression of an hour's sober formation had been too much. He was diving, engine on, at the ground. He pulled out at about ten feet and zoomed up to five hundred or so on the momentum; but his pull into the zoom was rough and sudden, and his turn at the top was yanked, uneven.

" Gosh ! " said one of the old hands, at my side, " that's the way to pull your wings off."

By now the machine had turned and was diving vertically, crazily, at the ground. Again he yanked out the machine with a terrible jerk, about thirty feet up. It seemed to stagger. Then there was a tear, a wrench, and one pair of wings folded back. Bits of wood and canvas flew out. The machine fell headlong, struck the ground with a terrible crunch, and burst into flames. We rushed out— it wasn't a hundred yards from the tarmac—to try and pull the man out. But the machine was an inferno. The flames crackled and roared up to a height of fifty feet or more. It was useless.

The next day I went off on week-end leave, putting my deputy in charge. In the afternoon he took up the Flight in formation. We had two styles of formation flying: an open, fighting forma- tion, in which the machines had at least fifty yards between them; and a close exhibition formation, in which the closer the machines could fly the better.

In the close formation turns had to be made cautiously, else the machines might foul each other; but in the open we had invented an about turn, which reversed the direction quicker than going round in a half-circle. The leader did a half-roll on to his back, coming out directly underneath, facing in the opposite direction, while the two machines at either side of him turned left and right about re- spectively, crossing each other, and so regained their correct positions facing the other way. It was a neat manœuvre, and the Flight did it pretty well.

My deputy was a canny Scotsman; but he wasn't used to leading. He had the Flight up in tight exhibition formation, and then must have lost his head, for he gave the signal for the about turn, and started his half-roll. The machine on his right, only about ten feet away, couldn't get out of the way. His propeller cut into the body of the leader, and the two machines, tangled up, spun down to earth. Both men were killed.

It was, I remember, one of those still mornings with high clouds massing when we carried them down under the Flag. The age-old village church adjoined the aerodrome. The graves had been dug, and the Padre conducted the short ceremony at the graveside. The riggers had made crosses from four-bladed props, cutting off three blades short and leaving one long, and embossed their names on copper plates, covering the hubs where the bolts went through. We listened to those final simple words with, for my part, a sort of numbness, a feeling that this couldn't possibly have happened, that these men I had talked and joked with a day or two back were not really lying cold and mutilated in those damp holes, the earth crashing down on their coffins. The valedictory volleys cracked and echoed in the still beauty of the morning. The Last Post rang out and echoed away, as if calling up into that vault of blue ; but the air that had borne them was as heedless as the earth that held them now. None but the few of us who knew them would remember or mourn. Well, we should all go that way. There was nothing to be done about it. I remembered the cynical war-time prayer : " O God —if there is a God, save my soul—if I have a soul."

I was not quite so cynical as that. I did believe I had a soul, a speck of radio-active divinity, a drop of the Life Force, within me. But it was only on loan, so to speak. When I had finished with it, that drop went back into the bucket, into the agglomeration of surplus vital energy we, for want of a better term, called God. I did not believe in reincarnation, the same drop inhabiting another body; the odds were against it. Besides, the drop merged back into the whole; it was not an entity that could be fished out and popped into another body. The Life Force was a blind instinct: God was not a conjurer.

And I renounced, with reincarnation, all other forms of personal immortality, sugar candy that the world sucked to comfort it, unable to face the cold fact that death was the end. What merit was in me, I asked myself, that *I* should continue? Had I such virtues, were the graces of life so arranged in me, that they were worth perpetuating? I could not so delude myself. I was an experiment, an essay in creation, to be discarded when worked out. A chemist does not repeat an experiment, he tries another. Not to do so would be to deny all evolutionary appetite in life. With the whole range of creation before me, from amoeba to ape, witness to this progress, was I to suppose that I, a human being, was the end? Was the whole majestic unravelling to stagnate in little me? Only a sublime conceit, or a monumental cowardice, could frame such a hypothesis.

Besides, wherever I went, whatever I did, I had to take *myself* about with me. I could not escape it. And often myself bored me. The older I grew, the better I knew myself, the more dissatisfied I grew with my sorry limitations. Was it this I wanted perpetuated? Was I to imagine an eternity of it? Men called that going to heaven, I called it going to hell. The angels, in the hymn, " casting down their golden crowns upon the glassy sea " —a sort of heavenly ice-curling—were the apotheosis of ennui. If, in heaven, my grosser qualities were to be purged away, leaving me all "good," so much the worse. The devil was the pepper in my curry; remove it, and how flat the dish would taste.

No, the conventional formula for a life to come did not bear examination. Might I, at least, be spared it! After life, of a sort there was—an after life in thoughts and deeds; but this was not eternal, it was merely a projection of personality, doomed to eventual oblivion. According to the greatness of your souls, so shall ye live! I could subscribe to this, for life and death were figments of the mind. As long as I remembered Christ, Bach, or Borgia they lived. Their influence, for good or evil, was not dead till the last man had forgotten them. The greater their imprint on the world, the more enduring their immortality. And so down the degrees of lesser men: remembered they would live, forgotten they would die. I was content to be so judged by my contribution to life, for could not the influence of a man's thoughts pass on down through the generations, progressively diluted, but ever present, until it was absorbed into the consciousness of the race? That was enough. Indeed, what better immortality could one ask than to live for ever in the minds of living men? Beside such faith, conventional belief was dross to be discarded, as adult men discard the fairy tale.

*

It was the time of the St Quentin push, the Hun had broken through on a wide front, retaken his

lost ground, and was heading for Amiens. I had
gone over to Brooklands to collect an SE to take
back to Rochford. It was a pouring wet day,
clouds at two hundred feet, no weather for flying.
But they were in dire straits the other side, machines
were urgently wanted for squadrons in France, and
Major Sarigny, commanding the Aircraft Accept-
ance Park at Brooklands, called for volunteers to
ferry machines to St Omer. I knew the way like
the palm of my hand, so I phoned the squadron, got
permission to go, and soon had an SE in the air,
heading for France instead of Rochford.

It was a filthy day. The rain poured down,
running off the planes, lashing my face like a
whip if I ventured out from behind the wind-
screen. The clouds were right down on the
Downs; but I managed to slip through the gap
at Reigate, found the Folkestone main line, and
followed it to the coast. Now for the Channel!
It was always rather a nervy business crossing the
water. No experienced pilot had much confidence
in new machines delivered from the Parks. The
engines were often in bad tune, electrical connections
and pipe joints had not, we thought, the same meticulous care and examination expended on them as
they got at the squadrons. So there was an added
tension, which normally would have been dispelled by getting high enough to be within easy
gliding distance of either coast. But to-day there
was no chance of that. I pushed out over the
water at about a hundred feet, on a compass course
for Calais. Immediately England was lost. I was
alone above the grey cold water, under a bank of
heavy cloud and a downpour of rain. I thought

this would get into the intake pipes and spoil the mixture; but the engine didn't seem to mind, and if it was going to cough out, it would have done so already on the way down to Folkestone. The fifteen-minute crossing seemed interminable. I was forced lower and lower, so that the first thing I saw of France was the white face of the cliffs near Boulogne. I was flying straight into them, below their summits, and turned vertically, getting round only a few yards short of the chalk, my heart in my mouth. Then I swooped for the sands, sped up the coast to Calais, found the main road to St Omer, followed it over the town, and slipped in over the water tower on to the aerodrome, drenched in rain. I strolled into the office.

" Where in hell have you dropped from? " said the C.O.

" Brooklands."

" God Almighty! On a day like this! What did you bring over? "

" An SE 5a. Here are the logbooks."

I got a tender to Calais, caught the Leave Boat, and was back for dinner in town by seven that night.

*

My memories of that year at Rochford are crowded. Something always seemed to be happening. It was while I was there that the R.F.C. and the R.N.A.S. merged into the Royal Air Force, and we all preened ourselves in beautiful new blue uniforms. It was here I did my first gas-mask drill, walking about in a room full of chlorine, trying to pretend it was fun. It was here my Pup caught fire in the air, the most terrifying moment in all my flying experience. Luckily it went out.

From here I went over to the Sopwith works to offer practical pilot's advice on their new types. The huge factory fascinated me. Camels were going through by the hundred. In the experimental shops stood the Hippo, a new back-staggered, two-seater fighter, and a Triplane with six guns and a three-ply body, which the end of the war put on the shelf.

At Rochford we did the first wireless telephony tests on scout aircraft. We tried to speak, not very successfully, from machine to machine. But to speak to the ground was easy. The tremendous implications of this passed right over my head. Years later, when I first heard of broadcasting, I did not connect it with those experimental tests in 1918.

One night, on a party in town, I met Lily Elsie. Her charm and beauty turned my impressionable young head. I flew over to tea at her little house at Kingston. Ivor Novello played ' Cupid, Cupid,' the song with which she was captivating London at the time, and she came downstairs singing it. " What would you do without me to make an entrance, darling? " he laughed. I think I never saw two more beautiful human beings together.

Then there were Sunday suppers with Bertram Jones of the Air Ministry, with whom I became fast friends ; a man so able and confident, one felt that if the heavens fell he would be there, smiling, dealing with the situation: dances in Southend, plenty of leave to town, with an occasional raid to give things a fillip. The Rochford days were good, and when the news came through that a new Night Fighting Squadron was forming and I was to go out with it, well, I could not complain after such an easy year.

But before that, one more idiotic experience with an aeroplane—the last, of any account, that happened to me during the war. Somehow or other—I cannot remember why—I was flying an old BE 2c across London. Fog came down. I got lost, and landed in a field to ask where I was. A passing butcher told me Hounslow, and I walked back to the machine to start it up. A pilot usually has some one to swing his prop for him ; but there was nobody about, so I set the throttle at tick over and walked round to start her up. But I had miscalculated the throttle position. The engine went off at about a quarter out, and before I could slip round the wing to the seat, the machine had gathered way. The rudder was hard over, so the machine started taxying round and round by itself. Now what was to be done? I was dressed in a heavy combination suit. It would have needed a first-class sprinter to get in the centre of the circle and make a dash for the seat, jump up it while it was going, and shut the throttle. However, this seemed the only thing to do.

There was the machine, in the centre of a biggish field, spinning merrily round in a circle, at about fifteen miles an hour, gradually working toward the hedge. If it could not be stopped, it would pile up in the hedge, and I should never get home that night. So I jumped in and made a dash at the cockpit. I failed to reach it, tripped, fell on my face, while the machine completed its circle.

One wheel of the undercarriage bumped over my back, and the tip of the prop whirled by a foot above my head. I'd seen a man killed by getting in the way of a prop, and this one was too uncomfortably close for my liking. I managed to scuttle out of the way before she came round again, and stood there watching the machine, getting my breath. It was a ridiculous feeling of impotence.

I tried it again. I tried it twice more, in fact, with the same result. I was panting, for the effort, in a heavy suit and flying-boots, was exhausting. Besides, as the engine warmed up, it ran a little faster, and the speed of the waltzing machine increased. Two or three onlookers collected, equally impotent. We stood there for half an hour, while the machine spun nearer and nearer to the hedge, and at last drove into it, damaging the propeller and wing. Of all the exasperating stupid things that ever happened to me with an aeroplane, that took the prize. I never started up a machine alone again.

VI

OVERSEAS AGAIN

NIGHT bombing was becoming a regular practice, and London was not the only objective. In France aerodromes, dumps, batteries, depots, headquarters, towns behind the lines were bombed nightly. It was a mutual activity. We had squadrons of Handley Pages and DH 4's raining eggs on the Hun. He did the same to us. Something had to be done to check these raids, and so Home Defence pilots, used to night flying on scouts, were formed into Night Fighting Squadrons, and prepared for overseas.

The machines we were to fly were special Camels, in which the positions of the pilot and the tanks had been reversed. This brought the cockpit out behind the main planes, and gave the pilot a better all-round view, though it somewhat impaired the flying qualities of the machine. Henty, who had trained with me at Gosport back in 1916, was put in charge of one squadron, No. 152, and I was his senior Flight-Commander.

On the 21st of October 1918 he entrained with the men for France, leaving me to bring the squadron —and his bull-terrier puppy—over by air the next day. The evening was busy, packing the last of our kit, saying our farewells, and giving the last instructions to pilots, some of whom were pretty raw. Here is the final memo to pilots issued that evening :

"The strictest care is to be exercised by all pilots in their flying on this trip out to France. Flights will take off in order, A, B, C. They will fly in a Vee with A Flight leading, B on the left, C on the right. The leading Flight will be composed of seven machines (as arranged) : the other two five each. The Squadron Leader will fly alone, fifty yards ahead of the A Flight Flight-Commander. Flights will take off and circle round the aerodrome until all machines are in formation. On landing at Lympne, Marquise, and Faukenbury (our destination), the Squadron Leader will fire a light, Flights will separate ; *but keep in their flight formation.* A Flight will then land first, followed by B and C Flights. ON NO ACCOUNT WILL ANY PILOT LAND BEFORE HIS TURN, *i.e.* NO PILOT OF 'B' FLIGHT WILL LAND UNTIL *ALL* 'A' FLIGHT HAVE LANDED.

"There is no need for any confusion if Flight-Commanders do not take their machines in to land until the Flight landing before them is all down.

"DON'T land if there is another machine in the way. You may not have room. Go round again.

"DON'T do 'S' turns coming in to land more than necessary : it may disturb a pilot behind you.

"DON'T stunt or show off by landing near the sheds or by fast taxying.

"The best way for the Squadron to show off is to land 18 machines at the Squadron aerodrome, all O.K. If pilots will help by bearing these points in mind, there is no reason why we should not all reach our destination without mishap."

And we did! The morning was inauspicious to start with, clouds racing along at five hundred feet; but it cleared later into a perfect October day, and after the usual telephonings, to find out the weather conditions at the coast and on the other side, to get the G.O.C.'s formal permission, and so on, machines were swung up at about 11.30. They all started splendidly, the squadron wheeled into formation, while I waited below, crammed the bull terrier into the little cupboard behind my seat, where it yowled pitifully (and then went fast asleep and only woke up at our destination), and climbed up to the head of the formation.

We sailed out over the river, receiving a parting salute of Very lights from the chaps left behind, and headed for the coast. The squadron was keeping beautiful formation, engines well throttled down, and we crossed the Kentish Weald in fine style. How beautiful it looked that morning! The golden woods, the blue smoke curling up from the cottages, the crisp healthy autumn air! After four years, it was still intact, undamaged, standing as it had stood for centuries. What a happy contrast to the hundreds of square miles of devastated France! What a lot we owed to that narrow strip of sea! It looked never so lovely as on that day when we were leaving it behind.

We all landed at Lympne O.K., and while they filled us up and made one or two minor engine adjustments we had a quick lunch at the Mess. This was Lympne Castle, overlooking the Channel, the finest Mess, I should think, in England. During lunch I had a query from Brigade Headquarters, asking how many of us had arrived and how many

245

crashes there had been. This is sufficient indication of what usually happened to squadrons proceeding overseas. I replied curtly: " All machines arrived safely and are proceeding at 2 P.M. to France."

Soon the white cliffs were fading behind us, the blue Channel was below, and ahead the bluff of Cap Griz Nez. I was sentimental enough to take a good many " last looks " at England. I saw the Leave Boat gliding in to Folkestone, with its escort of destroyers and the little airship hovering above, alert for submarines. And then my thoughts turned to the seventeen fellows behind me, each tucked into his scout, and I wondered if any of them were taking their last looks too. For some of them, I thought, it would be the last look, for we couldn't expect, all of us, to come back. But, as it turned out, I over-dramatized the situation, for the Armistice came in a month, and we did not lose a man.

By this time we were over Griz Nez. I counted the whole seventeen still behind me. Murmuring a short prayer of thanks that none of them had had to swim for it, I shut off and we came down at Marquise. Here we stopped for tea, maps, and permission to proceed. It took longer than I thought, and not until 3.30 did we get in the air again.

The calm autumn day was closing in, and, as on many such days, with the evening came thick mists, reducing the visibility along the ground and making path-finding difficult. The aerodrome we were heading for was just across the road from the one I had been stationed at with 56 the summer before; but landing at Marquise instead of St Omer made

the route to it strange. Northern France is featureless compared to England, owing to the quantity
of small villages and the comparative lack of outstanding landmarks. Also their maps were not as
clear and accurate as ours. Of course, I had told
all the pilots that I knew the way like the palm of
my hand, to give them confidence; actually, five
minutes after leaving Marquise I was completely
lost!

Now it is always unpleasant to be lost in the air,
but if you are alone, you can twist this way and
that to pick up a landmark. But, at the head of
seventeen machines, had I suddenly started twisting, the formation would have been all over the sky,
direction lost, confidence shattered, and our fine
flight come to an ignominious end. So I edged
cautiously round, hoping they were not aware I
was lost, picked up a likely wood, and set off along
it, only to find my compass showing North-East.
As our general direction was South-East, that must
be wrong. The sun was setting, twilight was
coming down, and I had a momentary horrible
vision of us all flying on, lost, night falling, and
machines landing anyhow, anywhere, crashing all
over France. This would never do.

I edged round till my compass showed South-
East, and the squadron followed, blissfully unaware
of the predicament they were in. I skewed round
my map till it pointed the way we were going, and,
peering into the mist, tried to recognize on the
ground the woods that were shown as odd-shaped
blobs of green on the paper before me. That one,
shaped like an hour-glass, it was so unusual, if I
could find that, there could be no mistaking it.

And there, by the grace of God, it was! On the wrong side of us, it's true, but still there. And there was the main road beyond. I wanted to shout with relief! Now it was all plain sailing. In ten minutes we were over the aerodrome, saw the men grouped round the sheds below, and came down, all eighteen still intact, at our destination.

Henty was surprised and pleased. He had only just arrived himself and didn't expect us—certainly not an intact squadron : it was too good to be true. Not many squadrons could boast of having achieved that, and I was proud that both I had led—56 and 152—had done it.

*

Extract from a letter written home a day or two after :

" Imagine to yourself a semicircular roofed hut of corrugated iron. At either end a door for people to enter by—also for draughts to enter by!—and on either side of these doors a window, making four in all, covered with canvas, none too air-tight. In the centre of the hut a stove, made from an old oil drum, with a chimney going up straight through the roof. At the sides, tucked away under the curved roof, two little camp beds, and about the rest of the hut towels on strings, tunics, overcoats hanging from hooks in the roof. In front of the stove there is a rough table-top—a piece of an old door—standing on two upturned petrol boxes. In the centre of the table a solitary candle, which, as you can imagine, does not light the hut. The shadows hang thick at the end of it, hiding its bareness;

but the stove is good and warm, and the candle gives enough light for me to see to write to you.

" The aerodrome is enormous, built for a complete Wing of machines. It is now deserted, owing to the rapid advance, and we are the sole occupants. Last night we crashed off to a neighbouring village for dinner—the sweet champagne would have been almost too sweet for you, I think—came back and turned in at 9 P.M. I woke up, frozen stiff, at 4 A.M.—a camp bed is a change after a year in a civilized one! This morning we spent scrounging stoves and coal, and this afternoon I went up to Lille, with two other chaps, and had a look round. It was comic, tooling round Lille at 1000 feet, where I had been Archied like blazes many a time at 10,000 feet! I located the disused Hun aerodrome where we are moving up to shortly. It looks pretty good; but the desolation! The enormous tracts of shelled and pock-marked country that were all fresh and green when I was out last year and have been blasted in the advance this spring!

"All squadrons are moving up, and we are more or less prepared to live in discomfort for some time. It will be canvas tents when we move up, they say. Canvas, in November! Ugh! "

*

We duly moved up to Carvin, our aerodrome near Lille, and billeted ourselves in the village. The place was filthy with the leavings of the Hun retreat; but a couple of days' work cleared it up, and we began to get comfortable.

Now we had heard, I do not know with what truth, that in some places the Hun had left delayed mines behind him, which would blow up on time fuses or on contact. So we were suspicious of everything, always on the look-out for these alleged mines.

I had an iron stove in my room, which was a small one between two others, each holding three officers. I lit the stove; when it warmed up it began to tick slowly and regularly like a clock. A mine in the stove! I called in one of the other pilots.

"Listen to that!" I said. He listened.

"Do you suppose it's a mine?"

"Might be." The thing went on ticking ominously. We called in some of the others. Soon the room was crowded with pilots.

"How long do they tick before they go off?"

"Sometimes for days."

Tick! Tick! Tick!... went the stove.

"Well, if it goes off now, it'll blow us *all* up. Let it blow Lewis up. It's his stove. He scrounged it," said one. And he strolled off. The others, moved by the logic of this, began to follow.

Tick! Tick! Tick!... went the stove.

The Major came in. He listened to it attentively.

"I think it's only the iron expanding under the heat."

"Well, if it blows me up, it'll blow you up, and the chaps next door as well."

"Yes, I suppose it will."

"Shall we put it out?"

We put it out. It stopped ticking. We lit it. It started again. By that time we were fed up with it.

" If it goes off, it goes off. To hell with it anyway."

Need I add that it did not go off?

*

Making night landings in France was a very
different affair from making them in England. The
German air activity made open paraffin flares, which
would give away the position of the aerodrome for
miles around, out of the question. We should have
been bombed at once. Another system had been
devised.

Each machine had a small signalling lamp fixed
on the under side of the body. When he returned
to the aerodrome, each pilot flashed his own particular
call sign. If it was all clear for him to land, he
was answered by an electric torch from the ground.
The aerodrome was in pitch-darkness ; but at the
edge of it was a small movable trolley pointing into
wind. On this were mounted three powerful Aldis
signalling lamps. As the machine came down
these were switched on, throwing a beam across the
ground. The machine landed in the beam. No
sooner was it down than the lamps were switched
off. The aerodrome was in darkness again.

We did practice patrols to get used to this very
tricky form of landing, and, later, pilots were sent
out farther afield to get the lie of their area. France,
at night, was absolutely dark : not a light anywhere.
We had to find our way about by beacons, small
lighthouses, which, all up and down behind the
lines, flashed different letters in Morse. It wasn't
at all easy.

On the first practice patrol one of the younger pilots
failed to return. His mechanics waited out for him,
but two, three, four hours passed, and he did not
come back. We feared the worst, but at four
that morning the telephone rang. He was safe,
but this is what had happened.

He had left the aerodrome, got muddled by the
beacons, and lost. For two hours he had wandered
round, from beacon to beacon, hoping to recognize his own, but couldn't hit it. At last he saw
the beam of the Aldis trolley right underneath him!
What luck! If this wasn't his aerodrome, it was at
least some aerodrome. He came down and morsed
his signal. The ground didn't seem to answer;
still, the beam was there, it must be all right.
He came down over the trolley to land; but somehow or other undershot. He went round again.
This time he landed, hit a telegraph pole and
crashed. He had landed in the beam of a moving
motor-cycle, on a road, one hundred and fifty miles
from the aerodrome! That he could ever have
made such a mistake shows the amount of light we
had to land by.

*

Our squadron, 152, had a sister, 151. This was
commanded by " Flossie " Brand, a very gallant
and devout officer, who was afterwards knighted for
his trip to the Cape. It was Flossie whom I met
one day with no eyebrows, and when I commented
on his singular appearance, he told me (in his modest
smiling way) that he had shot down a Hun which
had caught fire. The flames from the machine
had singed him. I leave the reader to imagine how

close Flossie must have been to that machine. With him were a crowd of fine pilots, Tommy Broome, Stan Cockerell, Armstrong, and Bill, my friend from Hainault.

I suppose every one who saw him would agree that Armstrong was the finest pilot in the Force. He was a past master at that most dangerous and spectacular business of stunting near the ground. He would take his Camel off and go straight into a loop. The Camel, if the engine held, gained about ten feet on it. If the engine spluttered or missed, he was for it. His luck held until now, only a fortnight, had we known it, before the end of the war. Then, one day, he was spinning down to the ground, with him a favourite method of descent; but he left it too late, pulled out, thought he had not enough room, jerked back the stick before the machine had flying speed, went into another spin, and struck the ground. He was killed outright. They found his tongue on the engine.

It was the day that I flew over to visit these chaps I heard this news. But there was worse to come. Bill had been killed too. And in such a senseless, useless way, that I remember, on hearing it, I stamped and shook my fists in impotent rage against the Universe.

He had been up on night patrol and came down, making a perfect landing. He was taxying up to the sheds rather fast, but forgot, in the darkness, a shallow ditch between the aerodrome and the tarmac. The Camel, which was very light, bounced in this ditch and turned over on its back. Bill got out, swearing at himself for being such an idiot as to forget the ditch, and started examining the damage to the machine. The prop was broken, the top plane dented, the cowling loose, what about the engine? He knelt down in front of it with a torch trying to examine the valve rockers. At this moment his rigger, who had struggled into the cockpit to make sure the switch was off, cleared one of the guns. It fired: Bill fell back dead, shot through the heart.

*

To increase the squadron's effective range, the Major detached me with my Flight and sent us up to Houthulst, a little village north of the Ypres salient. I was glad of this chance to hold a small independent command, and we set off. It was lowering, heavy winter weather. We had to fly at 300 feet over the devastated areas, and I shall never forget the sight. The Somme, after the bombardment, had been pretty well wrecked, but it was nothing to Ypres. For square miles in all directions there was nothing but a featureless landscape of contiguous shell-holes. Now, with the winter, they were mostly filled with water, and in the evening light looked dun, rancid, slimy—an abomination of desolation. Beyond this awful tract, to the north, the ground recovered something of its normal contours, though it was badly pitted. We found our aerodrome, where the men had just arrived and were erecting our canvas hangars. A Chinese Labour Corps stationed in the village helped us on the ropes. By nightfall we had the machines snugly away and had quartered ourselves in a house in the squalid village street.

We all flew about a bit next day, getting our bearings and practising landings on the aerodrome, which was small. On the 9th of November we did a patrol, the last of the war. It was a gorgeous star-lit night. I saw fires and dumps going up lower down the line, but no Huns came over. They seemed to have given up the war. Next day, the 10th, came orders for us to cease operations. We heard vague rumours of the German High Command coming through the lines to sign the Armistice. The next day it was confirmed. The war was over.

We were cut off in this little village miles from anywhere, and though we felt the occasion demanded some celebration, it was impossible to hold one. There was nothing to drink in the whole village and nowhere to go to. All we could find was a dump of Hun Very Lights, of all colours, left behind in their retreat. With the help of the Chinese we made a bonfire of them. This pyrotechnical display was all we could contribute to the gaiety of Armistice night.

So it was over. I confess to a feeling of anti-climax, even to a momentary sense of regret. We were a new squadron, fresh overseas, we wanted—particularly the new pilots—to justify our existence, to carry out in action the thing we had been training for. Moreover, when you have been living a certain kind of life for four years, living as part of a single-minded and united effort, its sudden cessation leaves your roots in the air, baffled and, for the moment, disgruntled. But the readjustment was rapid and soon we began to explore the possibilities of peace. Where should we go? What should we do?

The first thing was to pack up and rejoin the squadron at Carvin. We hung about there for a few days, kicking our heels. I got fed up with this and decided to make an unofficial trip to England. I got permission to spend the week-end with another squadron, but instead headed the old Camel for Rochford, docked her in the sheds there, and turned up in town, much to the delight of some one who was not expecting me. On Monday morning I flew back without mishap, and nobody who was not in my confidence ever knew I had been home at all. It was the last lunacy of those days.

Then the squadron retired to its old aerodrome at Estrée Blanche. As senior Flight-Commander I was the first to get leave. A fortnight later I was in town. I went to Bertram Jones for advice as to what I should do. He sent me to General Caddell of the Vickers Aviation Department. Caddell took me on. Within another fortnight I was demobilized with a good civilian job. I was twenty years old.

VII

CIVIL FLYING

EVERYTHING which now follows will be, I fear, an anti-climax. Peace is not so exciting as war : that is one of the difficulties in maintaining it. Up till the Armistice, flying had filled full the page of my life ; but now it was only a job there were margins, and, because life itself was new and untasted, those margins began to be more absorbing than the main print. If the years just after the war are the most romantic and idyllic in my life, it is because of what was written in those margins, with which this book has, properly speaking, nothing to do. Largely because of this, I suppose, the end of the war left me with no feeling of flatness ; indeed, the change was a stimulus. Other men might shake their heads, having pre-war days to remember. I was not going back to things previously known. Everything was shining new. Besides, although the war was over, the attitude to life it had provoked continued. It was a sort of hang-over. Everyday existence was like those snatched weeks of leave from the front ; incredibly hectic, gay, and careless. No doubt the general feeling of immense relief was bound to vent itself thus in an orgy of exuberance and irresponsibility. An era of false prosperity set in. Nobody stopped to examine the real situation. A million men had been killed ;

billions of pounds had been blown away. The waste had been terrific. The world must be poorer; but nobody would face it. Had we pulled in our belts and disciplined ourselves for four years to proceed with caution and circumspection now, when we were victors?

At Versailles, those few who prophesied disaster were never heard. Who could hear such a whisper in the tumult? Hang the Kaiser! Make Germany pay! Take away her colonies, split up her empire! Rearrange Europe and give each of the victors a share of the spoils! These were so many strokes of the pen. And if some economist advised moderation, pointed out the absurdity of making a state bankrupt with one hand and demanding it should pay in full with the other, he was swept aside. The public wouldn't stand it, was the answer. And that, indeed, was true. It is easy to be wise after the event and condemn those who drew up that Treaty, but, at the time, it is difficult to see what else they could have done. The world had no experience of treaties on such a scale to go on, so its statesmen did the obvious and popular thing. It was too much to expect jaded and middle-aged politicians to realize that the whole economic structure of the world had changed overnight.

If believing in good times could bring them, the post-war years should have been the most prosperous the world had ever known. The spirit of those days was, in fact, as I remember it, immensely liberal. Everything was to be rebuilt on a bigger and better scale. Of course, it might not pay at once; but, later, things would improve. It was not until ten years after, when the looked-for prosperity had not materialized and this delusion had almost wrecked the world, that we suddenly pulled up all standing and found ourselves bankrupt. To-day, whether there is a way out is still in question. Probably the next, now rapidly preparing, cataclysm may provide an emotional solution to a problem insoluble intellectually.

*

As far as flying was concerned, we really started in after the war with a great advantage; that of having no experience or tradition to jettison. The immense stimulus of the conflict had advanced flying from being a crazy trapeze act (without a net) to an everyday occurrence no more hazardous than track-racing. But to get it beyond this point, to make it a safe means of transport, was another, and equally great, advance. It involved a complete change of outlook in design, and, since experiment could not be indulged in on the lavish war-time scale, it would take longer.

Fighting machines must sacrifice everything to performance, commercial machines to safety. Passengers take up more room than bombs, and this, among many other things, means radical changes in construction. Economy too, unheard of in war, became of prime importance. How far could a machine be made to fly on a given quantity of petrol? Obviously the greater its range, the more petrol it would need, and therefore the less useful load it could carry. This useful load—passengers, goods, mails—represented the gross earning capacity of the machine; but from it had to be deducted

overheads—maintenance, repairs, ground organization, depreciation—before an effective nett payload
figure could be determined. Eventually all this
could be reduced to a formula : the cost of operation
of a machine per seat mile. This figure was an
index to the efficiency of the type.

I have presented the problem simply ; it was (and
still is) vastly complex, depending on a number of
related factors continually in flux ; but, in 1919,
the finer shades had to be brushed aside : a start
must be made somewhere. But where?

Most of the existing material was no use at all.
Machines and engines, efficient enough for war
conditions, were useless commercially. They were
for disposal by the hundred, and could be bought
for a song ; but nobody wanted them. They were
so much junk. Yet nothing existed to take their
place.

Of course the designers were on to the problem,
but what sort of aircraft were they to produce?
And for what market? Now there was no Government panicking for hundreds of machines to be
delivered the day before yesterday, there were only
a few tentative buyers prepared cautiously to consider initiating air services in various parts of the
world, provided they were reliable and would bring
in a safe return on the outlay. Some demanded
large passenger machines, some flying boats, some
amphibians, and whatever was offered did not seem
exactly to meet their requirements. Handley Page's
had converted their double-engine bombers into
passenger-carrying machines and supplied them to
Imperial Airways for the London–Paris Air Service.
We converted the Vickers' "Vimy," a smaller

machine with two Rolls-Royce engines, for similar services elsewhere.

For the first few months I spent nearly all my time drawing up schedules of capital expenditure, running expenses, and possible profits to be derived from starting air services in various parts of the world. Most of the projects came to nothing, for the truth was that machines were too costly to buy and expensive to run to make such services worth while. The world was not yet air-minded. Commercial Aviation hung fire.

*

Then, partly for publicity and propaganda, but more, I suspect, to satisfy that peculiar, but innate, desire to break records—one of the few outlets for the pioneering spirit in modern days—long distance flights began. The most spectacular and daring to attempt was obviously the Atlantic. John Alcock and Whitten Brown, the former a splendid pilot and the latter an observer with a knowledge of navigation and wireless, came forward to make the attempt.

The Vimy was a good choice for such a flight. She was fast, as such machines went then, compact, could carry the necessary petrol, and was fitted with Rolls-Royce engines. Probably she was the only machine in existence at that time fit to make the crossing. That particular Vimy, the first aeroplane to cross the Atlantic, now stands in the Science Museum at South Kensington, and I am proud to state that if you ask the Curator to show you the logbooks, you will find my name on the front page,

for I flew that Vimy from Upavon to Brooklands
before she was converted for the great flight.

The trip, as every one now knows, was a triumph
of endurance and navigating skill, for the wireless
broke down almost at once, and the machine en-
countered fogs and storms almost the whole way
over. However, helped by a strong following
wind and a course that was, under the circumstances,
uncannily accurate, the machine landed in Ireland
(in a bog) in 15 hours 57 minutes, setting up a
record that stood for many years.

★

To take up civilians in war-time had been strictly
forbidden. Few had flown in pre-war days. Must
there not be a public dèmand to go up and see what
flying was like? We decided to start a small flying
circus to find out.

Walking down Piccadilly to the club, I ran into
Tommy Broome and Stanley Cockerell.

" Want a couple of hot-stuff pilots? " they said.

The answer was in the affirmative, and they forthwith joined me. We bought some Avros from the
Aircraft Disposal Board and fitted the rear cockpit
to take two passengers, roped in some good Air
Mechanics from the Rochford days, and set off
light-heartedly to make the great B.P. air-minded.
Light-heartedly, because it was impossible to be
anything else in the company of Tommy and Stan.
Known to all, and each other, as Grock and Pard,
they were inseparable and had that sort of Potash
and Perlmutter humour which was irresistible
because it arose naturally out of their reactions to

one another and was quite unforced. But for all their apparent frivolity, they were both extremely skilful and steady pilots. Our passengers could not have been in safer hands. Later they attempted the first flight to the Cape ; but engine trouble foiled them. When they returned, they took up testing for the firm, and continued this work for some years until, one winter day over the Solent, the tail came off a boat they were trying out. The machine dived headlong into the sea. Tommy came to the surface first and looked about for Stan, who was nowhere to be seen. Suddenly up he popped like a cork through the waves. " Bloody hot in Africa, Pard," was his first remark. It was in this spirit that the two took all their adventures and mishaps. On that occasion they were very lucky to escape with their lives. Tommy's hair went white overnight, and he was put on to less strenuous work.

So, with suitable advance publicity and ground staff, we started out. We visited Cardiff, Birmingham, Sheffield, Newcastle. The municipal authorities and the local press backed us up and gave us facilities. When the weather was good we did quite well ; but the public was cautious—particularly up north. Flying was still something of a miracle. " On the ground you know where you are, but in the air—well, where are you ? " To fill up the time we gave exhibitions, impersonated Providence at garden fêtes, dropping balloons and confetti on the crowd below, while the children sang " All good things around us are sent from Heaven above." We were available for advertisement or special charter. During the Great Strike we flew loads of daily papers to provincial centres. But, on the whole, although we had a lot of fun out of it, the circus was not an unqualified success, and with the coming of winter it was abandoned.

★

But all that summer long, when Saturday came, dropping a suitcase into the back seat, I took off and headed south with an eager heart. Wherever we happened to be, my destination was always one of two great country houses in the south of England. I put down the machine in a neighbouring field and walked up to the house. Then life began.

There were many young people at those house-parties, and after dinner we would go roaming over the quiet lawns. From the mellow windows that opened on the gardens would come the sound of music; a wonderful voice, singing. Those magic notes, charged with such passion and such longing, unloosed in one, at least, an ardent and adoring heart. The song said Love was bitter and set down an aching joy. It was not true. There was a rose without a thorn. With us it would be different, for we had found our way, threading the secret labyrinth, into the shining presence of perfection. Was it not now about us, dark-eyed and still, closer than breathing, here in the dusk? Grief was a ghost that dared not steal out of the yews where the sad song had lost itself; joy was on tiptoe, waiting to be clasped, else it would fly and leave us lone for ever. Was it a dream? If this was dream, what was reality? If this was unreal, all was unreal; it was the peak of life, the aim, the end, the crown upon the brows of youth, the coronation of desire.

The last notes died away and left us stranded on a hush. The goddess was created, here in the gloom, carved from a fair white silence. Then music came again : a waltz, an old slow waltz, that swung us out in couples on the turf. The journeying was over, the wandering was done ; we had come home. Would there not always be, as now, a rhythm we both heard and moved to, lightly, firmly held? Should we not find, as in these mazy silent steps, a common path to last us to the end?

The big magnolia grew up about my window, drenching the room with scent. A sign, a whisper from the balcony, and then we crept, pillow and coverlet, down the great stairs, out of the listening house, towards the rose garden. The moon laid silver on this silent world ; but in the shadow of the ilex where the hammocks hung, darkness and mystery. Sleep not to-night ! There will be many nights when that secure release will come ; and many, many, when, however wooed, it will not come at all. What dream to-night can equal the reality? Our whispers, like a single voice in two tones, rose and fell so gently that they hardly sent a ripple up the shore of silence. A huge toad passed with gawky, hesitant stride, lumbering primeval to its lair ; a blackbird called, and while the moon was setting golden in the dell, the sun came up, and two lights made the morning.

We plucked the peaches sun-warmed from the orchard wall. Gaily we set out, a company on horse and foot, through woods and lanes, up beyond No-Man's-Land, to picnic in the heather. We laughed, we danced, we lazed, we loved. This was the bread and wine of life—the days of innocence, so kind and carefree to us that we never paused to savour them and say, This is the best. We passed from joy to joy as youth will, headlong, feckless, wrapped in the golden moment like a bee in amber.

Monday meant parting, and to see below the pattern of the house, girdled in summer woods, with one white figure waving on the lawn to speed me as I passed alone in the wide skies; and all the week was longing for the next time.

But autumn came. The magic circle snapped. The bond was broken, and the door of the great London house was shut to me. Ah, me! What was, what might have been, what never will be! Had you but been surer then, you might have saved yourself and me so many barren days! Together, so it seems, we might have made a nobler thing of life. Perhaps not, who can say? We cannot put it to the proof, alas!

The days dragged by and prison winter brought no comfort. Everything was dead. One evening I stood alone gazing over rainy roofs towards the house where she was moving, breathing, talking to others, and myself not by.

" Would you like to go to China? " said a voice.

I turned. It was the General.

" Yes," I said.

VIII

THE VOYAGE EAST

THE night train clattered out of the Gare du
Lyon. It was dark when I awoke, and I lay
there in the little berth, thinking. The last days
had been a rush, getting the kit together, selling the
car, getting tickets, passports, visas, money, and saying the sad farewells. Now we were off, bound
for the Far East. Forget the past! Another adventure had begun. The whole world lay before
me. I was twenty-one, and yet—I laugh now to
record it—I felt so very, very old!

The Peking representative of Vickers Ltd. had,
after months of negotiation and tortuous wangling
through his compradore (a sort of Chinese manager,
employed, by reason of his knowledge of the language, his contacts, and his understanding of the
Eastern mode of doing business, to put through
deals for Western firms, which they could never do
unaided), pulled off a big aviation deal with the
Central Government in Peking. It was for the
supply of sixty training machines (Avros) and forty
Commercial Vimys, with the necessary spares, extra
engines, etc., to form a training school for Chinese
pilots, and, out of this, to develop, with the Vimys,
a regular air service between Peking and Shanghai.
With the machines were to be sent a crew of riggers
and fitters to erect and run them, and two pilots to

test them. I was one, and Patteson, snoring away in the berth below, was the other.

The mechanics, eight of them, were all picked men, with a special knowledge of the engines and machines they were to work on. They had studied the erection of Vimys at the Weybridge works, and been to Rugby for a course on the Rolls-Royce engine. Now they were all on board, somewhere down the train, rolling south across Europe with us in the early morning. Pat was a good fellow; we should get on well. A good pilot and a good mechanic, too. Soon he would wake and we could order tea, and gossip. I had never been south of Amiens before. Paris had enchanted me, and the sun setting behind the Arc de Triomphe, with the great sweep of the Champs-Elysées rising up to it, was the first of many memories I should retain for ever. Soon it would be Switzerland: mountains, chalets, and chocolate; then Venice: churches, and gondolas; then the ship: Suez, India, the East. The prospect opened wide before me. Out of the word-pictures of my friends I had evolved a sort of composite image—lacquer, dragons, dark inscrutable faces, palms, turbans, pagodas, a pantomime fairyland of exotic scenes, nothing like the real thing, and far, far less romantic, but in contemplation, what a day-dream!

The train halted. I pulled aside the curtain and looked out. A foaming torrent boiled beside the track. Beyond, the steep slope of a pine wood. Through the wood, a track winding precipitously between the trunks, and on the track a little boy in a black cloak and long pointed hood, minute under the great trees, toiling uphill. Was he real? No, he was a goblin from a fairy tale. If I blinked he would be gone. I called Pat to look, pulled down the window, leant out. So this was Switzerland! Such mountains, such clean, crisp, resinous air, with the sound of hurrying water ringing through the silence. A gong said sweetly, Pong! Ping-pong! What land was this where even trains received melodious invitations to proceed? I was entranced. Dress! Dress quickly, not to miss a moment of the world! The train ran on. A tinkling bell went hurrying down the corridor: Déjeuner! Petit déjeuner! What coffee, butter, rolls, and cherry jam! It was like eating health. What prospects from the windows, what lush fertility! Surely this world was new: it had been born last night, and now lay smiling like a baby at the sky. On, on! Lausanne, Montreux, Vevey, the great lake; then the climb up the Rhône valley to the Simplon. Here came Napoleon, planting his poplars along his straight-made roads. Here, on this day, came sun, blue sky beyond that shining congregation of great peaks, where to the south lay Italy.

I have done the journey many times since then, and never lost the thrill of coming through the Simplon to run down that rocky valley, twisting from side to side under the tunnelled arches, to the lake. The air is warmer, sweeter; it has welcome in it, and the mountain villages, the quarries, and the fields are somehow unpremeditated, easier, more living and less organized than any other landscape that I know. At length, with evening, came Maggiore, ringed with its mountains and its lovely hills. Pink villas, flat pitched roofs, the first palms, the first camellias!

Who can forget the spring there? Scilla and prim-
rose, snowdrop and anemone carpet the woods,
the palm nods golden plumes, still water laps the
rocks, the poplars flutter into bronze, the opening
hornbeam is a miracle of green. That evening the
sky surpassed itself. High drifts of pink arched
over it, the lake was amethyst, the very air was rose,
flattering everything, till the castle at Arona as we
passed shone like a jewel on its crag. I never
dreamed the world could be like this, and stood at
the window gaping, drunk through the eyes. Some
day to this I must return, however far I journeyed,
for I felt instinctively what good fortune would
afterwards make true, that I had roots here.

As midnight struck, we came out of the Venice
station, down the steps to the black water where
the gondolas were waiting. Our hotel was an old
palace on the Grand Canal, and to reach it the gondolier cut through the smaller waterways. We
glided under hump-backed bridges, up narrow and
mysterious vistas where the tall houses lost themselves in the night above, turned sharp corners,
with a deep-throated warning " Hé ! " from the
gondolier, the delicate prow seeming to inquire of
the further water whether all was well, feeling its
way, like a protective serpent, thin before us. But
nothing moved over that sheet of ebony, and our
soundless swaying motion went on, a ghostly progress in a ghostly city of sea-lapped marble, so timeless, so detached, it might, I felt, now it had once
begun, go on for ever. To complete the magic
there was music; a guitar, a voice, seeming to
come from nowhere, following us like a spell,
till we emerged into the broader waters of the

Grand Canal, and slid to rest against the leaning mooring-poles.

It was the first day of that voyage, and, though there were many wonders in store, nothing after ever equalled it. It was an initiation into the lust for wandering, and such a potent one that ever since, maps and travel-books and time-tables provoke a fearful itch to pack a suitcase and be gone, hoping to recapture the gold of that day, and usually being fobbed off with very small change.

*

There was a performance of an opera by Mascagni at the Bernini Theatre. We could go by water. It seemed the most romantic way to approach the most romantic branch of musical art, so we went. I cannot remember the title of the work, which was of unequal quality; but at the end of the second act, the tenor, clad in a leopard skin—and little else—sang an immense aria. As he reached the climax, a property goose drifted across the stage on a string. The tenor, metaphorically pulling his bow and arrow out of his hip pocket, transfixed the bird, which dropped obediently to the stage, took a high B♭, and brought down the house. Cheering and clapping. Encore! Encore! He nodded to the orchestra. The goose was hauled off over the dusty boards, the band struck up, and the aria began again. The veins in the tenor's neck swelled, the music rose; would it appear on time, that melancholy bird? Of course! Correct to its appointment the amiable creature drifted by; another proof of musical marksmanship, another and finer tenuto on the B♭, and the house rose at the singer in a roar. I cheered louder than any. In London such a song would never have been encored because of the difficulty of the goose. You had to keep up the illusion. But here, in the home of opera, that was a trifle. What they wanted was that B♭ to send shivers up their spine. The goose was part of the situation to provoke the effect. Nobody laughed when it was hauled off and re-appeared at the critical moment. I found such naïveté delicious and remembered Shaw: " When a thing's too silly to say, you can always sing it."

*

After three days' exploring, a lazy water-borne wandering over the city, the ship steamed in and anchored off the Santa Maria della Salute. She was a Lloyd Triestino steamer, the *Innsbruck*, and when we went on board we thought everything well laid out, airy and cool. By the time we reached Shanghai I was describing her as a dirty, insanitary, badly provisioned ship; but that, I suspect, was due to the length of the voyage and the frightful boredom of being cooped up with the same people for six weeks, and unable, except in a stuffy cabin, to get away from them. They were a mixed bag, seventy-five per cent foreigners—Germans, Italians, Austrians, Spaniards, Norwegians, Danes—all bound for some port on the route anywhere between Port Said and Tokio.

The siren went. The façades of the palaces threw back the cry to us. The anchor came up, and under a pale Caneletto sky, with the church bells murmuring across the water, we steamed out into the Adriatic.

Such a voyage would make a good study for the psychological novelist. The first few days, as we went down past Brindisi and Cape Matapan over the blue sunny water, were a time of getting acquainted, amusing struggles in foreign languages, a sorting out, a setting to partners, so to speak; all extremely tentative and *comme il faut*. But, Port Said left behind, the clammy heat of the Red Sea began to shorten the temper and warm the blood. Definite cliques began to form, bridge fours, and dancing partners, while the warm nights and warmer days discouraged our energetic walking of the deck and prepared the way for those interminable conversations, leaning over the side, watching the swirl past of the water and the rising of the moon. Aden, with its magnificent and barren peaks, where the buzzards soared interminably on still wings, released us from the oppressive damp; but the temperature itself rose still higher. Partners were now definitely set. At least one love-affair was well alight, and other fires were laid ready to go off at a touch. It was a beautiful example of the effect of temperature on temperament. Drinking rose steadily in volume and violence, for there was nothing to do day or night. Idleness and the maddening propinquity so worked on vows of chastity or fidelity that, by the time the ship was half-way across the Indian Ocean on her ten-day course to Colombo, morals were at a discount and scandal could not keep pace with the rapidity of developments. Couples came together brazenly, violently, and as rapidly flew apart, hearts were broken, men rowed and threatened to throw themselves overboard, girls burst into floods of tears when offered cups of afternoon tea. A few married couples, mostly English, old hands and used to the scene, looked on tolerantly and retained their integrity; but the rest of the ship was all to hell and rather enjoying its dissolution. I personally escaped the worst of it, owing to my passion for writing poetry. At that time fame as a poet was all I cared about. The poetry was incredibly naïve and sentimental, full of clichés and borrowed ideas; but it had a virtue which I never suspected at the time : it gave me something to occupy my mind.

Colombo was the first real sight of the East. Here were the first rickshaws, barefooted coolies, naked to the waist, their dark backs running with sweat, torsos of living bronze. They stank of garlic, betel-nut juice dribbled like blood from the corners of their mouths, and they pulled us, shouting strange words, over the red roads to the hotel, where, to escape the ship, we had decided to spend the night. We wandered in the bazaars, were disgracefully fleeced buying moonstones and opals, played tennis, melting under the heat, and then plunged into the Galle Face swimming-pool, while the sky beyond the surf turned to a cloudless dome of orange, against which a few palms stuck out of the sand like gigantic pins. Here I tasted the first real curry, sat under the first punkah, slept under the first mosquito net, and first smelt that warm indefinable smell which, whenever it recurs (prisoned in curio or roll of silk), evokes the distant scene. Then, with a swift intaken breath, half thrilled, half saddened by the scent, comes back that vague nostalgia: Ah, the East! The East!

Schools of porpoises and shoals of flying-fish accompanied us on to Penang, where to escape the ship again we took the train down through Malay to Kuala Lumpor to see the jungle, the rubber plantations, and partake, even for a night, of the life of the people who made their home there. Penang was a study of blues, sea, mountains, skies, with fishing villages high on their poles above the water, and such white sand. The jungle was monotonous and disappointing; but the cultivated streets and gardens of the capital, the spacious bungalows, the doorless rooms, the huge earthenware bathing-tubs, the fireflies, all wrapped in an almost tangible garment of heat, delighted me at first. Only later did I understand the curse of that heat, the unescapable monotony of landscape and life, and admire the men who stuck it for a lifetime.

Then dusty Singapore, Hong-Kong with its junks and street of flowers, and so north. Now it was cooler again, and we began to walk the deck with Mediterranean energy. The *Pilsna*, a sister ship to ours, passed, and we saw from the stern a great red blanket waving—the crews of both ships were red-hot communists. Fog and rain met us in Shanghai. It was, I thought, a horrible city, neither East nor West, and full of U.S.A. Here we packed the men off to Peking by train, and taking the heavy luggage, boarded a local ship and ran up the coast, past Cheefoo, Wei-hai-wei, to Tientsin; caught a train, and reached Peking one night at 7.30. The men met us. We were rushed off to the Grand

Hotel to meet the other members of the firm and their wives—" things began to get cheery, got cheerier and cheerier and cheerier, till at last Pat came home on the bonnet, and we drank prairie oysters and eventually retired at 4 A.M. Pretty full day ; but thank God the journey is over."

IX

TEACHING THE CHINESE TO FLY

THE heading is anticipatory. In fact, my problem becomes increasingly difficult as it proceeds, for, though we arrived in Peking on April the 6th, I did not actually get a machine into the air until December the 17th—a nine months' delay. The hold-up was due to interminable arguments about certain clauses in the contract unacceptable to the Chinese, which automatically delayed the delivery of any machines. During this time we lived in Peking on a very handsome salary with practically nothing to do. Here then is a difficulty, for I set out to write about flying in a sort of autobiographical way, and now there is a big gap. The main print fades out entirely, and the margins to which I referred earlier absorb the whole page. To skip the period entirely would be to pass over days that were to me of absorbing interest, for Peking is a city of endless fascination; yet the reader may feel defrauded. But, after all, it is easy to turn a page, and those to whom life in the Far East is of no interest can pick up the thread later on.

The first thing, when we recovered the morning after our arrival, was to go to the office and get the lie of the situation with regard to the contract, to meet the Chinese compradore, and to receive our first cursory initiation into the tortuous and complex methods employed in doing business with the Chinese. Nothing, we learned, could be approached directly; all was oblique, often inverted, and depending for its success on the " squeeze " (rake off) which those who held the key positions could secure. But before we had been long at this the " Tai-tai " appeared. The Tai-tai —honourable gentleman's wife, or wife of an official—told us we were to consider ourselves engaged for the next two or three afternoons to " drop cards."

The complicated etiquette of European society in foreign parts (for I believe it is not peculiar to Peking) was strange and, at first, amusing to me. Being a minister's son, I had not been brought up to take any account of social status, and the war, which graded men according to prowess and ability, and not by blood or money, had confirmed the view. Wealth or position were no criteria of virtue. I made friends with people because I liked them, because I had ideas and feelings in common with them, or because I could respect their ability or learning ; never because they held elevated positions or because it was " done " to be seen in their society. This I found prevented my being a social success—it still does—but flying (and natural instinct as well, no doubt) had taught me to tackle things alone. I had no herd instinct. Being in the swim meant nothing to me. I felt it was a sort of opportunism to take advantage of your social connections to improve your position. The world was run that way, of course, but I preferred to rise or fall to whatever level my character and merit found for me. It was not conceit that made me take this view. It was a sort of stubborn or quixotic belief in worth as opposed to self-interest—no asset to any who worship the bitch goddess, Success. I have on occasion deserted this standard and done things for kudos or gain, and always the event has proved what the instinct foretold, that no good could come of it, and that the essential self would emerge somehow degraded and soiled. Society, no doubt, was composed of many worthy and estimable persons, with all sorts of qualities I did not possess, yet being by nature separate, aloof, a lover of solitude and contemplation, it was oil and water : I could mingle, but not mix. Life was so full of interest, activity, and effort—and so unbearably short—there was no time to waste on fools who had no appetite for it, nor to suffer them gladly.

But the first thing the newcomer to the Far East had to do was to establish his status and obtain admission to Society. His ticket was his visiting-card, which he dropped at the houses of those by whom he wished to be recognized. There was a recognized hierarchy. At the top was the British Minister, then his Legation and Consular satellites. Next came the bankers, the advisers, and administrators to the Chinese, the heads of reputable commercial firms, and after these a nondescript selection of people who might be useful, members of foreign Legations, travellers, writers, sinologues, etc. The nondescripts (the only interesting ones) did not really matter. The upper levels would ensure your admission to the Club and establish your bona fides. But the joke was that these calls were merely a formula. You expected, and indeed arranged the time of your visit, to find people not at home. If

they were so tactless as to be in, you muttered Damn !
and entered, hoping to get away as soon as possible
—the afternoon was passing and you had many
cards to drop. When you were presented, your
sponsor, who chaperoned your visits, unobtrusively
but firmly labelled you ; your job, your age, married
or single, social assets (if any), they were all trotted
out. You were sized up, catalogued, pigeon-holed,
and would be invited, according to your status, to a
dinner, lunch, tennis, or cocktail party in due course.

I played up at first, partly out of curiosity, partly
from a sense of loyalty to the firm, partly because
it was all new and I was too young to realize immediately what a crashing bore the whole show was.
For what was this social round? It was the life
of a small provincial town in England—slightly
more spacious because money went farther—but
with the same narrow outlook, restricted round, and
interminable gossip. Here, in the capital of the
oldest civilization in the world, in a city whose
beauty and antiquity were breath-taking, whose
tradition, custom, and daily life were so fascinating
and diverse that a lifetime would hardly suffice to
explore them, these superior "foreigners" went from
office to club, from tennis to cocktails, from dinner
to bridge, and from bridge to bed. For variety
they would train ponies for polo or the races, play
billiards or poker, and dance. To escape the hot
weather they would go to bungalow seaside resorts—
inferior Margates without the good air and the
winkles—and perhaps the very adventurous would,
once or twice a year, spend a week-end in a Chinese
temple in the hills ; but this was something exceptional, to be remembered. The Chinese themselves

were niggers in all but colour, they spoke an impossible tongue-twisting language, they were dishonest, they were dirty, they were " heathens," and they ate disgusting food. Any one who really studied them or found sympathy with their point of view and interest in their life was at once labelled " queer " : to become a sinologue was equivalent to going native, hopelessly *déclassé.*

This was the average point of view, and its high-nosed, ill-informed superiority bored me. No wonder the Chinese called us Foreign Devils. I stuck it for a month or two and then slipped out, for I had begun to find that tucked away obscurely in that little community were people who really loved China, who responded to its culture and civilization, who spent their time wandering in the Chinese city, visiting the innumerable temples, markets, and fairs, and delighted in the never-ending pageant of its life. Most of them were not English, most of them had no " standing "; but it was with them, I resolved, I would associate, and let the snobs go hang.

*

There were several possible aerodromes outside the city, all drill grounds, level wastes of foot-beaten mud, and one of them, Nan Yuan, was already in use as an aerodrome. There were sheds and machines there. We were taken to see them. The place was huge and desolate, fringed with a few blocks of tumbledown barracks, and at one side the flying school, three wooden sheds, a cluster of grey-roofed, single-storied houses, meagre, dirty, bare— the whole thing looking somehow blasted.

General T'ing, in charge of Chinese aviation—
he knew about as much about flying as a caterpillar—
accompanied us, with his A.D.C., a slick American-
educated Chinese with a rapid flow of imperfect
English and a broad Yankee accent, and two inter-
preters. The prospective pupils, the nucleus of
the future Chinese Air Force, emerged from the grey
buildings to meet us. Their long silk coats swept
in unbroken line from shoulder to ankle, their hands
were hidden in their sleeves, and as they bowed,
timid and smiling, the little red buttons in the centre
of their black skull-caps nodded brightly at us.
They were introduced—Mr Ma, Mr Lu, Mr
Ch'ing, Mr. Chen . . . each one proffering a
delicate hand, which emerged magically from the
long sleeve, then, clasping the other, disappeared
again.

" They are greatly honoured to meet their illus-
trious teachers, and hope, with your help, to learn
many things."

Remembering my own early days, how my instructor was a sort of God to me, I smiled reassur-
ingly at them; they were so eager and so young;
but, all the same, in their long robes they looked
frail and somehow out of place : to teach them to
fly would be wrong, incongruous—like expecting a
moth to manage a torpedo.

We trooped out to inspect the machines. I do
not know what comment they expected; but faced
with them, standing in a row outside the hangar, we
burst into laughter. They were pre-war Caudrons,
with three-cylinder Anzani engines—" real antiques,
made by them ancient Greeks." The fabric, rotten
and yellow with age, hung in festoons on the planes,

the bracing wires and turnbuckles were red with rust, the tyres had gone long ago, and had been replaced by pieces of stout rope, wired on to the rims. Perhaps we would like to give them a flying exhibition? We politely but firmly refused—the only occasion, I think, on which I declined to take a machine into the air—explaining that, although they were very nice machines, the type was unfamiliar to us. Soon the new machines would be here, and we would teach them everything. The new machines! Their eyes gleamed for a moment through their impassivity—ah, yes! The new machines! The tour over, they conducted us back to the school and regaled us, Western fashion, with sweet champagne and fly-blown biscuits. Then, with much bowing and expressions of mutual esteem, we got back into our Fire Wagon (motorcar), and returned towards the city.

Peking stands on an alluvial plain, and the Western Hills, where the Great Wall begins its three-thousand-mile journey, encircle it to the north and west. Running up the road from Nan Yuan, it lay before us, backed by the mountains. The City, actually, like Troy, an agglomeration of many cities, is set out, four-square, in the most modern manner (so old is novelty), its streets running north and south, east and west, with mathematical precision. Its main axis lies exactly on the magnetic north and south—the Chinese discovered the compass—and if all the gates and doorways were to be opened simultaneously, it would be possible to see through the whole length of the city along this axis. First the outer gate of the older Tartar City, then the Chen Men, the South Gate of the Manchu City, then the

entrance to the Imperial City, after it that of the
Forbidden City, then the outer Palace gatehouses,
across the Dragon bridges, through the doors of the
Throne Room, where the line, bisecting the navel
of the Emperor himself, sitting on his throne in
the centre of the world, would pass on, through innumerable other doorways and gates, and at last
emerge in the open country, beyond the last wall.
It was a marvellous piece of architectural symmetry,
city within city, wall within wall, gate within gate,
growing more secret and more magnificent as it
drew to the kernel, which was the very body of the
Son of Heaven.

On either side of our road stretched the plain, flat
and fertile, everywhere cultivated with rice, maize,
gowliang, liberally manured with human excrement
(there is no drainage system, everything is carried
out of the gates in wheelbarrows), and irrigated with
much fresh water. Wherever you dig, at a depth
of ten to fifteen feet, there seems to be water—as if
the whole plain were only a skin over an immense
subterranean lake. This water is raised by primitive
wheels or endless chains of buckets, operated by
diminutive rotating donkeys (blindfolded to stop
them going giddy) or human treadmills. At
intervals we passed tombs, set in their pine groves,
and small clusters of grey mud-brick houses, very
poor and sordid. Along the roadside, grovelling
in the dust, were innumerable beggars, displaying
fearful self-inflicted sores, arms paralysed from holding them for years above their heads, atrophied legs,
monstrous goitres, all bobbing and begging piteously (but professionally—there is a union) for
coppers from the rich who passed in rickshaws on

their way to a certain temple to burn joss for easy childbirth.

At the outer gate were deep hovels in the bank-side around a pool. In these primitive and age-old refrigerators the ice is stored : it remains frozen all through the spring, to be sold to the thirsty in the piping summer months. For the climate is one of extremes ; a bitter winter, a sudden, short-lived spring, great heat with a stormy tropical rain, and a languid and exquisite autumn. Except during the rains, it is dry and brittle, very hard on the nerves : blue succeeds blue, a crystalline procession of perfect days, unbroken save for dust-storms—opaque as London fogs and as yellow, swirling maelstroms that penetrate everywhere—and the occasional, and how welcome, high overcast day.

Once within the gate begins that long processional way, a road of marble slabs, between the great Temples of Heaven and Agriculture, which flank it right and left, leading up towards the city gates proper. It was laid by Ch'ien Lung, but is now in sad disrepair, one block missing meaning a foot-deep pot-hole, so the Fire Wagon turns and runs along beside it over the hard mud, raising a long plume of dust. Now we are at the outskirts of the " Chinese " city, which clusters close under the main walls. Here stand the theatres : huge structures of matting and bamboos seating thousands of people, who go, *en famille*, to sit and watch a play which lasts sometimes for days. They eat pink jellied sweets and spit sunflower seeds, talk, feed their babies, and in hot weather call for scalding towels to cool themselves. These, taken from a bucket, are flung by an attendant with uncanny accuracy high over the auditorium and drop pat into the hand of the customer, even though he be a hundred feet away. The play continues, mindless of the hubbub, the orchestra with cymbal and stick-tap pointing the scenes, the actors in florid costumes and grotesque make-up strutting and posturing, seeming to squabble like so many tropical birds.

The road is broad. At either side stretch dusty wastes as wide as it again. Here pass camel trains with baskets of coal, dirty dignified processions, tied nose to tail; shaggy jaded mules, six to a team, drag-ging heavy loads, perhaps come down a thousand miles from the deserts of the north; Peking carts with blue cotton hoods and white well-groomed beasts; shiny broughams with trotting Mongol ponies, very mettlesome and fine; barrows piled with fruit or vegetables, the huge central wheel groaning and the sweating coolie straining his shoulders to balance the heavy pannier loads; cars, sedan chairs, bicycles, a multitude of rickshaws, and all the drivers, bearers, runners shouting, greeting, abusing each other, while weaving in and out between them the watermen fling great ladlefuls of the cool stuff underfoot to lay the choking dust.

From the shops which flank it all comes the sound of hammering: coppersmiths at work on bowls and saucepans, ironmongers, blacksmiths, and silver-smiths. Tea-houses, shoe-shops, food-shops, shops for clothes, umbrellas, harness, lanterns, grain, joss, coffins, jewellery, gramophones, or jade. Some have Western plate-glass windows, but most wooden shutters, paper-backed, raised or removed to leave an open front. All display a trade-mark, sign or streamer, a long blue pennant with white characters upon it, so that the whole vista, swirling with traffic, its banks fluttering with swaying flags, is like a torrent, gushing out under the ornamental p'ai-lous, and dominated beyond by the great mass of the Chen Men Gate.

Within the gate. . . . But I could go on for ever, for this is a scene as full and varied and interminable as life.

*

The compradore wished to entertain us to Chinese Chow. Would we visit with him the Peony Temple and take tiffin there?

" If you are wise," said a friend, " you will take some envelopes with you."

" Envelopes! What on earth for?"

" To put the food into."

" But I like Chinese food."

" I dare say; but take some envelopes, all the same."

The temple was quiet and unassuming, the courtyards full of beds of peonies, scarlet and white, just breaking into bloom. We were entranced : it was so typical of the Chinese to dedicate a temple to the growing of a favourite flower. We wandered round admiring, till we were called to eat. The table was circular. Our host sat at the south side. Opposite to him, on the north, sat the chief guest, the less important grading round to east and west, while the insignificants sat immediately on his right and left hand. The compass again ; not only for the lay-out of the city, but for procedure in a banquet. In fact, I soon found the words Left

and Right hardly existed. You directed your rick-
shaw coolie to turn East or West. The house doors
were all on the south side, the north wall was a blank,
a disgraceful wall, used only when a hole was broken
in it to eject a worthless bride. Your caddie on
the golf-course to help you to locate a lost ball would
cry out: 'North! A little more to the North! A
pace to the East!' It was strange how soon you
grew into the habit of carrying a compass always
with you in your head.

Soon the food appeared. It had, of course, been
ordered in advance and sent out to the temple,
complete with cooks, coolies, and Boys; but even
in the city you would never walk into an eating-
house and expect to sit down to a meal. Food was
a serious matter, to be pondered over. You informed a restaurant you thought of honouring them
with your custom. They sent a headman to talk
to you about it, some days before. You discussed
the temperature, the guests, the dishes in season.
There would be regulation numbers, eight, twelve,
or more. *A la carte* did not exist. It was real *table
d'hôte*, and the host gave himself infinite pains to
see that you should like his table. Then the wine,
the price per head, the date, the time. It was a long
and delicate business, requiring great aesthetic sense :
a meal should be a poem.

Of all this we were informed as we consumed a
variety of unexpected but delicious hors d'œuvres.
When such a lot of trouble had been taken on our
account, we certainly could not be discourteous;
besides, the dishes were good, we did justice to them.
But, alas, these were nothing; mere appetizers; the
meal had not yet begun! Already more than half

replete, we began to look the big bowls askance. They were set down centrally on the table. The host with his own chopsticks helped the guests he wished to honour, the rest helped themselves, dipping their private chopsticks in the public dish. It was impossible to refuse the host's proffered morsels; saying " No " was mere politeness, a formula that no one dreamed of taking seriously. Dish after dish! All the usual delicacies were brought forth, and many that I cannot now remember. It seemed interminable.

It was a sign of appreciation to make noises as you ate, to suck up your soup like a walrus, say ah !, belch loud and long to the table at large. It was equally proper to rise without leave, walk up and down, talking or chewing sunflower seeds from a side table. This was an interval, helped to settle the food, and whetted the appetite for the next dish. At last, after some eighteen dishes, the sweets! Well, it hadn't been so bad, we hadn't had to use the envelopes after all! Premature relief; for our host explained that in a Chinese meal the sweets come in the centre, a custom left over from the days when meals were really meals, when banquets lasted all day long, and guests ate sweets in the warm noon. We smiled wanly, hiding our extremity, and fingering the envelopes in our pockets. For you could not refuse, you could not leave things in your bowl, yet when you cleared it surreptitiously into the paper in your lap came the immediate response: ' Ah, you like this dish? A little more! Come, this is the last dish! (It was the thirty-sixth.) Please ! "

At last it was over. We were groaning, distended, bursting, speechless. And then the rice appeared! Great lacquer bowls of steaming rice. A helping as big as a Christmas pudding was placed before you. This was not the meal. This was just a chaser, to fill up any vacant crevices : " Eat a little. Please! It is healthy to end a meal so." And the good man laughed, and continued to discuss his piles, a subject he seemed to find of outstanding interest.

Among the Chinese to have a " da doodza "— big stomach—is a sign of wealth and well-being. Perhaps we should grow accustomed to it, for it was really a question of ventral distension. There was little sustaining in the food. After three or four hours we were ravenously hungry again.

At last we got away with effusive expressions of delight and gratitude, climbed gingerly into the cars, because of pockets bursting with well-filled envelopes, and lay back, exhausted. Though there was no wind, the peonies were swaying in the court-yard.

*

Soon the swift spring was over and sweltering summer began. I fell ill with an obscure swelling in my left ankle and right wrist. It was, they said, a sort of rheumatic fever, and it confined me to bed for two months of tropical nights and days with everlasting aching throbbing pain. We shared a room, Pat and I, in the Hôtel de Pékin. It was, at that time, the only tall building in Peking, and our room looked west, over the Forbidden City to the hills. I had my bed pulled to the window.

The prospect was broad and fine. Below, the city, grey single-storied houses, almost hidden in a sea of green trees, on which floated the golden roofs of the Forbidden City. Roof beyond roof, they lay like inverted boats, separate, shining royal in the sun. Beyond them the western wall with its tall gatehouses, and beyond again, at the foot of the hills, the Jade Fountain Pagoda, whose marble finger shone white, upraised through the early morning mists.

I slept little. In the night I would hear the tap-tap-tap of the watchman going his rounds. His object in advertising his presence was not to catch the thieves, but to drive them away. Then, with the first light, the herons would rise from the yews in the Palace courtyards and sail, like grey majestic ghosts, silently overhead down to their feeding grounds in the reed lakes beyond the walls. Soon the first street vendors would begin their calls. I heard the water-carriers pass, the wheels of their barrows creaked when they were laden, empty they made no sound. To his spokes the coal-seller fastened little bells, so that his wheel passed with a jingling that brought customers to their doors. The knife-grinder had pieces of metal that jangled together hanging at his waist; the barber a sort of tuning-fork, which, plucked, emitted a long dying note. These, and many more, I heard below, mingled with calls and cries and camel bells: the confused mutter of the waking city, an indistinct persistent murmur, like sea-sounds from a shell.

Sometimes Chinese military bands would pass, playing Western instruments with Eastern harmony, a blatant comical braying that would have made

Hindemith blush for his orthodoxy. They were preceding a fire engine to a fire. The matting and bamboos of a market were blazing; but, all the same, there was order and ceremony to be observed. True, the hand-pumps could not throw the water twelve feet high; true, by the time they got there, even London's Fire Brigade would have been put to it to dowse the roaring mass; but what of that? Their water would squirt finely till it was exhausted, the fire would then be left to burn itself out; and the gallant Brigade would return, something attempted, nothing done, the bands playing louder than before.

On propitious days there were funerals. A long procession lined each side of the road, while the traffic passed unheeding between it. Innumerable mourners and musicians, hired for the occasion, blowing sobbing notes from golden horns; the hearse, a ponderous catafalque, draped and hooded with crimson embroidered with blue and gold, borne slowly by on the shoulders of a hundred coolies, with one ahead tapping two sticks to mark the time. Then the Chief Mourner, all in white, sitting on the shafts of a Peking cart, head in hand, a pensive attitude of ceremonial grief; behind him other mourners, walking, white-robed, spitting thoughtfully from time to time; after these, effigies of wives, houses, furniture, motor-cars, all in paper, to be burnt—relic of the days of suttee when a man's wives and goods were really destroyed with him.

Another day would come the quicker rattle of the executioner's cart, the victim strapped standing in it, naked to the waist, and the soldiers' ponies trotting cheerfully before and behind. After the

madness of the summer wars, rebels were executed,
sometimes twenty at a time, beyond the walls.
They did not seem to mind. When they were
made to kneel in a row, hands tied behind them,
they watched those who went before and laughed as
their heads rolled off, struck with the great two-
handed sword.

Or it would be a wedding procession. Little boys
carrying gifts in glass-topped cases, showing them
through the streets. Crimson tubular umbrellas
preceding the bride in her hooded lacquered palan-
quin, going secret to her unknown husband; the
bridegroom's family waiting to receive her, and, if
all was well, displaying the next morning at the
street doorway on white silk the scarlet evidence
of her virginity. (But the wise women, it was said,
knew tricks with pigeon's blood to counterfeit such
things.)

At last the sun would set behind the hills, night
would come down, and behind the paper windows
lights would glow. The city quieted. At half-
past nine the great gates were swung to. None now
might enter it till morning.

At last I was able to get up, hobbled on to a train,
and went down to Tsingtao, where the sun, sea
water, and the hospitality of generous friends healed
me. When I returned to Peking in September the
heat had gone, and the perfect golden days of
autumn had set in.

*

We were dancing. She was tall and dark, a
passer-by, a traveller, seeing the world. We were

dancing, talking, close, released under the spell of the music, and the thoughts came out, chiming, like bells over water, distant yet mingled.

How you were alone. Always alone. How there was always something to come, and yet, after it, loneliness and the sad thoughts moving. Have you known this too? Then the lifted head: Are you Columbus? Do you imagine you alone have made the discovery? I tell you that others before you, others, nameless before you, have known it, have seen that desolate landfall. I, too . . .

How they said that the real thing lasted; but the rind it was that lasted, and the rind was bitter, though the fruit had been soft on the tongue and the taste lingered a little. But always after, dark, only the stars moving, and you alone, far from the constellations. And love was a secret mystery, only the fortunate found it. Yet there were other fires, brighter, consuming, and the moment too was a lifetime. . . .

There was jade-stone lapping her finger, lucent as sea pools at sun-fall. We were dancing. We looked at each other and wondered.

And the ring was there on my finger! Waking, I felt it. Still half dreaming, knowing the skin's touch, pressing the palm up under the weight of the shoulder, watching the love leap, big as a lark from a boy's fist. It was there!

And she was gone, nameless, and I alone with the morning.

And the years passed, like the shadows of wheel-spokes moving, till another (far from the Palaces), not knowing the secret, wore it. And it slipped from her finger to lap, and she rose, and her skirt swinging flung it, she careless, unmindful, into the glow of the fire.

In the heart of the fire I found it, glowing red circlet, and saved it ; but the fire had consumed it : dun, cracked, and lifeless it lay in the ashes. So I took it, crooking my thumb, and flipped it out through the window into the London gutter. I heard it hop, twice, clean and ringing. I closed up the window and sat there.

Are you Columbus? I tell you that others before you, others, nameless before you, have known things, as you have. . . .

★

A Chinese house, like a Chinese city, is planned four-square, its doorway facing south. Its court-yards open one out of another, first one for the servants and kitchens, then another for dependants or relations, then the living quarters themselves, behind these the sleeping quarters, the chief wife's pavilions, the place for the concubines. The beauty and complexity of the courts varies with the extent of the house and the riches of its owner ; each is flanked on all four sides with low grey-roofed pavilions into which the light comes through patterned shutters, backed with rice paper ; each, in wealthy houses, is decorated differently with lily pool, ornamental bridge, flowering shrub, or queer-shaped rock ; all in a lovely house stand under the shadow of great trees. Of all this nothing can be seen from the street. Passing along the narrow hutungs, under the blank walls, you would never guess what beauties lay behind the tall red lacquer doors. It is all mysterious, very secret, a perfect plan for privacy.

We are accustomed in the West to judge the grandeur of buildings by their mass. The size, extent, and eminence of structure excites our admiration. But Chinese buildings, where uninfluenced by the West, are all, house, temple, palace, single-storied, separately roofed, framed on wooden pillars, and therefore must be, as a mere matter of stresses and strains, strictly limited in size. The largest that I know, the Throne Room of the Forbidden City, could be put, roofed, into Westminster Hall. Yet these comparatively puny buildings give an impression of magnificence unequalled by the mammoths of the West. The secret of our satisfaction, faced with masterpieces such as the Temple of Heaven or the Forbidden City, lies, I think, in their perfect sense of value of emptiness. No other builders have ever framed nothing in a little something and produced such harmonious serenity.

When you approach Hampton Court, St. Peter's, Rome, or the Empire State, the effect is immediate. The building is there before you, you see all of it (more or less) and can walk round admiring it from various angles: not so in China. They will not display a beauty blatantly. It must be a gradual approach, a slow revelation, courtyard after courtyard, vista upon vista, a delight not to be hurried, a consummation to be savoured delicately through stages of initiation which attune the mind to receive the ultimate perfection. Also the architect has taken care that you should see his work from only one point of view. He encloses your vista, he circumscribes the angle of your vision. You cannot wander around viewing, say, the Temple of Heaven from every angle. There is only one approach : the south (I think it is the most perfect approach in the world), and from that angle, and that angle only, can you view the marvel.

I had long wished to own a Chinese house, and at last managed to acquire one. It was small but had charm, and even some Western comfort. The next thing to do was to furnish it ; but here arose the question of language. Chinese is, as every one knows, a tongue of extreme difficulty. The complexity of the written language is such that scholars only master it after much study ; the spoken word varies all over China. To such an extent does it differ that when my friend's Boy from Shanghai wished to communicate with my Boy from Peking on the neutral ground of Tsingtao, he had either to write down what he wished to convey or resort to pidgin English ! The Northern (Mandarin, official, and educated peoples) language has four tones. Thus the same *sound*, such, for instance, as of " ka," can mean a mosquito, a pair of spectacles, smoke, or blue, according to the intonation given it. To the Chinese the word does not spell itself " ka " as it does to us, it has a separate and distinct hieroglyph for each of its meanings, so it is useless to try to get an uneducated Chinese to see that " ka," level inflexion, and " ka," downward inflexion, are the same sound. To him they are not. Once, entertaining Chinese to dinner, I thought to air my Chinese by telling my Boy to bring another chair : " Nah eedza li." But I said " eedza " in the wrong tone, and the Boy reappeared a moment

later with a cake of soap! Besides this the voca-
bulary is endless. The educated Westerner em-
ploys, I believe, on the average, about eight to
ten thousand words. The Bible has a wider
range, and Shakespeare tops the English vocab-
ulary with about twenty-five thousand. But a
Chinese writer may easily go up to forty thousand,
and, as the characters are composite, hyphenated,
so to speak, he can go on increasing these almost
indefinitely. At the other end of the scale the
coolie gets along with two hundred to three hundred
words. Some of those three hundred I had
managed to acquire. At any rate I knew enough
to find my way about and buy and bargain for what
I wanted. So the furnishing of the house became
an amusing and educative adventure.

Originally the different trades had their shops all
grouped together. And although this was then [1]
breaking down, you still found all the furniture
in Furniture Street, the lantern-makers in Lantern
Street, and the workers in jade, gold, embroidery,
kingfisher feathers in their respective streets. It
was convenient to be able to inspect everything of
a kind without journeying here and there. So I
set off daily to the Chinese City—Chen Men wei
—and began my furnishing.

I bargained over blackwood tables, watching the
men polishing them by holding a shovel of red-hot
charcoal above the wood and applying the wax
underneath, so that it went in hot. Shovel and
hand moved back and forth over the surface till it
shone like a mirror—and would not mark, as our
" french " polish will. I haggled over curtains and

[1] I speak throughout this part of the book of 1920-21.

298

cooking-pots, lanterns, rugs, and divans. I spent hours at the Imperial Goldfish Ponds, selecting exquisite banner-tails.[1] I visited temple market fairs, the night markets, flea markets, thieves' markets, picking up crockery, porcelain, pictures, curios, and despising much at the time I would now gratefully own. It was not only the pleasure of buying and bargaining, it was the teeming life about the stalls that never ceased to fascinate and charm. Tall Manchu women, with their flawless enamel-like make-up, their high black headdresses, and their shoes with the heels beneath the insteps, making them walk as if on stilts; Mongols down from the north, thoughtfully chewing a sugared necklace of red crab-apples as they bargained; children with their four stiff plaits, like dolls round the toy stalls; old men with long thin drooping moustaches, fanning themselves, reflective over the pictures; sober peasants in stolid black, or gay tea-house girls in their short tunics and bright trousers; all life was there, from satin to cotton, from childhood to dotage, and it was all happy and genial. By the time it was over I knew every quarter of the city, and had shop-keeping friends in every street.

Meanwhile, back at the house the plasterers were touching up the walls, the windows and ceilings had all been repapered, the vine and wistaria had been safely buried against the hard winter, a jobbing carpenter was making good the shutters. He was a strange man, that carpenter, the symbol of that age-long tradition of China where things are still

[1] It was said that the ponds froze solid in the winter with their fish, and that in the slow spring thaw the fish came alive out of their crystal coffins none the worse.

made as they were three thousand years ago. And this is why.

I had bought a " crackled ice " screen. It was really four window-shutters pieced together. The crackled ice design is one of the oldest and I think the most poetic of Chinese designs. You may see it on cheap ginger jars, on old porcelain, on embroidery, in shutters and windows. Some artist once saw a lake thawing and cracking in the spring and almond blossom falling on it. Out of that he created a design : a background of irregular pentagons and hexagons, with carved, engraved, or painted blossoms at the joints. My screen had four such patterns, each different, all badly broken, one with a great hole in the centre, and each with several pieces missing. I spent some time examining the design, trying to find some general formula which would keep it in balance while allowing it to vary in detail ; but in spite of measuring angles and lengths of the " cracks," I could find no rule : it seemed a real improvisation. I asked my Boy whether we should not get in a cabinet-maker to repair it. No, he said, this man would do it. So I watched. The thing was swiftly, deftly done, without hesitation or measurement. Each piece fell into place, and when all four panels were complete, it was impossible to tell which was new and which old. The four patterns, all different, had each been perfected. To what jobbing carpenter in England, I thought, would you entrust the repair of damaged Chippendale ?

At last I moved in and stood, one late autumn evening, surveying my own courtyard. The Boy, the cook, the coolie, the motor-man, the rickshaw-runner were all below there, turning in, chattering before they rolled up on the k'ang, their stone dais of a bed. Behind, the lights glowed through the paper windows. Within were all the things I had collected with such zest and care. I was a very proud and contented householder at twenty-two.

*

It was Armistice night. A large dinner-party had been held by all ex-ranks at the Wagonlits Hotel in the Legation quarter. It had developed, as such parties will, into something of a drunk. Later, some of us decided to go on to the other hotel. I offered all and sundry a lift in my car, a large two-seater. We got three in the front seat, three in the dickey, three of our mechanics on each running-board, and set off. The road that leads out of the Legation quarter has a double bend in it, right and left, where it emerges, because the protecting wall overlaps here to prevent enfilading. Beyond the wall there is a bridge, crossing a dry moat which surrounds the foreign reservation within the city. We sped down the road and approached this double turn. At the first one, the centrifugal force threw one of the men, Bill Rumsey Williams, outwards, so that he drooped over the steering-wheel and the wind-screen, and, being somewhat the worse for good liquor, remained there unable to recover himself, right in my line of vision. Therefore I had to take the second corner blind. I missed it, hit the concrete bridge rails, and the car came to rest hanging half over the moat.

We had been singing down the street, but after

the sudden crash there was an ominous unnatural silence while we all collected ourselves, felt ourselves all over, and decided we were not hurt. Then some one noticed that Bill had disappeared. We searched around in the darkness ; he was not there. We looked under the car, down into the moat, no sign of Bill.

"Where's ole Bill?" they said. "Lumme, where's he gorne?"

I switched on the spotlight and pointed it down into the moat. There, covered with bits of the bridge, lay a figure, face down in the bottom of the gully.

"It's Bill! Gawd, it's poor ole Bill! 'E's dead! Look at 'im, 'e's dead." And the more sober proceeded down the moat and picked him up. I must say they did it in style. They lifted him on to their shoulders, six of them, just as if he had been in his coffin going to his funeral, and climbed up the slope, one of them singing the " Dead March in Saul "—it was that kind of an evening.

Half-way up, the corpse woke up. " Lemme go ! Lemme alone. I'm alri," and he kicked away his pall-bearers and walked up to the top, dazed but unaided. We always said it was that especial Providence that watches over the servants of Bacchus that made him fall, quite limp, down a twenty-foot drop, with lumps of concrete as big as footballs all round him and on top of him, and still remain unhurt.

But observe the wonder of Peking. Within ten minutes fifty coolies collected round the car. With much Yo-hoing they pulled it back on to the road, and pushed it, both back wheels being locked solid, half a mile to the garage—and all for five shillings.

*

At last, in December, the first machines began to arrive. The mechanics were given quarters at the aerodrome, and the huge crates unpacked. After all this time it was exciting to see an aeroplane again. We had almost forgotten what one looked like. The Avros arrived first. They were quickly erected and tested, and off we crashed, into the air again. It was over a year since I had been up, and I wondered if, in the interim, I had forgotten how to fly, if I had lost the feel of it or should be hesitant or clumsy in the air. The doubt was soon dispelled. It was second nature. I could fly as well as ever.

In parenthesis, it may be of interest to those who have stopped flying and wonder whether they could handle a machine still, if the occasion arose, to know my experience of this. I gave up flying finally in 1921, and did not touch a stick again until the summer of 1935—fourteen years later. A friend took me up in a Moth, a machine I had never been in before. It had dual control, and he let me take over. In under a minute I was doing vertical banks with perfect assurance. All the other stunts I could ever do, rolls, loops, half-rolls, Immelmans, followed without anxiety or hesitation. I felt perfectly at home, as if I hadn't been out of the air a week. I therefore conclude that flying is a matter of balance, like riding a bicycle, and once you have acquired it, it does not, unless you have lost your nerve, subsequently desert you.

Soon we had three or four Avros in commission and started instruction. Eight pupils were allotted to me. Before taking them into the air, we gave some lectures on the ground. I tried to explain such mysteries as horizon, bank, engine torque, and so on—all, of course, through my interpreter. Such Western terms were, I should imagine, extremely difficult to translate, for no Chinese equivalent could possibly exist. With the aid of a blackboard, I amplified, drawing diagrams of thrusts, pulls, turning moments; trying to brush up half-remembered diagrams of schooldays, parallelograms of forces, explanations of centrifugal force, anything in fact which might help to give my pupils some general idea of what made an aeroplane lift, fly straight, turn, or glide. I often wonder how much they understood, for my interpreter, though eager and fluent, must have been as much mystified by it all as they were.

At last we went out and I took them up in turn, trying on this their first lesson to teach them to fly straight and keep the nose on the horizon. It wasn't a great success. The day was wintry, misty and overcast, so that, as it happened, there was very little horizon to be seen. This flummoxed them completely. As soon as I released the pressure on the rudder, round she went under the torque. As soon as I took my hand off the stick, up went the nose like a lift. Now what was to be done? How to explain? We had no telephones between the cockpits, and even if we had, they would have been no use. Imagine trying to say in Chinese in the air: " You must use left rudder to counteract the torque. You are not applying it sufficiently.

Can't you feel the machine slipping? Can't you feel the wind on the side of your face? That means we are sliding outwards. Put on some left rudder. More! More!"

My pidgin Chinese, good enough to purchase a yard of silk or a pair of candlesticks, couldn't begin to cope with this sort of thing. The only alternative was to switch off and shout some phrase you had learned by heart: Rudder! More rudder! Straight! Keep straight! But if the pupil heard it, he could not tell you so. Besides, in the effort of shouting you might have used the wrong tone and perhaps unknowingly insulted his mother, or inquired about his boots. It was a predicament. The only thing to do, as we soon found out, was to land, explain the difficulty to the interpreter, wait while it was translated, and then start off again. The effect was either nil or else to send the pupil to the opposite extreme: he jammed the rudder hard over and the machine whisked round like a kitten after its own tail.

Besides this there was a curious opacity, a sort of wooden-headed fatalism, a streak of national temperament, that stepped in. One pupil so constituted did what was the equivalent of losing his head, and locked both feet on the rudder bar, pressing them against it so hard that I could not move it and thought for an anxious second that the controls had jammed. I switched off at once and yelled something: "Take off your feet! Let go!" Useless. It meant nothing. There was the rudder locked central, the machine dithering and slipping, and what could I do about it? Luckily I was stronger in the leg than my pupil, so I got the

machine down by main force. But it was unpleasant.

So the instruction went on, day after day, in a
temperature about ten degrees below freezing-
point; round and round the desolate aerodrome,
coming down frozen to explain to a frozen pupil,
through a frozen interpreter, how, say, to keep his
wings level. Couldn't he see he was flying one
wing down? Couldn't he see they were not parallel
with the horizon? Off went the wretched interpreter in a torrent of angry-sounding Chinese, while
the water dripped steadily from his nose. You
waited, slapping your numb hands on your thighs.
You expected perhaps some reason, some ade-
quate explanation of his idiocy. The conversation
stopped. The interpreter turned. "He is very
sorry. Next time he will make great efforts to do
better." It was pathetic. You took off again, let
him take over, and down went the wing, just the
same as before.

Unquestionably ignorance of the language slowed
up instruction; but we soon formed the impression
that the Chinese were not natural aviators, certainly
not for light aeroplanes. They were slow and ham-
fisted—strangely, for their hands were so delicate
one would have thought that over-lightness would
be the fault—and had sluggish reactions. This
question of the speed of the hand's response to the
thing perceived by the eye, the lag between im-
pulse and reflex, is, as every pilot knows, the
essence of good judgment; instantaneous reaction
is an absolute necessity in putting a light aeroplane
down successfully. A split second too early or too
late, and you land well above the ground or fly into

it. Our pupils, when they went solo, often landed cheerfully twenty feet up. " He is very sorry. Next time he will make great efforts to do better." It was a formula. In such circumstances " better " seemed hardly the word.

*

At the winter solstice, the shortest day of the year, one of my pupils invited me to his house to witness a firework display. The Chinese were the inventors of gunpowder and, with characteristically civilized instincts, put it to no other use than to make crackers. These crackers in my boyhood were obtainable in London for the 5th of November, skeins of small scarlet tubes with their fuses plaited together. They could be detached and set off separately or lit as a whole, when they exploded in a series of reports like a young machine gun. Such crackers have still a serious function in China, for they are used in temple ceremonies.

The great bronze cauldron is piled high with golden paper discs, prayers, whose words in smoke and flame will fly upwards and be received in heaven ; but, since the occasion is an important one, it is as well to make sure that heaven should be warned and be on the look-out for them, so round the court are skeins of crackers tied to the trees. The prayers are lit. The flames rise in the sunlight. In front of the cauldron the suppliant kneels, bowing his forehead to the ground. Now the crackers are set off. Smoke, flame, and a cheerful crackling fills the courtyard. " Look, God ! They are coming up, my prayers ! You will not, I know, omit to give them your distinguished attention. The matter is of some importance to me. Pray forgive my troubling you." The crackling ceases. The flames die out. The suppliant rises and moves off happily through the full moon doorway. There! That's all right. Impossible that the Master of the Universe should have slept through that racket. No further need to worry.

There were quite a company collected to see the display. It was the first time I had been in a truly Chinese house, owned by a Chinese, and at first I was surprised at its simplicity and austerity. (For much of the junk that is sold to tourist and foreigner is specially manufactured for the market and quite alien to the people.) The walls were bare, hung here and there with a few scrolls, four or five large characters on a plain white ground. These were poems which appealed, not only on account of the beauty of the thought expressed, but also because of the actual caligraphy. In the West some of us admire fine handwriting; but it is no longer an art in itself. It would not occur to us that the beauty of a stanza could be enhanced by the writing of it. Not so in China. The outward clothing of the thought is a supplement to the thought itself: an ornament to beauty.

These scrolls are not permanent decorations as our pictures are. Many are kept in chests, and when the whim takes the owner, he lifts down the one on view and substitutes another. So, in this way, it is possible to clothe the walls with sentiments fitting to the occasion or the season of the year.

At the sides of the room against the walls were

pairs of stiff blackwood chairs, a small table between each pair, on which stood an ornament, a vase, or perhaps the diminutive teacups, little bowls holding a tablespoonful of golden liquid, a teapot at their side. Sometimes, in spring, growing flowers were to be found on these tables. A flat oblong dish, about an inch deep, of pale green porcelain, would be filled with fine gravel and covered with clear water. A single narcissus bulb, but one carefully selected having three corms, had been placed in the dish. Its roots had grown out, a tenuous white net through the gravel. Its three green shoots had lifted in a lovely pattern of leaf and flower. The size of the dish seemed exactly proportioned to the height of the slender stems, and the whole had a simple unity of perfection. Standing by such a flower I once observed a very old Chinese. His hair, plaited into a long pigtail, was almost white. He was clad in a white silk robe from ankle to throat, in his hand he held a large golden fan with a poem inscribed upon it. Unaware of my presence, he was standing, wrapped in contemplation of the flower, and very slowly fanning the scent of it towards him.

But this evening the decoration of the room was the people in it. There were many, mostly young. Some were dressed Chinese fashion, some incongruously wore the lounge suits of the West, some combined the two, wearing Homburg hats, horn-rimmed spectacles, and satin robes. The girls, their shiny black hair caught in a single plait, a fringe in front, wore gay silk coats, buttoning at the side, with long tight sleeves and straight-up military-looking neckbands. These coats fitted tightly to their waists. Below were ridiculous and charming little pink trousers, reaching to half-way down the calf, where they finished in a lace fringe. Black stockings and bright pink embroidered shoes completed a captivating effect. But some of the girls, too, affected the Western blouse and skirt, to their detriment, and one successfully outdid all others by displaying a fine pair of whalebone stays, reaching from bust to thigh, tightly laced *outside* her blouse.

The fireworks were to be let off in the courtyard outside. We were called to the window. Coolies staggered in with large flowering trees, standing in their tubs about four feet high. When they came closer I saw they were all made of paper, blossoms, leaves, stalks, trunks complete. At first I did not realize that these were the fireworks. But soon they were lit with tapers. The paper flowers became fiery blossoms. As they subsided their stalks burned, emitting showers of sparks, leaves spurted and hissed, golden rain and Roman candles gushed from the trunk, and, at last, the whole tub blew up with a gorgeous and shattering report. The girls laughed and clapped their hands. Then another tree was lit, and the naïve setpiece repeated itself.

Such scenes as this belong to the life of a civilization that is rapidly changing. They have an innocent, spontaneous air about them that cannot long survive the train, the motor-car, the radio, and the press. We can therefore congratulate ourselves that we have destroyed them, for our flat, stale, unprofitable civilization has seduced them from the natural springs of their own ways, so that now they

even blush at their own customs, so anxious are
they to ape ours. Yet which is more civilized?
To use gunpowder for crackers, or for murder? To
listen to the radio, or take your pet thrush out under
the willows by the water that it may be happy and
you may hear it sing? To rush about madly over
the face of the earth in car or aeroplane seeing
nothing, or to spend hours in the contemplation of
a single flower? We should have little difficulty
in choosing, I think, if the general fever to " do "
something, to " save time," did not possess us.
(And what will you do with the time when you have
saved it? ask the Chinese.)

In any event, whether we congratulate ourselves
or not, nothing will now stop the Juggernaut. The
Foreign Devils have come with their ships, shells,
and aeroplanes, sold them to the East, and taught
it their use. The thing has caught on like a deadly
virus. There is no antitoxin. A general con-
flagration is at hand, and it will only be poetic
justice if we are hoist with our own petard, for we
started it and they are far more numerous than we.
But whoever goes under in the all-round cancelling
out, I am certain that China will survive. They
know about conquest, they have been conquered
before. The Tartars conquered them and were
absorbed, the Mongols, the Manchus, even the
Jews, have all invaded China in various ways ; and
always, like a buried tortoise, the shell slowly, pon-
derously, lifts and emerges again. So I believe
Japan, the quickest and most malevolent copyist in
the world to-day, will find in the immense inertia of
China's four hundred millions a sort of python grip
that will ultimately swallow her whole. And then

when it is all over some one will set out to recover the lost values and set up the forgotten standards. Civilization is an inward, not an outward thing.

★

Spring came in a sudden riot. One day you were pulling down your ear-flaps and burrowing into your fur coat, and the next the almond tree in the courtyard had tumbled into flower, the willows had let down their hair, the cherry blossom was bubbling and bursting along the twigs. The temperature had risen twenty degrees: it was as if God had suddenly relented of some punishment against the earth and lifted His hand to let the spring gush forth. In a fortnight everything was in full leaf; the vine had been dug out of its winter mound, the peonies thrust forth their bronze shoots, the lilacs were labouring day and night to perfect their heavy trusses—never have I seen such lilac as Peking can show in May.

Our instruction continued steadily, and now much more comfortably. Some of our pupils had gone solo, some showed signs of developing into decent pilots; but, generally speaking, they were very slow. I often wonder now how those first batches were selected, whether the best type of man had been found, or whether, since, a class more fitted has come forward. For, as far as we could see at that time, the chances of a competent Chinese Air Force were extremely slender.

My best pupil was Mr Ma. I grew very fond of him, for he was more alive and eager than the rest. He had a fine sensitive face, full of expression,

312

not bland and impassive as many Chinese faces
seem to us to be. His broad square brow was surmounted with a close-fitting cap of hair that stood
up on end, short and straight, somehow pleasantly
pugnacious, his eyes were level and steady, his
cheeks a little drawn, nose (for a Chinese) on the
long side, and his mouth and chin trim and firm.
He had acquired a few words of English; but,
though that made it easier for me, he didn't really
need them, for he had the right feel, a something
every instructor instantly recognizes, the natural
ability of a born pilot. It was a pleasure to teach
him, and I soon got him off solo. By the summer
he flew well, and was the first man we trusted with
a Vimy alone, and later he accompanied me on my
one and only trip to Tsinanfu.

When the summer wars came on—there was
some sort of a small war every summer, it seemed
a function of the temperature—he was sent up in
a Handley Page. The machine was nothing to do
with us, so how or why it happened I never knew;
but the great lumbering thing caught fire in the air,
and little Mr Ma was burned to death.

*

The evening started badly. I lost my temper.
It was the heat, the nervous irritability that an
Englishman, bred to frost and fogs, sometimes gives
way to when he lives in the atmosphere of a Turkish
bath. To be in a state of copious perspiration day
after day, night after night; to feel your shirt sticking to your back, your collar to your neck, your
hand to the paper on which you write—all this

lacerates your mental balance and, quite suddenly, you rave over something perfectly insignificant. So it was in this case.

I was late back from the club, due to dine out, and drove recklessly along the narrow, dusty streets, pulled up at my front door all standing, and ran in for my white evening kit. Jo, my Boy, had not put it out. I yelled across the courtyard for him to do it now, at once, and why the devil hadn't he done it before? He hurried in and I jumped into a cold tub. By the time I was rubbed down, everything was lying out on the bed. Now, if you will believe me, the Boy had been idiot enough to put me out a stiff shirt. A stiff shirt! With the thermometer at a hundred in the shade! Any one with a grain of sense would have known I wanted a soft shirt. There were no soft shirts. Well, why not? Why hadn't he seen to it that there was a soft shirt when I wanted one? I had not enough soft shirts. Who was he to tell me how many soft shirts I ought to have? His business was to produce a shirt when it was wanted. And more in the same vein.

I managed to get hold of one at last, and rushed out of the house, strapping up my cummerbund as I ran. Jo stood looking after me. He had a great deal to put up with; but he served me devotedly, with a touching dog-like affection, and when at last my train steamed out of Peking, he stood on the platform, clasping his hands to his heart and holding them out to me, for he spoke very little English and felt, I suppose, that he could not tell me what his whole being showed, that part of his heart was there in his hands for me to take and keep for ever.

I arrived late for dinner. The other guests were drinking a second cocktail in the courtyard, we were to dine out of doors. Two huge lanterns stood like golden balls on the paved ground. The grey brickwork, the vermilion shutters, the paper windows were all overlaid with a fine tracery of tree shadows. Through open doors a distant candle lay mirrored in the polished floor, like a lily in a pool. The sickly scent of flowering trees intoxicated the air, which hung heavy and languorous below the tilted eaves. We sat down. Two Boys stole silently about the table. Dishes appeared and disappeared as if by magic. From time to time above a pale sculptured shoulder of the West a yellow impassive face of the East would peer, turning a menial service into a mystic rite. Dinner wore on, and I began to feel the house, the court-yard, the guests, the ghostly servitors had all been conjured into life for this one moment only and would presently dissolve. Conversation flagged. The last blue plate vanished into the shadow. Cigarettes began to glow, lighting for a moment some smooth forehead, shining into eyes that saw nothing, so deep was their repose. Silence came down like something palpable, too heavy to be lifted by a word. Upon one lantern a huge moth explored laboriously the curved surface of its golden world, trembling with wonder at the joy within. Some-body sighed. It was so still I heard my own heart beating.

" If there were only music! " said a low voice at my side; and immediately, as if obeying her will, from the big Blüthner within the first notes of the *Liebestod* bloomed in the night.

The stage, you perceive, was set. On such a
night something was bound to happen. Looking
back on it now, I cannot always persuade myself of
its reality. Perhaps it was no more than a dream
within a dream, and the greater dream itself only a
fitful waking in some profound unending sleep. I
do not know, and, anyway, it does not matter.
The voice which seemed to have command over
the spirit of music was entirely strange to me. I
had never heard it before, and I am fated never to
see its owner clearly. The shadows and the candle-
light confused my sight. I know the head was
dark and shapely, the mouth tragic, the hands cool.
So much I retain ; but no more. The whole thing
is elusive. It might never have happened.

The Walls of Peking stand square about the city.
They tower fifty feet into the air, and on their
summit thirty men could march abreast. Upon
their backs the huge gatehouses, gloomy, forbidding,
frown over the plain. In olden days those towers
garrisoned ten thousand men, and at the alarm of
danger they would pour forth to defend the Son of
Heaven.

Now the heavy velvet of age-long dust lies upon
the floors where the warriors slept, the tumbling
roof-tiles make a perch for the falcon, and from the
painted rafters hang rows of dreaming bats.

The Walls, too, once polished with the tread of
many feet, now lie deep in weeds, and where once
the archers, thumb-ringed with jade, stretched their
tall bows, there wanders between tall grasses and
flowering nettles a little twisting footpath trodden
by few but the curious, the idle, and the solitary.

It was here we came walking when midnight had

struck. Within the city a few late lights showed
the house-roofs, strange twisted shapes, like the
backs of a herd of sleeping cattle; without stretched
the vast plain on whose horizon the sky cloth rested
lightly, pricked with many stars. Framed in the
gatehouse pillars, musty, camphor-scented, the
round moon fell slowly to the earth—a drop of
honey from the mouth of God. . . .

Enough! Words are like sweets; too many
of them make you sick. In the face of any
deep emotion we choose rather a look, a gesture,
or a silence, than the bathos of blundering words.
At best they only enkindle our thought, at worst
they kill it. So the magic of that too short hour
eludes my capture. Words did not make it then,
and cannot make it now. There was a curious
communion, an understanding without speech, up-
lifting us to certain knowledge. We could do great
things; life was a tool, it lay to the hand, obedient
as a chisel in the grasp of Michelangelo. A
vision of the heights we might attain, a revelation
of our purpose and our power, did we not falter,
transported us and held us high, secure, complete.
We *knew*.

The moon went down. We left the high places,
came into the streets, and in the courtyard of a
strange house we parted. A gracious wind cooled
the sultry night a little, silvered the poplar leaves
and made them whisper. I bent over her hand
and kissed it. It lay passive in mine for a moment,
then, with an incomparable movement of head and
shoulder, she turned and went in.

I drove home in a trance. Life had meaning,
order, purpose—and it was good. Ugly things,

most of all Death, were blotted out; yet the sombre angel had been close at my elbow all the night.

I knocked, and the coolie opened, letting me through into the courtyard garden. A breath of perfume from a clump of japanese lilies rose at my feet. The house beyond was dark, and I paused for a moment to look up at the night sky through the close-leaved cherry trees. Then, out of the corner of my eye, I caught sight of something white moving in the shadow of the veranda. I spun round quickly, startled, and called out, "Who's that?" No answer. I ran up the steps. The white ghost came out of the shadows and seemed to crumple and sink to a heap at my feet. Half a word, half a sigh came from it. It raised two hands and a pale stricken face. It was Jo, my Boy. "Get up! Get up!" I lifted him. He stumbled to his feet, then hid his face.

I took him inside. No need of words now. Least of all now. The white mourning robe and the heavy turban told their story. But still he blundered: "You know, Master. My father makee die." He paused, strangely impassive, terribly moving. "You know, Master. He one very good man." I did what I could; little enough; gave him money for the funeral (for a man's place in the world is judged by the pomp of his burial), comforted him in some fashion, I hope, and sent him to bed.

The night was far gone and I had lost all hope of sleep. The order in the shape of things had broken. The brief transfiguration of an hour ago was gone. The veils of mystery, bewilderment came down again and I was back on the old path, groping. A thousand times I reproached myself for stupid anger against a man who, even while I was railing at him, must have been struggling in the depths of bereavement and grief. A thousand times I tried to understand why a moment of revelation had been granted to me, who had no crying need of it, while to him such consolation had been denied. If I believed in Divine Justice or Personal Immortality some balance might at last be struck; but I did not believe in either, so I could not find that easy panacea—fobbing it off on God. It was too great and intricate a pattern for my solving. I knew a vivid conscience could be worse hell than any priest or poet could devise. There stood the limit of my understanding.

At last the shutters turned grey. Day was breaking. I heard the gate open, and knew that Jo was starting on his journey to some little group of pine-shadowed tombs, peaceful in the hollow of the hills. I dressed quickly and passed out, following at a distance. Upon the Hatamen, a spacious avenue that runs north and south the whole span of the city, a little group of men were waiting. They were dressed in dull green coats with queer black hats, a red feather peaked up from the crown. Some carried banners, others gilded horns. They looked pale and tawdry in the early light, a mockery of grief, clowns aping sorrow. There was no great catafalque with its pall of crimson and its hundred men; this simple box of pine went high on the shoulders of twelve coolies, who stepped out firmly, singing as they went. Behind, a white-covered Peking cart, a white mule, and, sitting cross-legged

319

on the shafts, the ghost of last night, shading his eyes with one hand, according to the ritual prescribed. I followed them to the gates, now thronged with barrows of fruit and vegetables from the gardens round about. Their wheels rumbled over the paved tunnel beneath the Wall as that pathetic little train moved out, and one priest clad in an orange robe flung discs of paper high in the air—prayers to defend the spirit of the departed from the menace of evil. I stood and watched them go.

So one more traveller passed beyond the protecting shadow of the dim, dawn-lit city, and young day waked smiling in the eyes of happier men. Beyond the limit of that vast crepuscular horizon the light grew, the earth became radiant with a certain promise of beauty and strength. Life went on! Sweet, truant life, who turns to each of us her face and shows us only what we wish to see, but is no less sorrowful because we laugh, nor less happy because we weep, who goes her own triumphant way, withdrawn, impassive and inscrutable at heart, bidding her guests find in her what they can.

A cloud of white pigeons wheeled above the Wall. Upon their backs the reed flutes whistled merrily. Could it be that same Wall where we had wandered with slow thoughtful steps among the weeds? On what white pillow lay that head? So close, so far away, so dear, yet so estranged by one brief step of time.

The great barrow wheels creaked piteously. The straining coolies, naked to the waist, struggled with their heavy burdens, calling to each other in sharp anxious voices. Then a load of egg plants overturned, and between the quarrelling men the rich fruit lay like globes of amethyst, shining in the dust.

*

From the outset it had been our ambition to inaugurate a commercial service, the first in China, between Peking and Shanghai. The distance was about eight hundred miles. We could do it in three or four hops. The one thing lacking was the aerodrome and the ground organization, and, though the thing was discussed interminably, it never seemed to mature.

I have already referred to the tortuous Chinese psychology, to the corruption of "squeeze" in official circles, and to the extraordinary lack of anything approaching Western executive or administrative ability. It was really impossible to get anything done, and when it was done you might be sure it would be beautifully bungled.

The whole Chinese system of government used to be based on the Confucian philosophy, ancestor worship, reverence for the head of the family, which, politically, established a train of respect or responsibility, according as to whether you looked up or down the scale, from the father of the meanest family to the village headman, from him to the head of the district, and so on, in widening circles, up to the Governors of the Provinces, who were directly responsible to the Emperor himself. The difficulties, owing to the vast size of the country and the teeming population, must have been many; but in the golden days of China's greatness it seems to have worked as well as any other political system, that is to say, adequately, with no more than the usual amount of corruption and abuse. But with the fall of the monarchy the keystone of this elaborate arch was knocked out. There was no final court of appeal or authority. Each provincial governor became a law unto himself, and these men developed later into the War Lords, tuchuns, each one maintaining a private army, and each manœuvring to gain the power (and thus the income) of some form of established government. Hence the continual summer wars. Only some one intimately acquainted with Chinese politics could possibly keep pace with the continual reshufflings and alliances. The intrigue was complex, continual, subterranean. No wonder an official in power feathered his own nest as quickly as he could. To-morrow he might be out. We often wondered whether the whole aviation contract was not a manœuvre for some one to acquire a substantial squeeze, for the obstacles, postponements, and lack of any serious attempt to organize seemed difficult to account for otherwise.

So the spring passed in rumours of the start of the service; but nothing happened. The temperature rose daily, the great heat and the two months' rains were at hand; evidently it would all have to be put off till the autumn. But not a bit. Some change occurred in the political position, some pressure had been brought to bear, and suddenly the service was to be inaugurated forthwith. Needless to say we were furious, for how could you expect to maintain any regularity through the worst period of the year? And what was the good of starting the service at all if you did not mean to keep it up?

The ridiculous lack of common sense revolted our Western habit of planned and progressive action. We pointed out that the rains would be hampering and dangerous, that the aerodromes would be flooded, that they had not completed the ground organization anyway; but it was useless. If the other aerodromes were unavailable, the first one, at Tsinanfu, was ready. If the service could not reach Shanghai, it could at least leave Peking. The great thing was to start it. Whether it ran or not was quite beside the point.

Now, the weather in North China is so regular, and has been observed and recorded by the Chinese for so many hundreds of years, that it is possible to say within a week when the rainy season will begin. They decided to start the service on the very day the first rains were expected! By this time the thing had to be taken as a joke, at which, owing to the temperature, we laughed somewhat shortly. There were the usual inaugural banquets during the few days previous to the send-off, interminable food, interminable speeches, press reporters, bands, flags all over the aerodrome, crowds of people, and at last Pat climbed on board the Vimy and set off on the first flight. Of course the thing was a farce, for there were no passengers, one small bag of mails, and two of our own mechanics in the cabin, while to give the thing more " face " (prestige), Pat took one of his pupils in the second pilot's seat. (I believe it was stated that this Chinese was really flying the machine, and that the Englishman was taken purely as a formality.) The rains held off. Pat reached Tsinanfu, stayed the night and returned the next day. On the day following that I left with Mr Ma, eight ounces of mails, and two mechanics.

Still the rains held off, and although the afternoon was very hot (about 105 in the shade), it was perfect, and at four thousand feet reasonably cool. It was my first and only cross-country flight in China of any extent, and quite an experience, for the ground was entirely devoid of any of the usual landmarks by which a pilot finds his way. Beyond the railway, the Grand Canal, and the Great Wall, there were, at that time, no outstanding features on the surface of North China. There were the Western Hills, which soon slipped behind, and beyond this nothing but a flat featureless plain dotted with innumerable small villages. No roads, no woods, no rivers, nothing but nets of cart-tracks radiating in every direction from each village and connecting it with those about it. A forced landing in such country would find you fifty miles or more from any modern method of transport or communication. Heaven alone knew how you would get yourself or the machine back to civilization. To dismantle it and return in carts seemed the only solution. So I thought as we sailed south-west on a compass course, but did not have to make the experience, for, after three hours, we sighted Tsinanfu, town, river, and aerodrome, came down, put the machine in its shed, and walked into the town to be received into the hospitality of the British Consulate. It was a perfect evening. Where were the promised rains?

They started that night. A violent thunderstorm and cloud-burst, a gushing rattling deluge that streamed from the roofs and slashed against the panes. This sort of rain has to be seen to be believed. Nothing of the kind ever visits England. It is as if there was water above the heavens, and some one had pulled out a slide, loosing a cataract solid on to the earth. At daybreak they stopped. The sun came out. The Consulate was well drained, so that the amount of water that had come down did not at first appear. I was warned against trying to get to the aerodrome. It was out of the question to fly, the rains would return in the afternoon ; but there was the schedule to be maintained, however futile the whole thing might be. If I possibly could, I must get the machine off and return to Peking.

So we set out. Soon the difficulties began to appear. The tracks were flooded, the fields were lakes ; but by making some detours, walking on the mounds by ditches, we progressed slowly for a little until we were brought to a real full stop. Through a slight dip in the ground ran a raging yellow torrent, about a hundred feet across, rushing past at six miles an hour. We stood there contemplating it, baffled. Evidently we should have to go back. There was no way across this except by swimming.

At that moment on the far side a coolie appeared, gesticulating and shouting something. He waded into the water, pushing a small tub, about the size of an earthenware bread bin, before him. He crossed towards us, the water up to his neck, reached the shallows, and emerged, chattering at Mr Ma.

" He invites you, sir," said Mr Ma, " to cross in this small boat."

The small boat was made of wicker, roughly

lacquered with mud, reasonably water-tight; but it was not big enough to float anything larger than a six months' baby. Now I weigh 13 stone and stand 6 feet 4. The " boat " would reach perhaps half-way up my calves, and my two feet, if curled up, might just find place on the bottom. I thought the thing impossible, and the idea of being tipped out into the swirling yellow water failed, at that moment, to appeal to my sense of humour. I suggested Mr Ma should make the experiment. He entered the tub without hesitation, while the coolie held it steady, and resting his hand on the man's head, was ferried across without incident. It was my turn next. If you have ever tried to stand upright in a small canoe, you know how it wobbles from side to side. This " small boat " wobbled that way in all directions. I half stood, half crouched, clutching the coolie's pigtail to steady myself, and we launched away. It must, from the way the two mechanics laughed, have been a ridiculous sight. My weight sunk the tub almost to the brim. The coolie, stepping uncertainly on the muddy bottom, slid this way and that, time and time again we were on the point of being overset. But he was a stout fellow that coolie. He pushed, he swore, he laughed, he slithered (and, Lord, how he smelt!); but at last we were safely across, and I stood triumphant on the far bank encouraging the others to follow.

Now the tub had been in none too strong a condition at the outset, and the journeys had weakened it, so that by the time Bill—he that had taken a drunken header into the Peking moat—came to cross, last, it was definitely leaky. Half-way across, the bottom fell out. Bill, with a curse, fell through to the mud beneath. The coolie hooted with laughter, but stuck on to Bill, assisting him through the shallows, and he emerged, wearing the tub round his middle, like a serviette ring, and using very colourful language. While he wrung out his ducks we paid off the coolie, to whom the loss of the tub seemed of no importance, and then proceeded. Soon we came to a small lake. "No more of them bloody tubs for me," said Bill. Then, from a house appeared, I have always wondered how, four Chinese ponies, saddled and bridled. Their owner invited us to mount. Now I had been bitten in my childhood by a horse, and therefore agreed with Maurice Beck, who, after twenty years in China, gave his considered opinion on the Mongol pony very succinctly: "Nasty vicious animals: one end bites and the other end kicks." However, once again there was nothing else for it. We mounted into the hard wooden saddles, stuck our feet in the heavy brass stirrups, and trotted off—I, like the White Knight, on the point of overbalancing at every step. At length we reached the aerodrome. It had taken us two hours to do our twenty-minute walk of yesterday.

Half the aerodrome was a soggy marsh. The machine, in the shed, was pretty well bogged. But there was a strip, higher than the rest, which might, I thought, serve to take off from, if we could get the machine to it. We started the engines up in the shed and managed to taxy out, but at once the wheels sank up to their axles, and full power from both engines (600-h.p.) refused to budge it an inch. A gang of coolies appeared—these things always seemed magical—and fifty were placed under the leading spar of each lower wing. They crouched and raised the spar with their shoulders, then, with both engines at full throttle, foot by foot, she moved slowly forward on to the better ground.

I suppose it was foolhardy ever to have made the attempt at all. On the other hand, the rains might last six weeks, and a week in this humidity and temperature would have been enough to turn the machine green with mildew, so leaving the men and Mr Ma to return by train, and taking advantage of every inch of run, I opened up. She crawled along, gradually gathering way, got up to about thirty miles an hour, and then we came to the end of the good ground. I closed the throttles, she sank, stuck, and turned up on her nose. So that was that.

We threw a rope over the tail and pulled it down. Luckily there was little damage, for the nose of the Vimy had a small wheel to protect it against such accidents. Laboriously we hauled the machine back to the start of the run again, and decided to leave it at that for the day. In the interim we got cinders put down, and the strip of ground stamped firm by coolies. But it was two days before the Vimy could be got off and flown back to Peking. And that, for the year 1921, was the end of the Peking–Shanghai Air Service.

★

The contract with Vickers Ltd. was running out. What should I do? I might seek another with the Chinese Government. But teaching the Chinese to fly led nowhere, as far as I could see. Besides, I had been flying for six years and my body was still in reasonable working order. It might be wise not to tempt Providence further. On the other hand, if I gave up flying, what was I to do? I was, as I said at the outset, untrained for any other career. Yet commercial aviation in 1921 seemed without prospects. I might have tried for some other work in Peking; but I felt that, although the place was unique, it was nevertheless a backwater, and if I remained there much longer I should get too firmly fixed in its easy ways. Lotus-eating either made a man relapse into a mindless vacancy or drove him mad: neither prospect tempted me. There was a wider sweep, could I but find it, back in the centre of things. And there were other reasons. . . . I decided to come home.

*

So the last flight came. I was up in a Vimy taking some friends to view the city from the air. It was perfect autumn weather, and we passed high over the pattern of the palaces northwards to the Great Wall. The flight had no significance for me. I did not know it was the last time I should pilot a machine. It just so happened that I never did again. Better so, for with what shrinking hearts do we approach the severing of ties. The last word, the last handshake, the last kiss, knowing that never again will the eyes meet so, nor the heart beat so, that something which once filled our lives has dwindled down to the pin-point of farewell and cannot be regained. Come back! Come

back! It will be different! We will start again.
I was to blame. I see it now. Forgive me! So
something in us calls, ready to promise anything
sooner than drink the cup, revolting that with life
itself so brief, the ties within it should be briefer
still. And yet we stand, like fatal oxen, mouthing
the bitter word, watch that which we most desired
to hold recede, and, waving, turn and go.

These are the wretched known farewells; the unknown slip by sometimes unperceived, and only after
many years do we look back and say: Why, that
was the last time! So with this. The fine engines
roared out there on the wings. The interference
beat was very slow, rising and falling like a deep
sea swell, so true were they in tune. There were
the Ming Tombs underneath; the broad way
up to them lined with its marble monoliths, dragons
and elephants, horses and watchmen, guarding that
sacred road by which dead Emperors went to rest
for ever in the valleys of the hills.

But had I known? Could I have seen it then,
as I do now, should I not have passed the whole
time in review? Should I not have thought, as I
do now, of my lost friends, companions of the air:
Pip blown to bits, Arthur brought down, Bill
coughing as he fell back at that single senseless
shot? They more than others I had known would
have been happy high aloft that day, to see below
the barren ridges of the hills and follow the Great
Wall, fighting its stubborn way up and down the
rises and the falls, lonely and strong, guarding the
desolation.

And hosts of other memories would have followed, crowding: a thousand skyscapes, day and

330

night, the gay or sombre garments of the blue; the way the earth looked, falling; the wonder at first coming out above the clouds; the rush of engines starting; swallowing to stop deafness in a dive; the scream of wires; shadows of clouds on hills; rain, sweeping like veils over the sea, far off; sunlight; stars between wings; friends, close in formation, swaying, hand on throttle, as they rode ten feet away a mile above the earth. And many others: grass blown down when engines were run up; the smell of dope, and castor oil, and varnish in new cockpits; moonlight shining on struts; sunset clouds, gold-braided; the gasp before the dive; machine guns; chasing wild duck; the feel of bumps, and all the mastery over movement, pride in skill.

And should I not, had I but known, have flung the machine this way and that, once more to feel it live under my hand, have sported in the sky and laughed and sung, knowing that never after should I feel so free, so sure in hazard, so secure, riding the daylight in the pride of youth? No more horizons wider than Hope! No more the franchise of the sky, the freedom of the blue! No more! No more! Farewell to wings! Down to the little earth!

No, the truth is, had I known, I should not have felt so. Life is more savoured in its after-taste. That distant day has a significance I could not give it then, and all those days now fall into a shape, this shape I have endeavoured to set down; some things with pleasure, some reluctantly, some ill; for words straining to catch emotion have a bursting-point, they crack into heroics, platitudes. Only the rarely gifted mould them to the thought's shape, docile, so that the reader scanning the cold print feels something stir within him and take fire, and gazes stupidly upon the page, seeing the ink blurred, uplifted by the music, hardly knowing why.

So we wheeled and came back south towards the city. There were the lakes, the palaces, the spirit ways mounting between the steps, so that the unseen world might have its own way up and down unhindered by the feet of mortal men ; there were the dyers' scaffolds where blue lengths of cotton cloth hung drying in the wind ; there was my little house ; there was the shop where I had bought an amber drop my unborn son would break. There it all was, the teeming world spread out four-square to see, and I should always be as then, apart, mostly alone, the self aside, however close the press.

The Temple of Heaven slipped by underneath, that perfect pattern in its ample park : the groves of yews, the long descending way to where the Altar, marble, white and triple-tiered, lay in the circle of its blue-tiled wall. Then the wide plain ruled to the far horizon. Soon the aerodrome.

Now shut the engines off. Come down and flatten out, feel the long float, and at the given moment pull the stick right home. She's down. Now taxy in. Switch off. It's over—but not quite, for the port engine, just as if it knew, as if reluctant at the last to let me go, kicked, kicked, and kicked again, as overheated engines will, then backfired with an angry snorting : Fool ! The best is over. . . . But I did not hear.

LONDON, BRABOURNE, LAS PALMAS,
1935-36.

Library of Congress Cataloging-in-Publication Data

Lewis, Cecil, 1898-
    Sagittarius rising / Cecil Lewis.
        p. cm. — (Wings of war)
    Reprint. Originally published: London : P. Davies, 1936.
    ISBN 0-8094-9004-5 (trade). — ISBN 0-8094-9001-1 (library)
    1. Lewis, Cecil, 1898- —Biography. 2. World War, 1914-1918—Aerial operations, British. 3. World War,
1914-1918—Personal narratives, British. 4. China—Description and travel—1901-1948. 5. Great Britain. Royal
Air Force—Biography. 6. Fighter pilots—Great Britain—Biography. 7. Novelists, English—Biography.
    I. Title. II. Series.
    D602.L4 1991   940.4'4941—dc20   91-6399 CIP

Cover photograph © Carl Purcell
Endpaper photograph © René Sheret/Air France